the
BEGINNER'S
COOKBOOK

Pamela Gwyther

p

This is a Parragon Book.
This edition published in 2005
Parragon, Queen Street House, 4 Queen Street, Bath BA1 1HE, UK

Copyright © Parragon 2001

ISBN: 1-40544-990-X

Printed in China

Designed and created by the Bridgewater Book Company Ltd.

Recipe Photography: Mark Wood, Ian Parsons
Home economists: Pamela Gwyther, Sara Hesketh

The publisher would like to thank Steamer Trading Cookshops
in Alfriston and Lewes, East Sussex, for the loan of kitchen utensils.

NOTE
This book uses imperial and metric measurements.
Follow the same units of measurement throughout; do not mix imperial and metric.
All spoon measurements are level: teaspoons are assumed to be 5 ml,
and tablespoons are assumed to be 15 ml. Unless otherwise stated,
milk is assumed to be full fat, eggs are large
and pepper is freshly ground black pepper.

Recipes using uncooked eggs should be
avoided by infants, the elderly, pregnant women, convalescents,
and anyone suffering from an illness.

AUTHOR'S ACKNOWLEDGMENTS
Thanks to family and friends for their support and encouragement,
and for eating and testing my recipes over the years. Particular thanks to
my husband, David Gwyther, for wine recommendations, to Mark Wood
for his photographic expertise, to Lorraine Turner for her professional editing,
and to my suppliers—butchers Andrew and Steve, and equipment suppliers
Kitchens of Bath and Kitchen Aids in London.

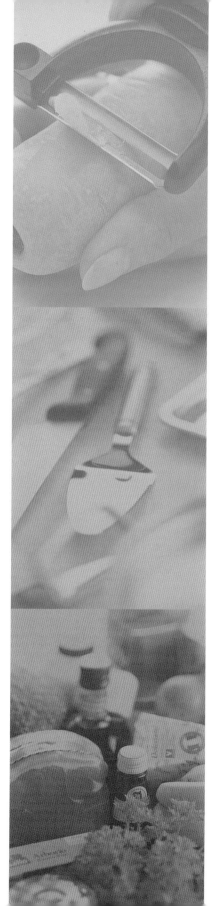

CONTENTS

Good eating

We are what we eat. But what we eat has been changing over recent years, under a range of influences. Foreign travel has broadened our tastes. Economic pressures have made us more aware of the cost and quality of food – of its value, in financial and nutritional terms. Busier lifestyles have given us less time to shop and prepare meals. But supermarkets now have a wider range of fresh foods – meat, fish, fruit and vegetables – and herbs and spices to add more exciting flavours. We can pull all these trends together under two keynotes of good eating: simplicity and healthiness.

SIMPLICITY

Today we are able to obtain raw materials at the peak of their quality, due to better production practices and improved transportation around the world. We can therefore enjoy food at its simplest, not overworked or overcooked – indeed quite often raw or lightly cooked. This way we are getting the best of flavours and of food values, with much less effort.

If we choose food carefully, there is no need to spend hours preparing it. Long, slow, cooking processes still have their place for some occasions but the newer, quicker methods like stir-frying and griddling are ideal for busy people at the end of a working day. Slicing and grating vegetables means that we can eat them raw in salads or quickly pan-fried. They do not need peeling; carrots and other root vegetables can just be scrubbed. Meat and fish can be prepared by the butcher and fishmonger, so that we have ready-to-cook, smaller portions rather than a whole joint or fish.

No longer do we have to disguise the poor cuts or 'off' tastes of foods that are past their best, by smothering them with overpowerful sauces. Food now is served unadulterated, leaving natural flavours to be enjoyed in their own right. The only exception is adding handfuls of fresh, readily available herbs and flavourings from all over the world – parsley, coriander, garlic and ginger – to bring a whole new range of natural flavours to old favourites.

Keep a good storecupboard of basic materials for good, quick meals – rice, pasta and lentils, oil, spices, a few tins of tomatoes and beans, and stock powder. These will quickly help to transform basic ingredients into delicious meals.

Cut down your consumption of red meat to reduce the chance of heart disease. If you do eat red meat, make sure it is lean and cooked by a healthy method, such as grilling. Eat more chicken and game because they are healthier options.

Eat fish at least three times a week. It is a good source of lean protein and the oily varieties give us essential fatty acids. All fish is very quick and easy to cook.

Eat at least five portions of vegetables, salads and fruit a day. One portion is an average-sized fruit like an orange, an apple, a pear, a medium banana, two smaller fruits like clementines or plums, a cupful of berries or grapes, or a large slice of melon or pineapple. A small glass of juice, about 150ml/5fl oz, is a portion but restrict juice to 1 glass per day. A small bowlful of salad leaves, tomatoes, cucumber, celery is a portion, or 2 tablespoons of vegetables such as peas, beans, spinach, sprouts or cauliflower. The more fruits and vegetables you eat, however, the better.

Restrict excess fat in your diet, particularly saturated animal fats from meat and dairy products. Resist spreading butter too thickly on your bread and piling it on your vegetables. In some cooking, oil can take the place of butter. Try adding olive oil to your mashed potato and enjoying the flavour. Lower-fat cheeses are available, or stick to the normal ones and reduce the amount you eat. The same applies to yoghurt and cream. Semi-skimmed and skimmed milk are a sensible option because they are lower in fat but still contain all the valuable nutrients of full-fat milk.

Hidden fat is the greatest enemy in prepared foods like cakes and snacks. Try to avoid these foods if possible, or read the label and try to choose lower-fat alternatives. Remember, though, that a low-fat diet is only a healthy option for those aged 5 and over – below this age a child needs easily accessible energy.

Eat more wholegrain cereals. Instead of white bread, eat wholemeal and wholewheat varieties and change to a high-fibre breakfast cereal or muesli. Try wholegrain pasta and brown rice – the latter particularly has a nuttier flavour.

Drink at least 1.5 litres/2¼ pints of water per day. You will feel healthier and your body will benefit. Limit tea and coffee because they contain caffeine, a stimulant that will keep your body in overdrive. Alcohol, in moderation, can lower the risk of fatal heart disease, but limit your intake to 1–2 units per day if you are a woman, and 2–3 units per day if you are a man. One unit is equivalent to a glass of wine, a half-pint of lager, or a pub measure (25 ml/1 fl oz) of spirits.

Always taste food at the table before you add extra salt. Restrict salt in cooked dishes and try to cook vegetables without any salt in the water. Too much salt can lead to high blood pressure.

Eating healthily will not stop you getting some diseases but it will affect how your body deals with them. A healthy diet will help you have a healthy life. In this country with so many people overweight, it really is time to question our eating habits and adjust them to ensure that we are getting the maximum benefits from good food.

LEFT Eating fresh, nutritious, simply cooked food is the best way to improve health and increase vitality.

BELOW To protect against heart disease, cut down on red meat and eat more fish, poultry and vegetables instead.

Part 1
Nutrition and Techniques

BASIC NUTRITION

In order to lead a healthy life we need to ensure that the body is receiving all the necessary nutrients to grow, maintain and repair it. Food is utilised by the body to produce movement, warmth, growth, protection, repair and reproduction. In order to do this efficiently, the body must have a good selection of foods that produce a balanced diet. We can break down the foods into five food groups: carbohydrates, proteins, fats, vitamins and minerals. No one food contains a single nutrient; foods are a complex mixture of carbohydrates, proteins and fats with very small amounts of vitamins and minerals plus water. Water is a very important part of the diet because it makes up two-thirds of the total human body weight.

CARBOHYDRATES

This group includes all sugars, starches and fibre. Sugars are referred to as simple carbohydrates because they have a simple structure and can be broken down by the body easily to give a rush of instant energy. Too much sugar is not good for the body, however, because it can increase the risk of diabetes, heart disease, obesity and tooth decay.

Complex carbohydrates are present in wholegrains like corn, oats and barley and in fresh fruit and vegetables. Their complex structure takes longer to break down in the body and provides a longer, steadier flow of energy in the bloodstream.

Fibre is not really a food because it cannot be digested by the human digestive system, but it is still very important in the diet because it provides bulk to assist the passage of the food through the intestines. In this way, a good intake of fibre helps to prevent constipation.

PROTEIN

Protein is essential for growth and repair of the body, and any excess can be used to provide energy. Proteins have a complex structure and are composed of amino acids. The ones that are necessary for the human body are called essential amino acids.

These are present in the correct ratio in animal proteins — in meat, fish, poultry, milk, cheese and eggs — and are said to have a high biological value. Vegetable proteins, known as incomplete proteins, provide only some of the essential amino acids and therefore need to be eaten in mixtures that complement each other. But there is such a variety available that it is unlikely that people not eating any animal protein would suffer from a deficiency.

FATS

Oils and fats are present in the diet as the most concentrated form of energy. They are available as visible fats, such as butter, margarine, oils, and fat on meat, but also as invisible fat in cheese, biscuits, cakes, crisps and nuts. Not all fats are bad. The baddies are the saturated fatty acids found in animal fats like butter and cheese and in animal products like sausages, bacon, pork, lamb, beefburgers, eggs and full-fat milk. Saturated fats are thought to increase blood cholesterol levels and therefore to be responsible for heart disease. Polyunsaturated and monounsaturated fatty acids, on the other hand, are believed to reduce cholesterol levels; these are available in corn oil, olive oil, soya and sunflower oils, and nut oils (not coconut).

VITAMINS

Vitamins help to regulate important body processes. Apart from vitamin D, all the vitamins must be supplied in the diet because the body is unable to manufacture them.

Vitamins fall into two groups, water-soluble and fat-soluble. Water-soluble vitamins include B1, B2, B6 and B12 and vitamin C; the fat-soluble vitamins include A, D, E and K. If a vitamin is not present in the diet, then specific symptoms of deficiency will be observed. For example, lack of vitamin C results in scurvy. Vitamins may be taken as supplements but they are expensive and if you have a well-balanced diet they should be unnecessary.

MINERALS

Minerals are inorganic elements needed by the body in very small amounts. They perform three main functions:

- Important constituents of bones and teeth (calcium, phosphorus and magnesium)
- Present as soluble salts in body fluids (sodium, chloride, magnesium, potassium and phosphorus)
- Aiding the process of releasing energy (iron, phosphorus and zinc)

Trace elements are also needed, such as copper, fluoride, selenium, iodine, manganese, chromium and cobalt, but in smaller amounts.

A well-balanced diet should provide all of these elements, particularly a diet rich in fruit, nuts, grains and green leafy vegetables. Supplements are widely available but should be used with discretion.

WATER

The most essential part of any diet is to drink at least eight glasses of water every day. Water is needed in the body for transporting nutrients, for digestion, for circulation, for body heat regulation and excretion. No matter how healthy your diet, if you are not drinking enough water the body will not function properly and you will feel lethargic and under par.

Sensible, healthy eating requires a good balance of food, which is low in saturated fats and simple carbohydrates. A reasonable amount of protein, vitamins and minerals, plus plenty of fibre and water, will ensure that the body continues to function correctly.

PREPARATION TECHNIQUES

*D*o not be daunted by all the different food preparation techniques and descriptions. The range of definitions given here will be all you will need.

BAKING BLIND

This means baking pastry cases without a filling so that the pastry is well cooked and crisp. The flan tin or pie dish is lined with shortcrust or sweet pastry and then lined with baking parchment or foil, which is then weighed down with baking beans (actual dried beans or you can buy ceramic or metal ones) to prevent the pastry bubbling up whilst cooking. The beans and foil are then removed and the pastry case cooked for a while longer to dry it thoroughly.

BEATING

This term refers to mixing food to make it lighter by incorporating air. You can use a fork, a wooden spoon or an electric mixer for beating. It is most often used for eggs, for an omelette and for making a cake, beating together the butter and sugar (this is also known as creaming). It is also used to beat a sauce or a custard, not to incorporate air but to make the consistency smooth and remove any lumps.

BLENDING

Blending means combining ingredients together, usually with a spoon. You can blend cornflour and water, for example, to a smooth paste before using to thicken soups and stews. Blending also refers to mixing soups and purées in a blender to reduce to a smooth liquid and remove any lumps.

CRIMPING

This means to decorate the edges of a pie in order to ensure the edges are well sealed. This is done by pinching the pastry with a finger and thumb of one hand and pressing with the first finger of the other hand, giving a fluted edge. Crimping is also used purely decoratively on shortbread or plate pies.

CUTTING

Cutting is a basic technique used to prepare meat, fruit and vegetables. Using a knife correctly is an important step in preparing food. Food that is correctly prepared will cook more evenly and have a more attractive appearance. A good knife and a firm board are essential. Make sure the knife is sharp because blunt knives cause accidents. Use the correct knife for the task, for example a bread knife for bread and a serrated knife for tomatoes.

CHOPPING

This is one step on from cutting. The food is divided into small pieces by more than one cut. To chop an onion, for example, you halve the onion from the top down through the stem and root, then you place the flat side of one half down on the board and cut the onion from root to stem into fine slices. Then you turn the knife and slice through the onion the other way ensuring that you have even, small pieces. Chopping herbs is another important skill. Hold the tip of the blade down with one hand and raise the handle of the knife up and down with your other hand as you chop into the herb, moving from left to right and back again so that you work all over the food.

Chopping can be done roughly or finely: roughly means pieces of food about 1 cm/½ inch, whereas finely means much smaller pieces. It is important to chop all the pieces to an even size. Sometimes a recipe might ask for food to be diced: this means pieces not only of the same size but of a regular shape; for example, diced cucumber should be small cubes.

CRUSHING

This technique is used for crushing herbs or garlic. To crush garlic, simply press down on the garlic using the flat side of a knife blade. Crushing is also used for making biscuit crumbs for cheesecakes or flan cases. To make biscuit crumbs, simply put the biscuits in a large plastic bag, cover the end and then crush with a rolling pin until they are reduced to crumbs. You can also crush garlic cloves with a garlic press or a heavy knife.

DREDGING

Dredging means sprinkling pastry with flour before rolling it out. The board and the rolling pin should be lightly floured to

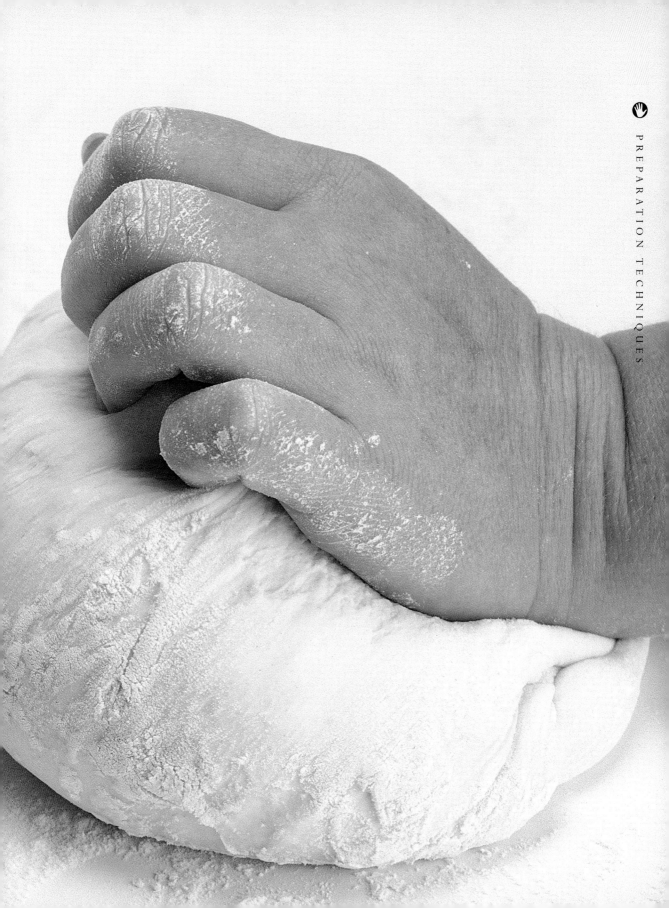

prevent the pastry sticking to them. The term can also be used for sugar and cocoa powder, for example, to dredge a cake with icing sugar. These days it is fashionable to dredge a plate with sugar or cocoa powder before serving a dessert.

FOLDING IN

The term used to describe how to incorporate flour into a cake mixture. It is a gentle movement, made with a metal spoon or a plastic spatula to cut through the mixture in a figure of eight movement, enabling the flour to combine without losing the air already incorporated. The same term applies to meringues and soufflés.

GLAZING

A glaze is a finish given to pastry and bread before baking. It can be simply milk, or beaten egg, or a water and sugar glaze.

Savoury pies are usually brushed with egg before baking to give them a rich, golden-brown, glossy finish. Sweet pastry products are often brushed with water and then sprinkled with caster sugar to give them a crisp, crunchy finish. Breads and buns can have either a savoury (egg) finish or a sweet (sugar) glaze.

You can also glaze a ham. In this case the ham is partly cooked and the skin then removed and a coating of sugar and mustard spread on. The ham is then baked further until golden and crisp in appearance.

GRATING

A grater is used to shred food into small particles. The two most common uses are for cheese and for citrus fruit peel. A box grater is useful because it has different-sized surfaces and can produce medium and fine gratings. A food processor can grate food very quickly and is useful if you have a large quantity to prepare.

GRINDING

Grinding means reducing foods to a powder or very small particles for use in recipes. For example, you can grind spices in a pestle and mortar until you have achieved the required texture. An electric coffee grinder will do the job quicker but you may get too fine a result. You will also need to keep it separate for the job because other flavours will ruin the coffee. A food processor will grind nuts and chocolate satisfactorily.

KNEADING

This technique is used in breadmaking. The dough is kneaded to develop the gluten in the flour so that it will hold its shape when risen. The dough is pummelled on a lightly floured board until it is smooth and elastic. Kneading involves a particular technique that uses the heal of the hand to pull and stretch the dough, which can be quite therapeutic. Kneading can also be done in a free-standing mixer using a dough hook.

KNOCKING BACK

This is the term for knocking the air out of the bread dough after its first rising. It involves literally knocking the air out of the dough and then gently kneading for 1 minute. The dough is then gently shaped before a second rising or 'proving'.

MARINATING

This involves allowing food to soak in a marinade, which will tenderise it and add flavour. Marinating is used for meat, poultry and game. The meat is covered with a mixture of oil, wine or vinegar and some added flavourings like garlic and herbs. The food can be marinated for a few hours or a few days. During the cooking, the marinade can be used to baste the food.

MASHING

This usually refers to potatoes and other root vegetables. Cooked vegetables are mashed, using a fork, a potato masher or an electric hand mixer. This makes them smooth and light and other flavours can be incorporated at the same time, for example, herbs, garlic and mustard. The addition of butter or cream makes them more luxurious.

MINCING

This means chopping food very finely. It is best done with a hand or electric mincer. A food processor can also be used to mince food.

PEELING

This is the removal of any unwanted peel from fruit and vegetables. Thick peel, such as orange rind, will require a

sharp knife, but for vegetables with a thin skin, such as a potato, it is better to use a potato peeler because you will have less waste.

RUBBING IN

This is a method of cake making where the fat is rubbed into the flour. The same technique is also used for pastry and breadmaking. The fat is rubbed into the flour using the tips of the fingers, lifting the flour high out of the basin so that the air will be trapped in the mixture. This technique makes the mixture lighter and ensures better results.

SCORING

A method of making light cuts on the surface of food to help it cook more quickly, to reduce fat and also to make the food's appearance more attractive, for example, scoring duck breasts before grilling.

SIEVING

This is a method of rubbing cooked food through a sieve to form a purée. The food is pushed through the sieve using a wooden spoon. Sieving can also refer to straining vegetables after cooking to remove the cooking water.

SIFTING

This is the same as sieving (see above) but refers to dry ingredients, for example sugar and flour, to remove lumps and to add air to the mixture. With these finer ingredients, however, there is no need to push them through with a wooden spoon.

TENDERISING

The technique of beating raw meat with a rolling pin or a meat hammer to soften the fibres and make the meat more tender before frying or grilling. This method is useful for steak that is not of the finest quality.

TRUSSING

This is the technique used for poultry and game whereby the bird is pulled into shape and then held with skewers or by string to maintain its shape during cooking. It is particularly useful if the bird has been stuffed because it prevents the stuffing from falling out.

WHISKING

This is another method used to incorporate air, but it is usually used for a lighter mixture, for example egg whites or cream. To make the task easier and more efficient, you really need an electric mixer for whisking. However, a wire whisk used in a large mixing bowl with lots of energy can perform the task adequately. Indeed, many chefs prefer to use their balloon whisks and a copper bowl for meringues.

COOKING METHODS

*A*gain, do not be daunted by the variety of the cooking techniques. Enjoy experimenting, particularly with some of the increasingly popular and healthier techniques like stir-frying and griddling. Here is all you need to know.

BAKING

This is the term used for cooking food in the oven by dry heat, for example, a baked potato or baked custard. It is also the process for preparing baked goods such as cakes, biscuits and bread.

BASTING

The process of moistening meat, fish or poultry whilst roasting in the oven. The cooking juices and fat are spooned over the food to keep it moist, to add flavour and to improve the appearance of the finished dish. If the tin becomes too dry then a little liquid, either stock or wine, can be added to the juices. Roasting vegetables are basted with oil so that they are well coated and will crisp evenly, and fried eggs are basted with hot oil to ensure the tops of the eggs are set.

BLANCHING

Blanching used to mean 'to whiten' and was used to whiten veal and offal. Today, however, there are two more usual meanings. The first is to immerse food in boiling water for a few seconds and then into cold water in order to remove their skins, for example tomatoes, nuts and peaches. The other is in preparing vegetables for freezing. You immerse the vegetables in boiling water for a short period, to destroy enzymes that will spoil the flavour and texture of the vegetables, and then into cold water to stop the cooking process. Blanching also helps to preserve the colour of the vegetables.

BOILING

This is cooking food in a liquid (water, stock or milk) at 100°C/212°F (known as boiling point). The main foods cooked in this way are eggs, vegetables, rice and pasta. Although sometimes fish and meat are placed in boiling liquids, the heat is then reduced and the food is simmered only. Continued boiling would render these foods lacking in flavour, shrunken in size and of poor texture.

BRAISING

A long, slow, moist method of cooking used for cuts of meat, poultry and game that are too tough to roast. Braised food is usually cooked in one piece and the amount of liquid used is quite small. The food is started off by browning in oil and then cooked with a quantity of vegetables in a casserole with a close-fitting lid. The dish can then be cooked on the top of the stove or in a low oven.

CASSEROLING

Another, more modern name for braising, taken from the name of the cooking vessel – an ovenproof casserole dish with a tight-fitting lid (this is often flameproof and can be used for the initial browning process, which cuts down on the washing up). The food is often served from the casserole dish at the table. Casseroling also includes stews, in which the pieces of food are often cut into small pieces and more liquid is used.

FRYING

The process of cooking food in hot fat. There are three main ways to fry food: pan-frying or sautéing, shallow-fat frying, and deep-fat frying. Frying gives the food a delicious golden-brown colour and a wonderful flavour.

PAN-FRYING

A more modern method of cooking, devised to cook food quickly and easily in a more healthy way. Some fatty foods such as bacon and sausages can be dry-fried because they contain enough of their own fat. Small cuts of meat, poultry and fish are cooked at a high temperature in a very little fat (half oil and half butter are ideal for this because the oil allows the fat to be hot without burning and the butter adds the flavour). The food is added to the hot pan, either with or without a little hot fat, and cooked on one side; the heat quickly seals the food and keeps it moist and tender. It is then turned over and cooked on the other side until cooked through. The food is then removed from the pan to a warm plate and a sauce can be made with the pan juices and a dash of wine or stock. Pan-fried food is served immediately.

SHALLOW-FAT FRYING

This method is used for coated foods, for example fish cakes and crumbed fish, or escalopes of meat and chicken, which are coated with flour or breadcrumbs. Use a vegetable oil such as corn oil in a shallow pan and allow enough oil to prevent the food from sticking. The thicker the food, the more oil you will need. Heat the pan and the oil to a high temperature and add the food: the oil will seal the food and hence will not allow it to absorb too much fat. Once cooked on one side, turn the food over and cook on the other side. Remove it from the frying pan with a fish slice or a slotted spoon, shake it gently to remove excess oil and drain on kitchen paper, which will absorb any remaining fat. Serve at once while still hot.

DEEP-FAT FRYING

With this method, food is cooked whilst completely immersed in hot fat. The choice of fat is important because you need an oil that can be heated to a high temperature without smoking. Corn oil and soya bean oil both have high smoke points – in other words, they smoke at a higher temperature – and are good for deep frying. However, groundnut oil is the best: it has one of the highest smoke points.

Foods need a protective coating when they are deep-fried and popular coverings are breadcrumbs or batter. The most usual foods to deep-fry are potato chips, seafood, fish, and chicken. For this method, you need a deep, heavy pan and a wire basket to lift the food out. It is quite a dangerous method of cooking because a very high temperature is needed and many housefires are caused by deep-fat pans catching fire. A better method is to have an electric deep-fryer, which is thermostatically controlled so it is safer and easier to use.

GRILLING

A very quick and easy method of cooking, which is also very healthy. The food is cooked by radiant heat, which ensures that the outside of the food is well cooked and browned whilst the inside remains moist. The food must be tender and of good quality, for example steak, chops, chicken, burgers, sausages and whole fish like trout and fish cutlets and fillets like salmon and cod. Vegetables such as mushrooms, peppers, tomatoes and onions are also suitable for grilling. The grill must be preheated and the food brushed with oil to give a little protection from the fierce heat. Barbecuing is the outdoor equivalent of grilling and is suitable for all the above foods though it produces a more smoky flavour.

GRIDDLING

A griddle was a flat metal plate, which was used on top of the stove to cook cakes and drop scones. Nowadays the expression 'to griddle' refers to a ridged griddle pan rather like a frying pan – it has a ridged surface, which gives the food attractive brown stripes. This item of equipment has become very popular due to its use by many television chefs. It does produce very appetising food and is a healthy way of cooking because the food only needs a light brushing of oil. Griddling is suitable for thin steaks, chicken, salmon fillets, squid and shellfish, and for vegetables such as aubergines, courgettes, peppers, fennel and onions.

POACHING

A gentle method of cooking food in a liquid at simmering point (see *Simmering*, below). Poaching is suitable for small pieces of fish, for example steaks or fillets, particularly for smoked fish like haddock and cod because the liquid absorbs some of the flavour and can then be used to make a sauce. Whole chickens can be poached so that the meat is succulent and tender and the well-flavoured stock can be used for soups. Whole fish like salmon can be poached to serve whole (see pages 118–19). Poached eggs are simple to cook if you use very fresh eggs. Fruit also lends itself to poaching because the long, slow cooking tenderises the fruit without losing its shape and you have a well-flavoured juice to serve with it.

SIMMERING

A method of cooking in liquid like boiling, but simmering is done at a lower temperature, just below boiling point. It is easy to control because you can judge it by eye. Boiling liquid has large bubbles and the surface is very agitated but liquid at simmering point just has a gentle stream of small bubbles hardly breaking the surface. The simmering method is suitable for vegetables, chicken, fish and fruit.

STEAMING

This technique involves cooking food in the steam of boiling water, either in direct contact or indirectly. Steaming is an

economical method of cooking because more than one item can be cooked at a time. It is also a healthy method of cooking because there is no immersion in water and therefore very little loss of nutrients.

The most usual foods to be cooked by steaming are vegetables; often potatoes are boiled in a saucepan and a steamer is fixed over the top and other vegetables cooked in the steam. You can buy 1–2 tiered steamers, which will fit over your saucepan and enable you to cook more than one vegetable at a time. The firmer vegetable should be at the bottom of the steamer and the more tender one at the top (where it is slightly cooler). The whole steamer is covered with a lid until the vegetables are tender.

Bamboo steamers are now very popular and inexpensive. They can be used for fish, poultry and vegetables. Just bring a small amount of water to the boil in a saucepan or a wok and stack up the steamers containing the food.

Another sort of steamer is the small, folding metal steamer. It is quite small and so not very difficult to store and will fit inside any saucepan. Bring 2.5 cm/1 inch of water to the boil in a saucepan and place the steamer and the vegetables in the pan, cover with the saucepan lid and steam until tender.

Steaming is also used for puddings. The pudding basin, well covered, is placed in the saucepan, on a trivet if you have one. The saucepan is filled halfway up with boiling water and the pudding is steamed for the correct time, checking the water level from time to time. Steaming gives a softer pudding than one that is baked.

ROASTING

This is a method of cooking food in the oven, like baking, but it is usually used for meat, poultry and vegetables (nowadays we roast fish as well). Roasting often requires added fat to protect the food and moisten it while it is cooked at a relatively high temperature. Roasted meats are cooked in a fairly shallow roasting tin to allow the air to circulate and the surface of the meat to brown. Large, tender cuts of meat and tender poultry and game are suitable for roasting. If you are in any doubt about the tenderness of the meat, braise or casserole it instead. The cooking juices can be used to make a gravy to accompany the meat.

The most popular roast vegetable is the potato but we can now roast all sorts of vegetables – parsnips, squashes, turnips, fennel, onions, garlic, carrots, sweet potatoes, tomatoes, peppers and aubergines – giving them a delicious flavour.

SAUTÉING

This method is similar to frying, but sautéing usually means 'moving' the food at the same time. The most common use of this method is preparing onions for stews or casseroles. You fry the onions in a little oil in a frying pan (or a sauté pan, which is slightly deeper) but you keep them moving because they are

finely chopped and need to be kept moving to prevent them from burning in the hot pan. It is this technique that has evolved as stir-frying.

STEWING

This long, slow method of cooking is very like braising, that is to say, cooking in a liquid. It is used for tougher cuts of meat, older chickens and game. In a stew the meat is usually cut up into small pieces and cooked in a large quantity of liquid. The liquid usually needs to be thickened or reduced before serving with the meat. Stewed fruit is often still referred to, but quite often the term 'poached' is now used instead. This is particularly so when the fruit is left whole, as in poached peaches. The term 'stewed apple', when the fruit is broken down to form a purée, is still used.

STIR-FRYING

This is a very quick way of cooking small pieces of food in a healthy and appetising way. It has become a very popular way to cook because it is seen regularly on television programmes and also the availability of woks (see page 30) has become

widespread. Stir-frying means sautéing a variety of foods together. In order to achieve this you need to prepare the meat or fish and the vegetables in advance. Make sure all the pieces are the same size so that they will cook evenly. If you do not have a wok, a large frying pan will suffice. Make sure everything is prepared before you start to cook because it takes very little time once started. Heat a little oil in the pan and make sure it is really hot before cooking. Only cook small quantities at a time because you need the food to fry and not to steam. In fact, I think stir-frying should only be done for 1–2 people at a time – any more and some of you will not have fresh, hot food.

The most successful foods cooked in this way are thin strips of beef or pork, strips of chicken breast, prawns, scallops, slices of salmon, plaice or monkfish and lots of vegetables that are popular in Chinese cooking such as pak choi, Chinese leaves (see page 163), cabbage, mushrooms, peppers and spring onions. Noodles are often added towards the end of the cooking time. Since this method of cooking mainly comes from the orient, suitable flavours are added, for example ginger, soy sauce and sesame oil.

KITCHEN HYGIENE

W hen preparing food, it is necessary to be absolutely rigorous about hygiene. Improper food handling is responsible for many outbreaks of food poisoning, the incidence of which is on the increase. Special care needs to be taken when you are preparing food for vulnerable groups, particularly young children, pregnant women, sick people and convalescents, and elderly people. Here are some basic rules.

Buying
Always buy from a reputable source where you have confidence in their food handling techniques. Buy the freshest foods and the best quality possible.

Storing
Keep food for as short a time as possible before cooking or serving, and ensure that it is stored at a safe temperature. A refrigerator should operate at below 5°C/41°F, so keep a thermometer in the refrigerator and check it from time to time to ensure it is working satisfactorily. Adjust the thermostat when necessary.

Cover all food with clingfilm in the refrigerator so that one food may not contaminate another. Be specially aware of any meat products, which might leak blood on to other foods.

Check 'use by' dates on packs of food before cooking.

Defrost frozen food thoroughly before cooking. Defrost it overnight in the refrigerator rather than at room temperature.

Preparing
Carefully wash any foods that need cleaning and dry well with kitchen paper – this is more hygienic than using a cloth.

Wash your own hands frequently with soap when preparing food. Use a separate hand towel, not a tea towel.

Keep work surfaces clean and use different chopping boards for cooked and uncooked foods, particularly meats. Wash them well and then rinse with diluted bleach between each use. Wash knives and other utensils in hot water and soap between each use.

Keep dish cloths clean and make sure that you change them often. Keep waste bins covered and empty them frequently, disinfecting regularly.

Cooking
Make sure food is cooked thoroughly and serve it piping hot as soon as practicable.

When cooked food needs to be kept, make sure it is cooled quickly, covered, and placed in the refrigerator as soon as possible. It is when food is kept at room temperature that food-poisoning bacteria multiply, so avoid keeping foods for long periods at this temperature.

Only reheat food once; if it is not used up then throw it away. It is safer than risking illness. However, never reheat a marinade, especially one used for marinating meat.

Part 2
Before you cook

UTENSILS

Before you begin to cook, you need to consider the utensils you will need. Everyone has a favourite tool for a particular job but there are a few basics you really need.

KNIVES

These are the most important things in the kitchen. With a good knife you can do most of the tasks you need to prepare basic ingredients. They come in all shapes and sizes and are made from different materials; do be prepared to spend in order to buy the best you can. A good knife will really last a lifetime. You do not need all the knives below: a cook's knife, a serrated knife, and a small vegetable knife would be a good start and then add any of the others when you feel you need them.

Care, safety and sharpening
Good quality knives are made from high-quality steel, which is virtually stainless. It is important that they are kept in a safe place, away from children and also to protect their sharp edges. A knife block is ideal and keeps them always handy for use. A knife roll can also be used but the knives are not so easily accessible.

A sharp knife is safer than a blunt one, so always make sure that the blade is sharpened regularly, either using a steel or a simple pull-through sharpener. It is a pity that the days of the knife grinder are gone, those men who sharpened knives on a revolving stone were very useful. If you have a friendly butcher, he might be persuaded to sharpen your knives for you.

Small vegetable knife

Serrated knife

Cheese knife

Grapefruit knife

Canelle knife

Small vegetable knife

A very small knife, usually only 5–10cm/2–4 inches long, used for peeling small vegetables and fruit. Traditionally this was used by chefs for 'turning' vegetables, that is, shaping them into even-sized small cigar shapes; not really necessary in this day and age. This knife could also be used for filleting meat and fish: work as near to the bone or skin as possible, taking care not to tear the flesh.

Serrated knife

This is an all-purpose knife, the one you reach for when you need to do a quick job like slicing tomatoes and preparing fruit.

Cheese knife

This is really a serving knife for the table. It has a straight, one-sided, serrated edge for cutting through the cheese and has a curved forked tip for serving the pieces.

Grapefruit knife

This is a very flexible knife with a curved, double serrated blade used to cut the flesh from a grapefruit or an orange. If you eat a lot of fruit for breakfast this might be useful. Skill is required in order not to waste too much of the fruit or vegetable. Again practice makes perfect. Luckily there are special peelers available (see page 24).

Canelle knife

This is used as a decorating tool for lemons and other citrus fruit by gouging out thin slices of peel, which can then be used for garnish or to make the sliced fruit look more attractive. It can also be used on cucumbers in the same way.

Cook's knife

This is the most important knife. They come in a range of sizes: choose one that feels comfortable. I have small hands and therefore am happy with a 20 cm/8 inch blade. Chefs tend to use enormous bladed knives but for home use one between 20–30cm/8–12 inches is more suitable. There should be enough space under the handle for the knuckles to sit comfortably and allow you to chop without hitting your hand on the chopping surface. Slicing and chopping are the most usual tasks for this knife. Make sure you keep it sharp and look after it when not in use by keeping it in a protective cover or in a knife block.

The main use of the cook's knife is to chop. The point of the knife is held down with the left hand, and then the knife handle is raised and lowered with the other hand, using enough pressure to cut through the food, repeatedly working in an arc from left to right and back again. A little practice and you will be very proficient and prepare finely chopped ingredients in no time. It is also useful for slicing and shredding. The cook's knife is also used for crushing, using the thick end of the blade on its side. For example, place a clove of garlic under the knife and bring the blade down firmly with enough pressure to crush the clove.

Bread knife

This is a long knife with a serrated blade, which is suitable for cutting through the crust and soft body of a loaf of bread. The art of cutting wafer-thin sandwiches is something our grandmothers were taught; unfortunately, with the wide use of sliced bread, this is now a lost art. However, we still need to cut through loaves when we want thick chunks for toast or for eating the wider range of different breads now available. A bread knife is also useful for cutting and serving cakes. Choose a well-balanced knife with a strong, slightly flexible blade.

Carving knife

This knife usually comes with a carving fork. The knife is quite long, about 30–35 cm/12–14 inches, with a pointed blade that allows you to cut round the bone of a joint. The fork has long, straight prongs, which enable you to hold down the meat so you can carve. The knife must always be kept sharp so that it can slice through the meat to produce neat slices without tearing the flesh. Carving is a lost skill. The head of the household always carved the Sunday roast in front of the whole family, but unfortunately it is becoming less usual for families to eat together and so the skill, passed on from one generation to another, has gone. Using a sharp knife and a good fork will make the job easier.

Palette knife

This is a long-bladed, flexible knife, which is often used to lift food from one place to another. It comes in various sizes. The smaller ones (10 cm/4 inches) are used for spreading butter, cream and icing.

Cook's knife

Bread knife

Carving knife

Palette knife

OTHER CUTTING TOOLS

Good cutting tools make life easier in the kitchen, though they are not absolutely essential if you have a good set of knives.

Mandolin slicer

Cheese slicer

Lemon zester

Apple corer

Vegetable peeler

Scissors

These are the most versatile piece of equipment in the kitchen. Not only are they useful for cutting rinds off bacon, they are wonderful for snipping herbs into a mug and spring onions into salads. They are also useful for trimming pastry and meat. Make sure the blades are fairly long and that the handles are comfortable.

Vegetable peelers

These make the job of peeling firm vegetables and fruit much quicker and more efficient. There are two main types, the traditional swivel-

bladed peeler, and the newer Y-shaped peeler. The Y-shaped peeler is very swift when peeling long vegetables like parsnips and carrots but tends to be more cumbersome and can nick your fingers when peeling smaller vegetables and fruits. Choice is personal, so try out a friend's before buying.

Lemon zester

This popular little tool has a series of small metal circles, which are attached to a handle. You simply scrape the tool down the side of a lemon (or orange or lime) and you

have lovely fine lemon zest, which is much more regular than if you used a grater. The zest can then be used for garnishing or decorating food. Its use also means that you get only the zest and no pith.

Apple corer

This is a specialised tool but because we eat a lot of apples in this country it is probably worth having. It is a cylindrical blade, which you use vertically to cut down through the fruit and remove the whole core in one piece. You then have a lovely

cavity to fill with sugar, butter and dried fruits before you bake the fruit. It is also useful for pears.

Mezzaluna

This kitchen tool has become very fashionable of late, due to its popularity with certain television chefs. It is a useful item because it chops herbs and vegetables quickly. It has a blade shaped like a half-moon, with a handle on either side. You simply rock the blade from side to side and cut through the herbs using the whole length of the blade. Some varieties have two blades, which

Kitchen scissors

Pastry cutters

Cherry stoner

Mezzaluna

make for even quicker chopping. Take care when storing because they are very sharp, and make sure you dry them well after use.

Egg slicer
A wonderful tool that slices hard-boiled eggs into even pieces. It consists of a series of wires held tightly on a frame, which cut through the whole egg to give perfect slices for use as a garnish or in sandwiches.

Cheese slicer
This allows you to slice cheese into very thin wafers, which is useful for sandwiches and for arranging cheese attractively when making a salad. It works best on softer, waxy cheeses like Emmental or Gruyère.

Pastry cutters
These are available in a range of shapes and sizes, fluted and plain. The most useful are the 7.5cm/3 inch size for lining 6cm/2½ inch patty pans for making jam tarts, and the 6cm/2½ inch size, which are perfect for the tops of mince pies. Make sure you wash and dry them well after use to prevent them rusting.

Mandolin slicer
The mandolin slicer is a flat piece of equipment with a slide that is pushed over a blade in order to cut vegetables into fine slices. It is a very good utensil to have in the kitchen if you tend to prepare a lot of vegetables. It allows you to slice vegetables into very thin, uniform slices quickly. There are three types available: wooden, metal and plastic. They also come in a range of sophistication. Some have several blades, both straight and rippled, to give different effects. The cost varies tremendously so you need to

assess how much it would be useful to you and how often you would use it.

Cherry stoner
Another specialist tool but one that works particularly well. It is a simple device for removing stones from cherries. You put the fruit in the tiny bowl and squeeze the prong through the fruit. Out pops the stone and you have stoned cherries quickly. It is probably only worth buying if you have a passion for dishes containing cherries, but it can also be used on olives.

Fish slice

Large wooden spoon

Small wooden spoon

Spatula

Ladle

Draining spoon

Basting spoon

SPOONS AND SPATULAS

A small selection of spoons and spatulas is important, and adds character to your kitchen.

Wooden spoons
These handy utensils are traditional and still most useful in the kitchen. You need a selection of sizes and shapes: a small, short-handled spoon for stirring sauces – the ones with one squared edge are good because they reach into the corners of the pan to ensure even mixing, a large, flat spoon is useful for creaming butter and sugar together in cake making, and a spoon with a very long handle is necessary when making jam.

Wooden spatulas
These are flat with a squared-off end, and are useful for turning food whilst cooking, for example sausages. They are also handy for stirring to ensure even cooking, for example, when frying onions. They are particularly good when used in non-stick saucepans because they do not scratch the surface. I would recommend using flat spatulas for stirring savoury foods and keep separate spoons for stirring sweet foods. In this way you will not run the risk of having onion-flavoured puddings.

Plastic and rubber spatulas
These are used for mixing and folding in ingredients in a bowl when baking and can also be used to reach the bottom of a jug or liquidiser to scrape out the last remnants of food. Care should be taken when using them in hot saucepans because they may not be completely heatproof.

Draining spoon
A very useful tool for removing larger items from liquids, such as boiled and poached eggs. You

can also use it for serving casseroled food, to serve the meat and vegetables before pouring over the sauce.

Ladle
You can buy ladles in various sizes. They are useful for serving soup and other sloppy foods. When making a risotto, you need a ladle to add the hot stock to the rice throughout the cooking process. A ladle is useful for sieving soups and fruit purées: the shape enables it to squeeze the contents through a sieve quickly.

Fish slice
This tool is used for lifting and turning fish during poaching or frying, and is also useful for transferring scones and pastry items from hot baking sheets. The flat, flexible, broad blade can be slipped under the food, which can then be moved easily.

Basting spoon
A large, metal spoon is very useful for stirring, skimming and basting. Try to find a good size, one that is larger than a tablespoon so that you can use it with large mixtures like your Christmas pudding. Also, if it has a good, long handle, it will be safer when basting large joints.

Measuring spoons
In baking where accuracy is important, these spoons can be a great help. They come in all shapes and sizes – usually ¼ teaspoon, ½ teaspoon, 1 teaspoon and 1 tablespoon sizes linked together – and can be made from metal or plastic. They are particularly useful for raising agents, gelatine and spices.

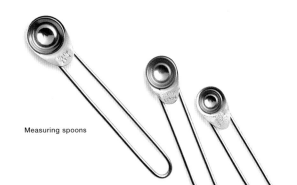

Measuring spoons

Not all of these items are essential: you can just buy them as you need them.

Rotary cheese grater

This is a handy little grater and works very well. It is at its best with medium cheeses like Cheddar. It is best to cut the cheese to the shape of the grater and put it in the container, press down with the lever and turn the handle to grate the cheese. It produces a good, fine grate and is also useful for nuts and chocolate.

Box grater

This is the traditional all-purpose grater. It has four sides for different sized gratings: coarse for cheese and breadcrumbs, fine for harder cheeses like Parmesan and lemon rind, a slicing side for potatoes, cucumbers and other vegetables, and a very fine grater for nutmeg. It is easy to use but can be difficult to clean; an easy tip is to use a pastry brush so that you do not waste any food.

Nutmeg grater

This is specifically for grating nutmegs. Nutmeg is a spice that is much better when freshly grated because it loses its flavour very quickly. Nutmeg graters are small, but some types allow you to store the nutmegs inside.

Nutmeg grinder

These are newer and work on the same principle as a pepper mill. However, I have not had great success with them because they seem to be reluctant to grind well.

Garlic press

A garlic press is useful when you want to use only the puréed garlic flesh. The pressure squeezes the garlic clove through the fine holes in the press, resulting in a smooth purée. Garlic presses can be very fiddly to wash, but they do keep your hands reasonably clean and fresh. If you do not have a garlic press, garlic can be crushed with a heavy knife quite easily.

Pestle and mortar

These popular tools have been used for centuries. They can be made of wood, glass or ceramic. The mortar is the bowl and the pestle is the rounded stick, which is used to grind seeds and spices. They are very satisfactory to use and the flavour of freshly ground spices exceeds those bought ready-ground.

Salt and pepper mills

Pepper mills have been around for years, particularly in Italian restaurants where they are usually of enormous proportions. But they are really useful – there is nothing better than the flavour of freshly milled black pepper; the ready-ground stuff has no flavour, just the sneeze. The traditional wooden ones work well and use a screwing action, which gives a fine grind. Salt is not so important for grinding but a salt mill is good to have on the table for use with salads and vegetables. There are newer mills available now, which work by squeezing two arms together at the top. These have two advantages: they come in a variety of colours and they can be used with only one hand, which is helpful when you have messy hands during cooking.

Pestle

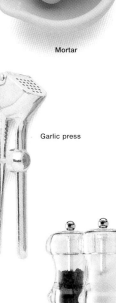
Mortar

Garlic press

Salt and
pepper mills

Nutmeg grinder

Openers

Here are the most useful openers.

Bottle openers

Crown cork openers are needed to remove fixed bottle tops. They come in all shapes and sizes and are quite often incorporated with a corkscrew. Every kitchen will need one if only to open the beer!

Corkscrews

There are many sorts available, from the simplest to the most expensive. If you are fit and strong, then the simple ones will suffice. However, if you have poor strength in your hands or find opening bottles difficult, it will help to pay more for one of the lever-type openers. If you are a wine enthusiast, then a special opener that has a device for cutting the foil round the bottle might suit you.

Tin openers

These tools are essential in this day and age. We eat and drink quite a few things from tins and need to have a simple opener. Some are easier to use than others. One type takes off the rim of the tin and leaves a sharp edge – beware. Make sure the opener has good handles that are easy to grip, and a firm and smooth action. You can buy electric tin openers but it really does depend how much you will use it to warrant the expense.

Bottle
opener

Combined
corkscrew and
bottle opener

Tin opener

Rotary cheese grater

Lemon wedge
squeezer

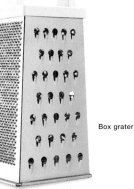
Box grater

EQUIPMENT

BAKING

Once you learn to bake fresh bread and cakes for yourself, and experience the enjoyment of all the enticing smells and tastes, you will need to buy some basic equipment. Here are some suggestions for the most useful items.

Pastry boards

These are not always necessary if you have good work surfaces. However, traditionally a large board made from wood was used to knead dough. It was also traditional to have a piece of marble on which to roll out pastry because of its cool qualities and its smooth surface, which allows the pastry to be moved around easily. If you are going to make pastry on a regular basis, it would be a sound investment to buy a specific board.

Rolling pins

In order to roll pastry well you need a heavy, smooth rolling pin. In emergencies a milk bottle can be used but it does not give an even rolling. Make sure the pin is of adequate length and has a smooth finish. Pins can be bought in a variety of materials: wood is traditional but you can buy metal and glass, which are cooler. Ceramic rolling pins used to be popular but seem to have gone out of fashion now. Rolling pins with handles have also become unpopular because they reduce the surface for rolling.

Pastry brushes

These brushes are useful for all sorts of jobs in the kitchen, such as brushing excess flour from the pastry and for glazing with egg or milk. They are also used for greasing tins and brushing oil on meat and poultry before and during cooking. They are available in all shapes and sizes and in various materials. Wood is traditional but plastic brushes are now available – make sure you

wash and dry them well or the bristles will start to fall out. Paint brushes are often used these days because they have a broad, flat brush, which covers the surface well. It is a good idea to have a very small one and a larger one for different tasks.

Baking beans

For years dried beans or rice have been used to weigh down greaseproof paper or baking foil. This technique is known as 'baking blind', and enables you to cook pastry without a filling until it is crisp; the filling is then added later. Today you can buy ceramic and aluminium 'beans', which have a good weight and will last forever.

Baking trays and sheets

A good, heavyweight baking tray or sheet is a must. It is not worth buying a cheap sheet because it will buckle in the oven and possibly spill the contents. Large baking sheets should have only one upturned edge so that you can slip a large or delicate item on and off easily. Trays with an edge all round are especially useful when making things like sausage rolls because they prevent the fat spilling into the oven. Make sure the trays are not too big for the oven – leave a gap all round in order for the air to circulate properly.

Cake tins

You need to decide what types of cakes you are interested in making because there are so many shapes and sizes of tins available. Perhaps the best

Baking sheet

Cake tin

Springform cake tin

Flan tin

Pie dish

Bun tins

starting point is two 20 cm/8 inch sandwich tins, which are at least 2.5 cm/1 inch deep. They can be used for sponge cakes and victoria sandwiches.

Loaf tins also come in many different sizes. I always use one 900 g/2 lb size and two 450 g/1 lb tins at the same time when making bread (it does not seem worth making a smaller amount of dough or having the oven on for less). They can also be used individually for tea breads and fruit terrines. Always buy the best quality you can afford: non-stick can be helpful but they still require a light coating of oil. Make sure you wash and dry them well before storing.

Bun tins

A set of 12 patty pans or a bun tray is useful for making small cakes, tarts and muffins and also for individual Yorkshire puddings. If you are going to bake quite frequently, or if you might make mince pies for Christmas, a second tray is helpful so that you can assemble one batch whilst one tray is in the oven, making for more efficient working.

Flan dishes

Tart tins, quiche tins, call them what you will, these items are very useful for sweet and savoury dishes. Always use steel tins, because those made from porcelain or glass do not allow the food to cook properly. Loose-based tins are the best because they allow you to remove the tin easily before serving; this is done by placing the flan on an upturned basin and allowing the ring to fall to the surface. You can then transfer the flan on the base to a serving plate. A 20 cm/8 inch flan tin is the most useful size but if you have a large family or frequently cook for six or more people, a 30 cm/12 inch tin would be helpful. Small, individual tins are also available and these can be used for packed lunches or picnics.

Pie dishes

Pie dishes need to be quite deep with a good rim so that the pastry will be supported. They come in a number of sizes, usually oval or round, and can be glazed ceramic or glass. Some are made from enamel and tend to be oblong in shape. Larger ones need to be used with a pie funnel to support the pastry in the centre.

Cooling rack

A cooling rack is particularly useful if you intend to bake bread and cakes. A rack allows the steam to escape from the baked items and prevents them from becoming too soggy. As soon as a cake is baked, turn it out of the tin onto an oven-gloved hand and then place it, base down, on the cooling rack. This way the attractive crust on the top is maintained. Cooling racks can usually be bought in rectangular or circular shapes.

Flour sieve

Sieving flour is important, not only to ensure there are no lumps but also to introduce air. A stainless steel sieve is best, of a medium size. The sieve can also be used to strain vegetables but make sure it is always cleaned and well dried after use. Plastic versions are also available. A very small sieve is useful for sprinkling icing sugar over cakes and desserts, or you could use a tea-strainer.

Flour dredger

A flour dredger makes it easier to sift flour onto a pastry board, pastry and rolling pin because it controls the amount of flour you use. I also find it useful for sprinkling flour into casseroles to prevent lumps forming.

Mixing bowls

These bowls are available in stainless steel, copper, glass, plastic and glazed ceramic. The choice is up to you. I have a large plastic bowl, which I have had for a very long time; it is particularly good because it has a rubber base, which keeps the bowl steady when mixing. A metal bowl is good for whisking egg whites because it keeps cool and the surface can be kept absolutely smooth and clean.

Basins

You will need a variety of sizes for different tasks, such as beating eggs and whipping cream. A selection of small basins is ideal for assembling your prepared ingredients before starting to cook. Some come with lids, which is an added advantage.

Cooling rack

Rolling pins

Flour dredger

Baking beans

Pudding basin

Mixing bowl

Pastry brushes

Baking trays

Griddle pan

Steamer

Individual soufflé dish

COOKWARE

You can start with one or two of the following items to get you going, then add to your collection as your skills develop.

Milk pan

A non-stick milk pan is preferable because milk pans without a non-stick surface are devils to clean. A non-stick milk pan is also wonderful for making sauces and scrambled eggs. Buy one that is well balanced, has a good pouring lip and a solid handle. Always use a wooden spoon or wooden spatula in it. Since your milk pan is likely to be well used, always buy one of a good quality.

Lidded pans

A set in small/medium/large is the best way to buy these. This set will cover all your needs: the small one for poaching/boiling eggs, one or two medium ones for vegetables and the large one for pasta, potatoes and rice. Make sure the bases are solid and flat, the lids are well fitting and the handles are comfortable and heat resistant. You can spend a small fortune on saucepans but you always get what you pay for in terms of quality and durability; good ones will last a lifetime. Choose from stainless steel, cast iron or enamel.

Steamer

This can be used with a medium/large saucepan to allow food to be cooked on the same heat at the same time. A steamer is a perforated, pan-like container, which sits on top of a saucepan and allows the food to be cooked by steaming. It is particularly good for steaming green vegetables over boiling potatoes or rice. Not only is this more economical but the vegetables retain more of their nutritional value cooked this way.

You can buy a steamer to match your saucepans or you can buy a 'universal' steamer with its own lid, which will fit a variety of pan sizes. A steamer is useful if you have limited stove space and want simply-cooked food.

Frying pan

There are many uses for a frying pan and your choice should depend on what you will use it for the most. If it is bacon and egg for one person, then a small pan will be sufficient, but if you want to cook larger quantities, you will need a larger one. Like saucepans, frying pans come in many materials but you must ensure that the base of your frying pan is heavy and flat so that it has good contact with the heat. A lid may be useful to enable you to continue to cook at a slower rate after the initial frying. A heat-proof handle may also be desirable if you want to 'pan-fry' a piece of fish and then place it in the oven to finish off. You can also choose a non-stick pan: opinions are divided as to whether they are of any benefit and whether they last long enough. I personally like a non-stick pan: it is easy to clean and allows the food to move around the pan without using too much oil and without fear of catching. However, treat it carefully so that the non-stick surface is not damaged.

Wok

These deep, rounded pans are very popular for stir-frying small pieces of food. They work best on a gas cooker. A large frying pan can be used instead of a wok.

Omelette pan

If you make omelettes regularly, you will need a pan that you use for nothing else (except perhaps pancakes), because if the pan is used for bacon or onions, it will make an omelette stick more easily. It should be a small pan, about 20 cm/8 inches in diameter, made from stainless steel or cast iron with a non-stick lining. Used carefully and treated well, your omelette pan should last forever.

Griddle

These are very popular at the moment. They are heavy, flat, cast-iron pans with a ridged surface to enable you to cook at a high heat. They produce attractive brown stripes on the food and help to develop a wonderful flavour. Griddles are available in circular or rectangular shapes – the rectangular ones are larger and fit over two burners and act rather like an indoor barbecue. The secret is to heat them to a very high temperature, oil the food well before placing it on the griddle and then leave it alone, without moving the food, for 2–3 minutes to ensure even stripes.

Casseroles

Casserole dishes are for braising or stewing food. I find that if you try to cook in a pot on top of the stove the food always burns a little on the bottom of the pot. A heavy-based casserole is better because it will enable you to start the cooking on top and then put it in the oven for a long, slow cook. Casserole dishes are available in different materials and come in different sizes. You will need a good size so that you can cook a whole chicken, if necessary. Obviously your choice will depend on the size of your household, but a large casserole enables you to cook double quantities and freeze

half for another day. Make sure the casserole has a well-fitting lid and that the two handles are large enough and comfortable so that you can lift the pot easily.

Roasting tins

These are necessary for roasting meat, poultry, game and vegetables. Choose one that is large enough to hold a large bird (for example a turkey) for all your household's needs and one or two smaller ones for when you only need to cook a couple of chicken joints. Make sure the tins are a good, solid weight so that they will not twist in the oven and that they have deep sides to prevent too much splattering. A shallow tin is also very useful for roasting vegetables as an accompaniment. A large one must not be too big for the oven, so allow 5 cm/ 2 inches of space all round to ensure good circulation of air.

Ramekin dishes

Ramekins are small dishes used for cooking in the oven and on the top of the stove. They are generally used for crème brûlée, crème caramel and individual soufflés. They can also be used for baked eggs. They come in a range of materials, including white porcelain, glazed earthenware and glass. They are particularly useful for holding prepared ingredients before you start cooking and are also good for serving small portions of butter and jam.

Soufflé dishes

Traditional soufflé dishes, made from white porcelain, are deep and straight-sided to allow a soufflé mixture to rise easily. They are available in all sizes, but the 1.7 litre/3 pint dish is the most useful and serves four people. A smaller one, 850 ml/1½ pints, is perfect for two people.

Saucepan

Milk pan

Frying pan

Large saucepan with lid

Ramekin dishes

Casserole dish

Colander

Metric/imperial
kitchen scales

Measuring jug

Sieve

Digital kitchen scales

Citrus squeezer

Balloon hand whisks

Double
potato masher

Large kitchen tongs

Small kitchen tongs

OTHER KITCHEN TOOLS

Finally, here are some suggestions for additional things that will make life easier and make you look like a real professional.

Colander

This is necessary for draining cooked vegetables, pasta and anything that has been cooked in water and needs straining. The best colanders you can buy are stainless steel, which are very robust and easy to clean. Make sure your colander is solid and stands on a firm base so that your hands are free to pour from the saucepan.

Sieve

This is sometimes necessary for draining finer ingredients such as rice. It is usually a good idea to keep a separate one for sifting dry ingredients such as flour and sugar, or, if you use the same one for draining and sifting, make sure it is completely dry before sifting.

Kitchen timer

A timer is essential in the kitchen. If you do not have one, you should go and buy one. There are many available, from simple to hi-tech, but make sure your timer is reliable and the ring is loud enough to hear above the radio.

Knife sharpener

In order to keep your knives sharp, you are going to need a sharpener. You can choose between a steel or a pull-through device to achieve a good edge. A steel is the professional way and takes a bit of practice but gives a sound result.

Measuring jug

This is important for liquid measurements when recipe quantities need to be exact. It can be bought in various materials, for example metal, plastic and glass. Metal ones are difficult to read, however, and glass ones tend to be rather heavy and of course can be dropped and broken. The newer plastic ones, which are made from polypropylene, withstand boiling liquids and have very clear print, making it easy to see the measurements. A 1.2 litre/2 pint size is the most useful.

Kitchen tongs

These are necessary for transferring hot food from the cooking utensil to the plate. They are also useful for turning food in a hot pan when cooking or barbecuing. They should be a good length and fit the hand easily. They are usually made from stainless steel so they are hard-wearing and do not discolour.

Citrus squeezers

There are many occasions when you will need the juice of a lemon or an orange, so a squeezer is a sensible piece of equipment to have. There are two different types. The first is a traditional squeezer made of glass or plastic, used by pressing a half of the fruit down onto the raised section and twisting it until the juice runs into the lower part of the dish; small, raised pieces of glass prevent the pips from joining the juice, or holes in the plastic variety allow the juice to drain through. The other type is a hand-held one (a reamer), which you can use over a bowl or saucepan directly; these are available in wood and plastic. You simply use a screwing action into the halved fruit and the juice falls into the receptacle; the only problem with this one is that you might get the pips as well.

Balloon hand whisk

There are many sizes available, from tiny (for whisking a mug of hot chocolate) to medium (for use in saucepans) and large (for whisking egg whites). Look for a good-quality, stainless steel whisk that will not discolour, and choose a size with a comfortable handle to suit your needs.

Potato masher

A masher is a valuable tool for making mashed vegetables, which are now very popular again. Choose a strong-handled masher because it will need to do quite heavy work. A comfortable handle is essential because you will have to put quite a lot of pressure into breaking down the lumps to make a smooth mash. A masher is also useful for stewed apples.

Scales

For many recipes you can manage to do without scales by using a measuring jug or by using cups and spoons. However, when you want to cook more precise recipes, such as baked items, then the accuracy is important and you should consider some scales. There are many types around: some cost modest amounts and some cost a king's ransom. Personally I use balance scales with weights, in both metric and imperial. There are also spring scales available, which have a bowl on top of the dial; make sure the bowl is large enough to weigh out bulky items like flour and pasta and that the dial is clear and large enough to read. Electronic scales are very hi-tech, both in use and in design – the weights flash up on the digital display and you can choose to weigh in either metric or imperial. They are very accurate but you may need to replace the batteries from time to time.

Chopping boards

A good knife is only as good as its chopping surface. Wooden boards have always been the traditional ones to use because they 'give' with the pressure of the blade and do not blunt it. A solid chopping board will cost you rather a lot but should last you a lifetime. Polyethylene chopping boards have become more popular because they can be sterilised and will even go in the dishwasher. They are probably a good idea for raw meat and poultry to ensure that everything is completely hygienic. Chopping boards are available in different colours, which are useful for ensuring you do not cut fruit on the same board on which you have just chopped garlic. In fact, a tiny board kept just for garlic is very useful.

Thermometers

Oven

An oven thermometer is useful if you are uncertain about your oven temperature, particularly if you are living or staying in a place where the cooker is unfamiliar. This thermometer is not essential but it could prevent disasters.

Oven thermometer

Meat

This thermometer is useful for checking if a large piece of meat is cooked through. It is particularly good for beef, because the temperature will tell you if it is rare, medium or well done.

Sugar

This is useful if you are making jam, marmalade or toffees. You can check the temperature during the process and ensure good setting.

Jam thermometer

Refrigerator

This thermometer checks that your refrigerator and freezer are working at the correct temperatures. It might save unnecessary food wastage.

Kitchen timer

Chopping boards

Sharpening steel

ELECTRICAL EQUIPMENT

There are all sorts of electrical equipment for the kitchen but all are rather expensive and many are for specific tasks. If we ignore kettles and toasters (they are not really 'cook's equipment') we can pick out two or three that will help take the hard work out of some food preparation.

Blender

Food processor

Standing mixer

Hand blender

Hand mixer

This is an inexpensive tool but very worthwhile. It enables you to beat and whisk very quickly, saving time and energy. It consists of an electric motor in the hand section and has two rotary beaters, which turn at variable speeds to incorporate air into mixtures. The beaters can also be used in saucepans to break down lumps and make purées. The whisks just slip out and are reasonably easy to clean, even in a dishwasher.

Standing mixer

This is a traditional mixer, which has a large bowl and a range of three basic tools – a wire whisk, a beater and a dough hook – so that mixtures can be whisked, beaten and kneaded. It is a very useful piece of equipment if you want to bake cakes and bread in quite large quantities. Some models come with a blender attached so that all kitchen tasks can be accomplished with one machine. The drawback of this machine is its expense and its heavy weight. It also needs to be kept out on the work top to facilitate easy use. However, once bought, it should last for many years and will take a lot of the drudgery out of cooking.

Blender

These can be bought free-standing and are essential if you want to make puréed soups, milk shakes and smoothies. They come in a range of prices and sizes, so choose one that will suit your needs.

Food processor

This machine performs many tasks, so it is really useful. It consists of a bowl placed on top of a high powered motor. It comes with one very sharp blade for general use but also comes with slicing and grating disks. It can chop, mince, slice, grate, shred, mix, blend, make breadcrumbs and knead dough. It is so versatile and has so many uses that it is worthwhile considering despite the high cost. Choose one with an adequate-sized bowl for your needs and make sure you store the blade carefully because it is extremely sharp.

CONVERSION CHARTS

OVEN TEMPERATURES

Celsius	Fahrenheit	Gas Mark	Oven Heat
110°	225°	¼	very cool
120°	250°	½	very cool
140°	275°	1	cool
150°	300°	2	cool
160°	325°	3	moderate
180°	350°	4	moderate
190°	375°	5	moderately hot
200°	400°	6	moderately hot
220°	425°	7	hot
230°	450°	8	very hot

SPOON MEASUREMENTS

1 teaspoon of liquid = 5 ml

1 tablespoon of liquid = 15 ml

OTHER MEASUREMENTS

Volume

Metric	Imperial
50 ml	2 fl oz
100 ml	3½ fl oz
150 ml	5 fl oz
200 ml	7 fl oz
300 ml	10 fl oz
450 ml	16 fl oz
500 ml	18 fl oz
600 ml	1 pint
700 ml	1¼ pints
850 ml	1½ pints
1 litre	1¾ pints
1.5 litres	2¾ pints
2.8 litres	5 pints
3 litres	5¼ pints

Weight

Metric	Imperial
5 g	⅛ oz
10 g	¼ oz
25 g	1 oz
50 g	2 oz
75 g	2¾ oz
85 g	3 oz
100 g	3½ oz
150 g	5½ oz
225 g	8 oz
300 g	10½ oz
450 g	1 lb
500 g	1lb 2 oz
1 kg	2 lb 4 oz
1.5 kg	3 lb 5 oz

Linear

Metric	Imperial
2 mm	1/16 inch
3 mm	⅛ inch
5 mm	¼ inch
8 mm	⅜ inch
1 cm	½ inch
2 cm	¾ inch
2.5 cm	1 inch
5 cm	2 inches
7.5 cm	3 inches
10 cm	4 inches
20 cm	8 inches
30 cm	1 foot
46 cm	1½ feet
50 cm	20 inches

THE STORECUPBOARD

*W*hilst different lifestyles mean it is impossible to decide what everyone
should have in their storecupboard, a basic range of essentials will at
least enable you to enhance your meals and also to produce a few quick and
simple dishes when time or fresh produce are in short supply. This will be
particularly important for people with limited accommodation. If you have
more space available, though, you can keep some really delicious and
interesting ingredients for meals and to keep in reserve for an emergency.

FLOURS

Storage
Always buy flour in the quantities you need. If you are going
to bake bread, buy flour in large bags, but if you hardly ever
use flour, buy the smallest pack. Store it in the dark in an
airtight container in a cool, dry place. White flour will keep
for 6 months or more, but whole-grain flours should be used
within a shorter period because they contain more oil and may
turn rancid. Check packs for 'use by' dates.

Plain flour

Cornflour

Plain wholemeal flour

Malted brown flour

Self-raising flour

Strong bread flour

Plain flour

This is useful for thickening casseroles, making sauces, coating food such as escalopes of meat and chicken before cooking, and rolling out bought pastry.

Cornflour

This flour provides a quick way to thicken sauces.

Wholemeal flour

Wholemeal flour is ideal for making bread and pastry.

Malted flour

This flour is used for breadmaking and crumbles.

Self-raising flour

Self-raising flour is used for baking cakes, biscuits and desserts.

Strong bread flour

This flour is used for breadmaking. It has a higher percentage of gluten, which gives the dough its elasticity. Bread flour can be white, brown and wholemeal.

SUGARS

Storage

Store sugars in airtight containers in a cool, dry place for up to 12 months. They may need sifting before use if slightly damp. Brown sugars may harden during storage; if so, place in a bowl and cover with a damp cloth for 2–3 hours or overnight. The sugar will absorb the moisture and will then be soft and usable.

Granulated sugar

This is the one sugar you need on a day-to-day basis. Use it to sweeten tea or coffee (if you take sugar). You can also use it on cereals and with fruits when they are too sharp. Granulated sugar is also useful for desserts and crumbles.

Caster sugar

This is finer than granulated sugar and is better for cakes, biscuits, and meringues. It dissolves quicker and is therefore used for syrups for fruit salad and for custards and sauces.

Icing sugar

A very finely powdered sugar, used for making icings and for sprinkling over cakes and desserts as decoration. It often turns lumpy in storage so it is essential to sift it before use.

Brown sugar

This is a moist sugar, which is available in varying shades depending on how much molasses is present. Light brown sugar is suitable for cakes and desserts, while flavoursome dark brown sugar (muscovado) is only suitable for rich cakes like Christmas cake or gingerbreads,

and dark puddings like toffee sponge where its pronounced flavour contributes to the overall taste. Dark brown sugar is also good where stickiness is desirable, such as in flapjacks and brownies, because its texture is more moist and heavier.

Demerara sugar

This is a partly refined sugar, which has some percentage of molasses. It is used mainly for its texture – it has large, crunchy granules, which give cakes, biscuits and crumble toppings their characteristic appearance.

Preserving Sugar

This sugar is specifically designed for jam-making. Its large crystals dissolve quickly, forming a clear jam with a minimum of scum.

Sugar crystals

These are used to top baked goods such as Bath buns. Brown crystals are also available, which are served with coffee as sweeteners.

Sugar cubes

These are available in white and brown. They are very decorative and are generally used for sweetening beverages.

Granulated sugar

Caster sugar

Icing sugar

Light brown sugar

Demerara sugar

Preserving sugar

Dark muscovado sugar

Crystallised sugar

Cubed white sugar

Cubed brown sugar

OILS

Good oil is important for many kitchen tasks – for frying, brushing foods before grilling, baking, making salad dressings and simply drizzling over food to flavour and garnish it.

Storage

Oils keep for 10–12 months if kept in a cool, dark place but sometimes will turn rancid. Check bottles for 'use by' dates. Once opened they will start to deteriorate. Buy specialist oils in small quantities.

Sunflower oil

A good, all-purpose oil, which can be used for all cooking methods. It is a light oil with very little flavour so it can also be used to make dressings (perhaps mixed with a little olive oil).

Olive oil

If you like salads, it is worth buying olive oil because dressings made with it are far superior due to the wonderful flavour. You can also cook with olive oil but of course it is more expensive.

Extra-virgin olive oil

This is the best olive oil you can buy, but it is expensive. It varies in colour from pale yellow to a rich green, often depending on its country of origin. Some people prefer Italian, others Greek; it depends on what kind of foods you eat. Experiment with small bottles and see which you prefer. Use it for salad dressings and pasta, and for drizzling over grilled vegetables (there is a wonderful Italian oil mixed with lemon flavour, which is ideal for this).

Corn oil

A cheaper oil with quite a strong flavour, which some people do not like. It is suitable for deep-fat frying, so if you often cook fried foods this is a good buy.

Soya oil

This oil is cheap and has a high smoke point (smokes at a very high temperature), so it is suitable for deep-frying. However, it has quite a strong flavour, which some people find unpleasant.

Groundnut oil

A light oil, which is suitable for all types of cooking. It has a very mild flavour and is good for mayonnaise and dressings.

Sesame oil

This is a dark, nutty oil frequently used in Chinese and Thai cooking. It has a wonderful flavour and aroma, sweet and very pungent. If used alone it will burn easily, so it is best mixed with sunflower oil for cooking. Alternatively, you can cook in olive oil and use the sesame oil to flavour the food just before serving, as I do. It also makes a superb dressing for oriental salads – just mix it with a little lemon juice and soy sauce.

Nut oils

Walnut oil and hazelnut oil have wonderful flavours for dressings. They are particularly good when served with a salad containing a few similar nuts. They can also be drizzled over vegetables and pasta and added to bread dough.

Nut oil

Corn oil

Basil-flavoured
olive oil

Olive oil

Extra-virgin olive oil   Sunflower oil

Vegetable oil

VINEGARS

Vinegars have many uses in cooking and there are many different ones in the shops. Each country has its own style, for example Britain has malt and cider vinegar, France has wine vinegars, Spain has sherry vinegar and Italy has balsamic.

Storage
Keep vinegars in a dark, cool place for up to 6–12 months. Buy small bottles so that you can use them up at their best.

Balsamic vinegar
This vinegar is very popular now. It originated in Modena in Italy and is the richest of all the vinegars, with a deep brown colour and a fruity sweet flavour. The best varieties are aged in oak barrels for up to 25 years, but can be very expensive. Good things are worth paying for, however, so treat yourself. Buy some on holiday in Italy if you can because it will be less expensive. Use it in dressings for salads with some interesting leaves and sprinkle it over simple fish dishes, pasta, roasted vegetables and soups. Plates can be garnished with small drops of this vinegar before arranging food on them – a neat 'chef's' trick.

Cider vinegar
A light vinegar with a slightly fruity flavour, used for pickling fruits and making dressings like the white wine variety. It is also used in recipes with apples.

Flavoured vinegars
There are many of these available, such as raspberry vinegar and walnut vinegar. However, unless you have a particular favourite, it is probably better to concentrate on a good olive oil. Fruit-flavoured vinegars were very fashionable but quite often stayed in the cupboard and lost their potency.

Malt vinegar
If you are a fish-and-chip fanatic or a pickle-and-chutney maker, this is the vinegar for you. Otherwise avoid it. The colourless variety is distilled and very strong (up to 12% acetic acid) and is used for pickling onions where the colour needs to be preserved. The dark-brown vinegar (available in fish and chip shops) is coloured with caramel and used to make chutneys. Do not try to make a dressing with this.

Sherry vinegar
This is used in Spanish recipes and salad dressings. Gazpacho (a Spanish cold soup) has sherry vinegar in the recipe and the vinegar can be used in sauces and other soups. It has a smooth flavour and can be used in dressings for salads with more robust flavours.

Red wine vinegar
Red varieties can be used in the same ways as white ones, although they have a more robust flavour. You need to try some different brands to decide which is the one for you.

White wine vinegar
A good, all-round vinegar, which can be used for dressings and sprinkling over food. It is mild and has a good flavour.

White wine vinegar   Red wine vinegar   Malt vinegar

Balsamic vinegar

SAUCES

You can have many sauces in the storecupboard for use in cooking and for use at the table – the choice depends on which type of food you enjoy.

Storage

Buy only those sauces you will use regularly – especially the oriental varieties – or you will have a cupboard full of out-of-date sauces. Keep them in a cool, dry, dark place; once opened, you might like to store them in the refrigerator. Check labels for information and 'use by' dates.

Tomato ketchup
This is a favourite for almost everyone, and goes particularly well with sausages, burgers, fish fingers and chips.

Brown sauce
This sauce is good in sweet-and-sour sauces and goes very well with bacon and egg.

Worcestershire sauce
This very spicy sauce has been a favourite in Britain for many years. Add it to casserole dishes and soups for a fiery flavour. It is also used in a Bloody Mary (a vodka-tomato juice cocktail).

Soy sauce
This is a popular Chinese sauce. It is used with all oriental foods, both in cooking and at the table. It adds a salty flavour, which is typical of this type of food. Soy sauce comes in light and dark varieties: use the light one with seafood and chicken and the dark one with duck and meat.

Sweet chilli sauce
This hot sauce made from chillis, vinegar, sugar and salt is traditionally used as a dipping sauce, although it is sometimes used in cooking. If the flavour is too strong for you, the sauce can be diluted with hot water.

Plum sauce
This is also traditional with Peking duck but it can be served with other dishes. It has a fruity flavour with a spicy overtone and is an instant dipping sauce for crab cakes, spring rolls and won tons.

Oyster sauce
A thick, dark-brown sauce consisting of oysters and brine and heavily flavoured with soy. It is used with all sorts of dishes – fish, vegetables and meat – where it imparts an oriental flavour.

Thai fish sauce (*nam pla*)
This sauce is used in many recipes in Thai cooking. It is rather like soy sauce; it adds flavour but also brings out the flavour of the other ingredients.

Brown sauce   Sweet chilli sauce   Oyster sauce   Dark soy sauce

Tomato ketchup   Plum sauce   Thai fish sauce

Worcestershire sauce

Pudding rice

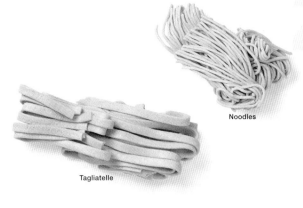

Noodles

Long-grain brown rice

Tagliatelle

White rice

RICE

A small range of different kinds of rice opens up a wide area of savoury and sweet dishes. A good basic rice to have in your storecupboard is long-grain rice. For a wider choice, try basmati rice, risotto rice, pudding rice, and brown rice. For more details see pages 181–2.

Storage
Store rice in airtight containers in a cool, dry place. Rice will keep for up to three years if stored correctly, so it is a good, long-term storecupboard item. If you have space and containers, it is a good idea to buy large packs because they are more economical (but only if you are going to use them).

PASTA

There are so many varieties of pasta available that you should stick to the ones you use regularly or you will end up with lots of half-empty packets. Spaghetti and macaroni are good basic pastas to have in your storecupboard. For a wider choice, try lasagne (sheets), cannelloni (tubes), fusilli (spirals), farfalle (bows), vermicelli (fine, hair-like pasta), tagliatelle (ribbons), conchiglie (shells) and stuffed pasta such as tortellini and ravioli. For more details see pages 180–1.

Storage
Dried pasta needs to be stored in a cool, dry place and will keep for around 18–24 months. The richer egg pastas will not keep as long as the plain varieties, so check labels for storage information. Fresh pasta should be stored in the refrigerator and eaten within 1–2 days.

NOODLES

Under this heading we are dealing with Asian noodles. They are fine noodles, which only need soaking in hot water or are quick to cook. Noodles in this category include egg noodles, rice noodles, cellophane noodles and Japanese noodles. For more details see page 181.

Storage
Keep fresh and dried noodles in a cool, dry place and use by the date on the packs.

Assorted dried pasta shapes

Spaghetti

Aduki beans

Red lentils

Haricot beans

Chickpeas

Red kidney beans

BEANS, CHICKPEAS AND LENTILS

These are all known as pulses and are a good, economical source of protein. They are available dried and in tins. Using tinned pulses cuts out the soaking and cooking time and makes them a useful, instant convenience food. Basic pulses to keep in your storecupboard include haricot beans, chickpeas and lentils. For a wider choice, try butter beans, cannellini beans, flageolet beans and red kidney beans. Other beans you might like to try include soya beans, pinto beans, borlotti beans, black-eyed beans, black beans, and aduki beans. They all have different shapes and colours and can be used to add bulk to casseroles and soups.

Storage

Buy dried beans, chickpeas and lentils in small quantities from a source that has a quick turnover. The longer you keep these dried pulses the longer you will need to cook them because they toughen with age. Store in airtight containers in a cool, dry place for up to 1–2 years.

GRAINS

It is useful to have both couscous and polenta in your storecupboard because they are quick to cook and are a good staple to accompany any meat or fish dishes.
For further details see pages 182.

Storage

Keep grains in an airtight container in a cool, dry place for up to 18 months.

Couscous

Polenta

DRIED FRUITS

Many fruits are available dried and can be used in a variety of dishes. Dried fruits can also be eaten as a healthy snack food. Traditionally, dried fruits meant currants, sultanas and raisins; then we had prunes, apricots and dates. Nowadays we have dried pears, peaches, apples, figs, bananas, cherries, cranberries, blueberries, mangoes, papaya and pineapples. All can be used in baking and savoury dishes. They can also be added to muesli for breakfast.

Storage

Buy only what you need because the shelf life of dried fruits is only 6–8 months. It is useful to buy them from stores where you can weigh out the amount you need, rather than buying them in a certain-sized packet. Store them in an airtight container in a cool, dry place.

Dried dates

Raisins

Almonds

NUTS

A few nuts are useful in the storecupboard to add texture to some dishes, but do not buy too many because they go rancid after only 2–3 months.

Storage

Nuts are best stored in a cool, dry place in an airtight container to prevent rancidity. Only buy small quantities when you know you will use them.

Walnuts
Walnuts are good in both salads and stuffings.

Almonds
These nuts are good for crumbles and fruit salads and are also useful in baking.

Pine kernels
These are actually kernels of pine cones and are wonderful tossed in salads or rice dishes. Their flavour is improved if they are dry-fried or grilled until golden brown.

Cashew nuts
These sweet nuts have a soft, crunchy texture and are often used in oriental dishes and in some Indian cooking. Add them at the end of the cooking time for the best flavour.

Chestnuts
These are popular at Christmas time, both for stuffings and as an accompaniment to Brussels sprouts. They are also used in desserts, most often with chocolate. Chestnuts are available

whole (with skins that are difficult to remove), dried (which need soaking), vacuum-packed (which are very convenient), or tinned. They are also available in purée form, both sweetened and unsweetened.

Hazelnuts
Hazelnuts are also known as cob nuts in Britain. They are small, round nuts, which are usually used in cakes, pastries and desserts.

Peanuts
These are best bought roasted or salted and can be used in salads and stir-fries with rice and pasta. They can also be ground to form the basis of a satay sauce.

Pistachio nuts
These attractive nuts can be used in cooking or eaten as a snack. They are available salted in their shells (for snacks) and also unsalted and shelled, which are the most useful for cooking. They are also used in pâtés, stuffings and as a colourful garnish.

Cashew nuts

Pine kernels

Pistachio nuts

Peanuts

Hazelnuts

Walnuts

Sweetcorn

Baked beans

Anchovies

Tuna

Artichoke hearts

Crab

Olives

Chopped tomatoes

Sardines

CANNED GOODS

Some essential foodstuffs come in cans and also one or two delicacies are available canned.

Storage

Cans have a long shelf life but it is easy to leave them at the back of the cupboard and forget about them. Check them regularly and use them before their 'use by' date.

Tomatoes

These are available whole or chopped. If you use them in casseroles, it will not matter if they are whole because they will cook down. However, if you want to make a quick pasta sauce, the chopped variety is better.

Baked beans

I cannot imagine many households having no use for this staple food. Baked beans are popular with adults and children of all ages: they make a healthy, quick meal or a useful addition to a simple food like sausages. They can be eaten hot for breakfast, lunch or supper, and do try them cold for flavour.

Tuna

A can of tuna is another useful standby. It can be eaten simply with a salad or used to make a pasta or rice dish. Tuna is economical and full of protein, and is a versatile storecupboard item.

Sweetcorn

Canned sweetcorn is easier to store and use than frozen and it is very versatile. It can be added to soups and casseroles as well as being a vegetable in its own right.

Artichoke hearts

These are useful for salads and starters, and can be added to a platter of grilled vegetables.

Bamboo shoots

Bamboo shoots make a good addition to oriental dishes, especially stir-fries.

Water chestnuts

These are used in Chinese hot dishes and salads.

Coconut milk

This is a popular ingredient in all Thai recipes, and is a very quick and useful ingredient. Coconut milk can also be used for cooking rice and in desserts.

Red peppers

These are wonderful when you have no time to grill and skin peppers. They are ready to add to salads, soups and casseroles.

Anchovies

These are used for pizzas, salads and garnishes.

Crab

A useful extravagance for pasta and quiches. Buy the best quality possible. You can often get better value if you buy it abroad.

Sardines

These make a delicious snack served with lots of buttered toast, or as an instant pâté with butter and lemon juice.

Olives

There is a wide variety of olives available; some are flavoured with herbs. Choose your favourites and keep them for nibbling and also for use in pastas and on pizzas.

Pulses

Canned pulses save lots of time in preparation and cooking (see page 42).

CONDIMENTS

Storage

Keep salt very dry because it tends to attract water and will solidify. Buy pepper as peppercorns and store in a cool, dry place. Dried mustard keeps well for 1–2 years in a cool, dry place. However, once jars of wet mustard are open, you should keep them in the refrigerator. They will keep for 6–8 months. Buy small sizes unless you are addicted to them.

Salt

If you have only one type of salt, make sure it is sea salt. It has more flavour than ordinary table salt and not only flavours food but is a useful garnish. Buy it in flakes, which can easily be crushed with the fingers or in a mill at the table. If you are cooking for a large number of people, then cooking salt can be used to salt vegetable water and water for cooking pasta and rice. It is more economical – keep it by the cooker.

Pepper

A wide range of peppers is available (see pages 54–55).

Mustards

English mustard powder

This has always been popular because it can be used in recipes as well as mixed to a paste with water to serve with steaks, beef and ham. It has a strong, pungent flavour and quite a kick.

Dijon mustard

The traditional mustard of France is now gaining in popularity because it has a milder flavour than English mustard and comes ready-mixed. It is delicious in ham sandwiches and is also good for glazing a ham joint. It can also be used wherever you might use any mustard.

Moutarde de Meaux

A whole-grain mustard, which is now also widely used in Britain. It does not have the strong flavour of English mustard, but it does have a wonderful texture, which makes it a good ingredient in sauces. Mustard sauce and mustard mayonnaise are made with this mustard. Try to buy a French brand.

English mustard

Moutarde de Meaux

Dijon mustard

2

OTHER ITEMS

Gelatine
This is used to set jellies, mousses and soufflés. You can buy it in packets of granules or leaf gelatine. It should be stored in a dry place.

Poppy seeds
These very tiny, blue-black seeds are often used as garnish, in salads or in baking. They have a mild flavour and add a nice crunch to food as well as an attractive colour.

Sesame seeds
These seeds are best if they are lightly roasted before use, either under the grill or dry-fried in a frying pan. Sprinkle them on top of salads or add them to bread mixes and dressings.

Cocoa
Cocoa powder is often used for baking and desserts, and can also be used for hot chocolate drinks. Keep it in a cool, dry place.

Sun-dried tomatoes
These can be snipped into salads and added to pasta sauces to give a vibrant flavour.

Pesto sauce
This is available in jars: red and green varieties are a good standby. Ready-made pesto is not as good as making your own, but it is a really useful item for making a quick pasta supper.

Stock cubes or powder
Different flavours (chicken, fish, meat and vegetable) are useful when fresh stock is not available. The powder is very convenient because you can add very small amounts. You can now buy organic stock, which has been produced without artificial chemicals.

Syrup
This is mainly used for baking biscuits and flapjacks and in treacle tarts and sauces. Sweet syrup is also delicious served with porridge.

Honey
Honey can be used as a sweetener in beverages, spread on toast, or spooned over yoghurt. There are many flavours available and the runny type is probably the easiest to use.

Coffee
There are many types available: keep yours in an airtight container or in the freezer.

Tea
Keep your favourite varieties – leaves or teabags – in airtight tins.

Maple syrup

Sesame seeds

Sun-dried tomatoes

Honey

Tea leaves

Cocoa

Red pesto sauce

Coffee beans

Stock cubes

REFRIGERATOR ESSENTIALS

Butter
Keep some butter not just for spreading but for cooking too. Unsalted varieties are available and are good spread on bread and also for baking cakes and sweet pastries.

Bread
There are many varieties available. A wholemeal loaf will keep for a week if well wrapped in plastic.

Milk
Ideal for adding to beverages and pouring over cereals. It is also essential for white sauces. Semi-skimmed milk is a good choice both for drinking and cooking. Milk keeps in the refrigerator for 4–7 days, but check the label for the 'use by' date.

Crème fraîche
This keeps in the refrigerator for far longer than cream (up to 2 weeks) so it is a useful standby and it does not curdle when added to hot sauces.

Eggs
Keep half a dozen eggs ready for use. You can then knock up an omelette or scrambled eggs on toast for a quick supper.

Cheese
Keep a small portion of Cheddar and a small portion of fresh Parmesan on standby in the refrigerator, both for nibbling and for cooking. Make sure you use the cheeses by the 'use by' date on the packaging.

Bacon
This is a good standby for a quick sandwich or as the base of a pasta sauce.

Chocolate
If you have some good-quality chocolate, you will always have the perfect end to a meal (with a good coffee), or a little indulgence now and again. Try to choose chocolate that has at least 70 per cent cocoa solids.

Eggs

Butter

Cheese

Bread

Milk

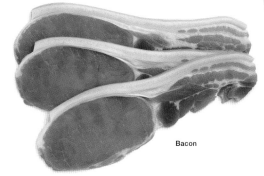

Bacon

Chocolate

FLAVOURINGS, HERBS AND SPICES

This is a range of the most popular flavourings you might need for your own cooking. You will not need them all to start with — your choice will depend on your own tastes. If you are a fan of curries, for example, you will need a range of spices, but if you prefer Italian flavours then a good supply of herbs will be necessary.

FLAVOURINGS

Capers
These small, green flower-buds of the caper bush grow all round the Mediterranean. They are pickled in vinegar or preserved in oil and are available in jars or tins. It is a good idea to rinse them before use. They have a sharp, sour flavour and are used in pizza toppings, pasta sauces and the Italian 'salsa verde', which is a strongly flavoured sauce served with fish. Buy them in small jars and store in the refrigerator for up to 2–3 months once opened. Make sure they keep covered with the preserving liquid.

Juniper berries
These are the berry-like fruits of a tree of the Cyprus family. The berries are small, dark-purple and wrinkled, but have a wonderful flavour that is associated with gin. They are very good with game and pork, in stuffings and also with cabbage, particularly red cabbage. The berries need to be crushed in a pestle and mortar or

with the end of a rolling pin before use to allow the oils to escape. They are now available dried and they keep well for 1–2 years.

Garlic
An indispensable ingredient for many savoury dishes. It keeps well in a dry, airy place.

Lemons
Lemons are one of the most popular flavourings in the kitchen. They can be used in sweet and savoury dishes and in a variety of ways, either whole, sliced, cut into segments, just the juice or just the grated lemon rind, which has an intense flavour due to its aromatic oils. Lemons are available all the year round, so buy them regularly and store them in the refrigerator for up to 10 days. Once cut, cover the surface with clingfilm to retain moisture. Freeze slices for use in drinks, which is a good way to use up an odd half. If you are using the lemon zest, try to buy the unwaxed variety.

Garlic

Juniper berries

Lemon

Capers

HERBS

A wide variety of fresh herbs is now available in supermarkets so you can use them all the year round. Alternatively, you can grow them in your garden or on a windowsill so that you can have them really fresh. It is always better to use fresh wherever possible but you can now buy frozen herbs, which are a great improvement on the dried sort.

Buy herbs as you need them so that you use them as fresh as possible. Choose herbs with bright colours and no wilting leaves. If you are buying pot-grown herbs, water them carefully and keep them in a sunny position. Snip the herbs from the pot and allow them to grow on before cutting again. Packaged herbs are best kept in the refrigerator, either wrapped in a plastic bag or in a small container of water. Dried and frozen herbs are available and can be useful whenever the fresh is not obtainable: use 1 teaspoon of dried instead of 1 tablespoon of fresh or frozen.

Basil

A delicate herb, which is very difficult to grow in Britain. It has a wonderful flavour and is particularly good with tomatoes and Italian recipes. It is also an important ingredient in Thai cooking. It has a sweet, pungent flavour with a touch of aniseed. The leaves are very tender and bruise and discolour easily. They should therefore be torn carefully and added to dishes at the last moment to prevent loss of flavour. Use them in pasta dishes, pizzas, with fish, Italian cheeses and salads, and particularly in tomato dishes and salad dressings.

Borage

A very pretty herb, which is easily grown in British gardens. It is mainly used for drinks and soups because the leaves have a slightly cucumber flavour; the blue flowers are an attractive decoration. The herb can also be used in salads.

Bay leaves

These long, oval leaves from the bay tree are used in stocks and many meat dishes, particularly casseroles because the long, slow cooking allows the flavour to permeate the food. They can be used fresh or dried and are one of the ingredients in a bouquet garni. They can also be used to garnish finished pâtés or terrines.

Bouquet garni

This is the traditional collection of herbs tied together to flavour stocks and stews. It normally includes parsley stalks, thyme and rosemary sprigs and a bay leaf.

Chervil

A very attractive herb with a subtle aniseed flavour. It can be used with fish, chicken and cheese, and is particularly good with egg dishes such as omelettes. It is also good in salads and its curly, delicate fronds make an excellent garnish.

Chives

Chives are very easy to grow and produce pretty purple flowers, which can be used for garnishing. It is a very useful herb: it is a member of the onion family and has a distinct flavour. Use it where a mild onion flavour is desired, with eggs, cheese, salads, soups, fish and chicken. A quick sauce can be made by adding chives to soured cream to serve with vegetables or poached fish. Always snip the chives with scissors, rather than try to chop them, and scatter them over dishes just before serving.

Coriander

A very popular herb today because it is not only used in Indian cooking but also in Chinese, Thai, South American and Fusion cooking (Australian/Asian food flavours mixed together). Use this herb with fish, lamb, rice dishes and stir fries. It can also be used as a garnish – its bright green leaves add colour to many dishes.

Dill

A very feathery herb, which is associated with fish. It has a pronounced aniseed flavour and has always been popular in Scandinavian countries. It is used in sauces and mayonnaise for serving with marinated salmon. It is also good with fish soups, potatoes and cucumber. Since it is an attractive herb, it makes an ideal garnish.

Fennel

This herb is very like dill but is much stronger in colour and flavour. Use it in the same way but when a more dominant flavour is required in sauces and stuffings for fish.

Marjoram

A Mediterranean herb that grows well in Britain but may need some protection from frosts. Use it in European dishes, casseroles, pastas and pizzas. It is also good with eggs, cheese, roasted vegetables and salad dressings. The stalk is woody, so just use the leaves and chop them finely.

Mint

This is a traditional herb, which grows easily in any garden, in fact too well because the roots will

Basil

Mint

Rosemary

Oregano

Sage

take over everything, so plant it in a large pot instead. It is used in classic mint sauce as well as to flavour new potatoes. It is also delicious added to risottos, couscous and salads. When chopped with parsley, it makes a good garnish for root vegetables, and whole sprigs can be used to decorate desserts, particularly fruit and ice creams.

Oregano
Like marjoram but slightly stronger in flavour, oregano is used in Mediterranean dishes, particularly pasta sauces where robust flavours are required. The leaves are removed from the stems and chopped before adding to the dish. It is this herb that gives pizzas their characteristic flavour.

Parsley
This herb is very popular in Britain and is used all year round for garnishes and in stuffings and sauces. It is quite easy to grow but can be slow to germinate. There are two main varieties, curly parsley, which is mainly used for garnish, and the flat-leaved variety, which has a stronger flavour. Use parsley to flavour all fish dishes, stuff whole fish with a few stalks and flavour sauces and butters with lots of freshly chopped leaves. Potatoes and other puréed vegetables are improved by the addition of parsley and so are mushrooms and onions. Throw a handful over salads, too.

Rosemary
Another favourite British herb, grown as a hardy bush, and available for use all year round. The spikes must be removed from the stalks and chopped very finely because some people find the spikes too hard and difficult to digest. Rosemary has a special compatibility with lamb and pork – its pungent flavour blends well with these meats. Greeks and Italians use this herb in their stronger dishes. Rosemary is particularly good with roasted and barbecued foods, and the stronger stalks can be used as skewers for pieces of fish or meat.

Sage
A very strong, slightly musty-flavoured herb, which can put people off if used in too great a quantity. The delicately coloured grey-green leaves are chopped and used in stuffings and sauces. Sage is good with rich, fatty meats like goose and pork, and goes well with cheese and sausages. Sage and onion stuffing is the traditional accompaniment to goose. The herb also goes well with apples, tomatoes, potatoes and some Italian dishes.

Tarragon
Tarragon has always been highly regarded by the French. It has a subtle flavour of vanilla and aniseed and its delicate leaves are used to flavour sauces like hollandaise, béarnaise and tartare. It is good with fish, shellfish, chicken, veal and egg dishes.

Thyme
Many varieties of thyme are available now. Common thyme is the most generally available, which can be very pungent so it should be used sparingly. Thyme is a small, woody plant with green-grey leaves, which need to be stripped from the stem before use. This herb is very good with all meats; roasts can be rubbed with the herb before cooking and casseroles benefit from its rich aroma during their long, slow cooking. Lemon thyme is less acerbic and has an additional lemon flavour, which is useful in stuffings, fish dishes and salads.

Bay leaves

Thyme

Dill

Chives

Parsley

Tarragon

Coriander

Paprika

SPICES

There is a vast range of spices available nowadays. In fact it is confusing because there are so many. Here are some of the spices you might need to flavour some of the dishes in this book. It is a good idea to buy spices in small amounts because they tend to lose their flavour, especially the ready-ground ones. Store them in a cool, dry place out of the light and check from time to time the 'use by' date to ensure you use them when they are at their best.

Allspice
This spice comes from the West Indies and is available as red-brown berries or ready-ground. It is very aromatic and has a flavour of cloves, nutmeg and cinnamon. Traditionally allspice is used in fruit cakes and Christmas puddings. It can also be used with chicken, beef or pork, as in Caribbean cooking. Allspice is best bought whole because the ground spice loses its smell and flavour. It is best to grind it with a pestle and mortar when needed.

Caraway seeds
These seeds are not very popular here but they are used in the northern European countries. The seeds are used whole in casseroles, soups, vegetable dishes and in baking. They have a warm, slightly bitter, almost medicinal flavour.

Cardamom
These are small, green pods, which contain tiny black seeds. They have the most delicious aroma and flavour. Cardamom is an eastern spice and is used in curry dishes and also in some pastry and sweet recipes. It can be used to add spice to vegetable soups and purées. To use, crush the pods with a pestle and mortar, remove the dried pod and add the

Chilli powder

Cardamom

Cloves

seeds to the dish. Always buy whole cardamom pods – the ground variety is inferior.

Chilli powder
This can sometimes be misleading because some brands have pure ground chillies but some contain a mixture of other spices, which reduces the intensity of the powder. The powder is usually made from a variety of chillies and can be very hot. You need to experiment to find the right amount to your taste. It is a good, red colour and is used in curries but also in South American and Mexican dishes where a fiery taste is required.

Chinese five-spice powder
As the name suggests, this is a blend of five spices, which is used to flavour Chinese dishes. The mixture consists of cassia or cinnamon, cloves, fennel seeds, star anise and Szechuan pepper. Use it in Chinese cooking, particularly vegetables, chicken and duck.

Cinnamon
This is a very popular spice. It has a warm, sweet, spicy aroma, which permeates the whole house when used. It comes from the inner bark of a type of laurel tree and is bought as cinnamon sticks, which can be used to flavour sweet and savoury dishes. Break off little pieces and remove before serving dishes such as poached fruits, Greek moussaka or mulled wine. A cinnamon stick can also be used to stir hot chocolate to give added flavour. In Britain, cinnamon is used in baking, particularly in Christmas cakes and puddings. You need to buy cinnamon ready-ground because it is impossible to grind the cinnamon sticks.

Cloves
Cloves are dried, unopened flower buds from an evergreen tree. They are used in Christmas baking, and to flavour bread sauce, mulled wine, pickles and chutneys. Cloves can be used whole (always ensure that you remove them before serving because a whole clove tastes rather nasty) or ground, which is best done in a pestle and mortar. The flavour is very pungent, so care should be taken not to make the taste overwhelming.

Coriander seeds
Little brown coriander seeds from the coriander plant have quite a different flavour to the leaves. The seeds have a warm orange flavour, and can be dry-fried before use to bring out their full scent. They are easily ground with a pestle and mortar and are best bought whole because their flavour fades rapidly once they are ground. This spice is one of the most important in Indian cooking. Ground coriander is used for curries, fish, meat, poultry, vegetables and some baking.

Cumin seeds
This is a very important spice, and another essential ingredient in curries. Cumin is also important in the cooking of Mexico and North Africa. The narrow, brownish seeds are quite soft and easy to grind. Their aroma is strong and spicy with a bitter flavour. Use them in curries and meat casserole dishes, and also with rice. Dry-frying before use will enhance their flavour.

Curry powder/paste
This is a mixture of different spices blended together for ease of use. If you make a lot of curries, it is a good idea to prepare your own mixture in a larger quantity and use as needed. Indian curry powder usually contains coriander, cumin, fenugreek, black mustard, black pepper, turmeric, ginger and red chillies. Commercial curry powder and pastes are available, and some are better than others. It is best to buy them from an authentic specialist Indian or Thai shop and try different brands until you find one that suits you.

Garam masala
Another Indian mix of spices, which is used to flavour curries, vegetable dishes and rice. It is often added at the end of the cooking time rather than at the beginning like curry powder. The mix includes bay leaves, black pepper, cloves, cinnamon, coriander, cumin and green cardamom. It adds a more fragrant flavour to food rather than a hot sensation of chilli. It is also available ready mixed.

Ground cinnamon

Garam masala

Coriander seeds

Cinnamon

Ginger

Ginger is a versatile spice and it comes in various forms. Fresh root ginger is easily obtainable, which has a fresh, spicy flavour and can be used chopped or grated. Stem ginger is preserved in sugar syrup and is very sweet – it can be used in baking or simply served with ice-cream. Ground ginger is used in baking, particularly gingerbread, to which it gives its characteristic flavour and aroma.

Mace

Mace is the bright outer casing of the nutmeg and is used in its own right in cakes, puddings and sauces. It tends to be stronger than nutmeg and should be used sparingly. Both mace and nutmeg have a warm, fragrant aroma. For baking, ground mace is best because whole mace is difficult to grind. Ground mace can also be used in pâtés and terrines.

Mixed spice

This is used for puddings and contains allspice, cinnamon, cloves, coriander, ginger and nutmeg. It is useful if you only cook occasionally because it allows you to have the six spices in one jar. It can also be used in biscuits, breads and cakes.

Mustard

Mustard seeds are available in white, black and brown varieties. The darker ones provide the heat and the pungency and the white ones the flavour. They can be bought whole and then you can grind them when needed. They are good roughly ground and mixed with potato for a slightly 'curry' flavour. Alternatively, you can buy the ready-ground English mustard powder and mix with water before serving with meats and sausages. Mustard is also used in cheese dishes and to flavour sauces.

Nutmeg

This popular spice is used all year round, not just in desserts but in many savoury dishes as well. It is available both whole and ground, but there is nothing like the freshly ground spice for flavour. Always keep a nutmeg close to hand with a small grater, so that you can add it to white sauces, pasta dishes and vegetables. Nutmeg is also delicious grated on top of hot drinks.

Peppers

Cayenne: this is a very hot, pungent pepper, which is made from a particularly hot variety of chilli. It has a distinctive colour and flavour but should be used with great care. A tiny pinch can add a hot fieriness to any dish. It is particularly good with cheese dishes, especially in scones and biscuits. It can also be used in sauces and curries.

Paprika: this spice is made from dried, sweet, red peppers, which are ground to give a deep red spice. Paprika's colour makes it an ideal garnish for savoury dishes. It can be shaken over pale-coloured food such as egg mayonnaise, or sprinkled on top of cauliflower cheese to add bite as well as colour. Paprika is quite a mild spice and is always used in Hungarian dishes such as goulash. Buy this spice in small quantities because the flavour deteriorates rapidly.

Peppercorns: this is the most widely used spice – it is used every day in cooking and at the table. It is not confined to savoury dishes either – a grating of black pepper is often encouraged with fruits such as strawberries and pineapple. Peppercorns have their own particular flavour and also the ability to improve other flavours. They are available in white and

Root ginger

Nutmeg

Paprika

Ground ginger

Cumin

Cayenne pepper

black. The white peppercorns are the kernels of fully ripened berries after the husks have been discarded, and the black ones are the whole green berries, which are picked whilst unripened and then dried until black. The outer layer of the peppercorn has the aromatic flavour. You can buy peppercorns either whole or ground. Freshly ground pepper is the only one to use for flavour and pungency; the ready-ground stuff is not worth buying.

Saffron

This is the most expensive spice. Saffron comes from the stigma of the autumn crocus. It is a bright yellow, and is used for its colour as well as its subtle flavour. Saffron is used in soups, paellas, risottos, fish stews, cakes and buns. You can buy it as tiny threads, which need to be crushed and soaked in a tablespoon of water before using.

Star anise

This attractive, star-shaped spice is really a fruit pod, and it is used extensively in Chinese cooking. It has a sweet, pungent, anise flavour and aroma and is used in both sweet and savoury dishes. It is good with chicken and duck and any stir-fries. It can also be used to flavour cakes and fruit compôtes. It is usually available whole, and must be removed from the dish before serving. It can also be ground with a pestle and mortar or in an electric grinder.

Turmeric

This is a brilliant, yellow-coloured spice. Take care with it because it can stain clothes and utensils. It is widely used in India, and comes from the ground root of a member of the ginger family. Its musky, earthy flavour is essential to curries. It is also useful as a cheaper substitute for saffron, purely for colour however because the flavours cannot be compared. Turmeric also adds colour to rice dishes and to some breads and cakes as well.

Vanilla

The pods of the vanilla plant give us one of the most popular flavourings. The black pods are sliced and the seeds extracted for use in sauces, custards, ice-creams and other desserts. The whole pod can be placed in a jar of sugar so that the sugar becomes flavoured with vanilla. It is also available as vanilla extract: make sure you buy this and not vanilla 'essence' or vanilla 'flavouring', which are inferior.

Turmeric

Peppercorns

Vanilla pods

Part 3
Recipes

SOUPS

Soups have always been good staple fare, but are really back in fashion. We have supermarkets selling soup in cans and packets and the new, chilled, 'fresh' varieties, which are very popular. They have introduced us to many new flavours and ingredients. At home we can make truly fresh soups using inexpensive ingredients and experiment with new flavours.

The base of a good soup is stock, so I have given two recipes for basic stock that can be easily made at home. You do not need to make stock, however. There are many brands of cubes and powder in the shops along with the new chilled stocks. The latter are quite expensive but can be useful when you want a particular flavour in a special soup. Some of the stock cubes have a very concentrated flavour and should be used in moderation. A good stock to try is the Marigold vegetable stock powder, which you can use by the spoonful and is excellent in vegetable, fish and meat soups.

Stock can be made quite easily from simple ingredients but can be time consuming. The results do add flavour to dishes and, as you can freeze the stock, it is a worthwhile exercise. There are a few rules to remember when making stocks:

- Use the freshest ingredients: there is no point in spending time making stock unless you have fresh ingredients.
- When preparing the stock, make sure the water only simmers; rapid boiling will result in a cloudy stock (you can boil it at the end of the process after straining it though).
- Always skim any scum from the top of the stock so that it will be clear.
- Make sure you strain the stock well through a fine sieve. This will ensure that you have a clearer, fresher soup.
- You can reduce the sieved stock by boiling to make for a more concentrated flavour. It is also important if you are to freeze the stock so you have a smaller volume to store. Always check seasoning after reducing because this intensifies the saltiness.
- If you have time it is a good idea to allow the stock to cool, then you will be able to remove any excess fat from the surface, thus saving unwanted calories.

Making soup at home can be as simple or as complicated as you like. Start with good, fresh ingredients and prepare them carefully. Vegetables need to be peeled but try not to waste too much. The green parts of leeks, for example, are not often served as a vegetable but are invaluable for soups because they give a good colour. Make sure all vegetables are cut to the same size so that they cook evenly.

Start by 'sweating' the vegetables in a little butter or olive oil. Butter is preferable for some root vegetables because the flavour is better, but for health reasons you might like to use oil. Then add stock and simmer; do not overcook at this stage or the flavour may be spoilt.

If the soup requires blending, use a food processor or a blender. This way you will have a very smooth finish. If the recipe is quite rustic and you do not want too smooth a result, you can blend only half of the ingredients and then add the chunky vegetables. However, if you want a really smooth soup, you might want to blend it thoroughly and then sieve it to ensure the correct consistency. Thanks to blenders we do not need to add any additional flour to thicken soups, we can rely on the puréed vegetable matter to do the job.

Serving soups for every occasion

Serving soup correctly is very important. If it is to be served hot, make sure the dishes are hot and the soup is at the correct temperature; if cold, ensure that the dishes and the soup are chilled. Accompany the soup with some good bread and an appropriate garnish. A good handful of chopped herbs, a swirl of cream, a few chopped nuts or a grating of cheese – all add colour, flavour and texture.

Soups can be delicate appetisers or robust, hearty meals, so here is a selection of recipes from across the whole spectrum: basic stocks, chilled smooth soups, puréed soups, and thick, chunky soups that can be served as a complete meal together with some fresh crusty bread.

BELOW Winter Bean and Lentil Soup

BASIC CHICKEN STOCK

You can make two sorts of chicken stock: a light stock made from raw carcasses and a brown stock made from a cooked carcass. It is more usual to prepare the latter because we often have a carcass left over from a roast chicken whilst it is very unusual to have a whole fresh carcass.

Makes about 1 litre/1¾ pints
Preparation time: 10 minutes
Cooking time: 1½–2 hours

INGREDIENTS

1 carcass from a roast chicken
1.4 litres/2½ pints water
1 onion, peeled and sliced
1 carrot, peeled and sliced
1 celery stick, sliced
1 tsp dried thyme
1 bay leaf
3 sprigs fresh parsley
salt and pepper

You will need a large, lidded saucepan (about 3.5 litres/6 pints), a cook's knife, a chopping board, a measuring jug, a wooden spatula, a slotted spoon, a large bowl and a sieve

METHOD

1 Break up the carcass and place it in a large saucepan. Add the water, vegetables and herbs. Season well and bring to the boil over a medium heat. Skim the surface if any scum forms.

2 Cover the pan, lower the heat and simmer for 1½–2 hours.

3 Remove from the heat, allow to cool a little and strain into a large bowl. Discard all the meat, vegetables and herbs.

4 Cool thoroughly, then remove all traces of fat from the top of the stock. If required, you can then reboil for up to 30 minutes to reduce the stock and give a more intense flavour. Cover the cool stock with clingfilm, and chill in the refrigerator for up to 1–2 days before use.

*Suitable for freezing. Chill thoroughly, pour into a rigid, lidded container, and freeze for up to 3 months. To use, allow to thaw at room temperature and use as instructed.

BASIC VEGETABLE STOCK

Makes 1 litre/1¾ pints
Preparation time: 10 minutes
Cooking time: 1 hour, plus reduction time

INGREDIENTS

1 tbsp olive oil
1 onion, peeled and roughly chopped
1 carrot, peeled and sliced
2 celery sticks, sliced
1 leek, trimmed and sliced
225 g/8 oz lettuce or cabbage, shredded
1.2 litres/2 pints water
1 bouquet garni (see page 50)
salt and pepper

You will need a large, lidded saucepan (about 3.5 litres/
6 pints), a cook's knife, a chopping board, a wooden spatula,
a measuring jug, a slotted spoon, a large bowl and a sieve

METHOD

1 Heat the oil in a large saucepan over a medium heat and
add the prepared vegetables. Stir well and cook for 3–4
minutes until the vegetables become slightly golden. This will
give the stock a good colour.

2 Pour in the water, add the bouquet garni and season well.
Bring to the boil, half-cover the pan and simmer for 30
minutes to 1 hour. The stock should reduce slightly.

3 Remove from the heat, allow to cool a little and strain into a
bowl. Discard all the vegetables and bouquet garni and use
the stock as required. If not used immediately, cover with
clingfilm and keep in the refrigerator for 1–2 days only.
Alternatively, reduce the stock by boiling for 30 minutes until
reduced by half, then cool completely and freeze.

• *Any vegetables can be used: cauliflower stalks, beans, broccoli, outside
leaves of cabbage and other vegetable trimmings. Do not use beetroot
because the colour will be too strong, and do not use potatoes or other
starchy vegetables because they will make the stock cloudy and also may
'sour' it.*

* *Suitable for freezing. Cool first, and then pour into a rigid, lidded
container. Freeze for up to 3 months. To use, allow to thaw at room
temperature and use as instructed.*

GIBLET STOCK

*This stock can be made with chicken or turkey giblets and is
essential when you need a good gravy to accompany the
roasts.*

Makes about 600 ml/1 pint
Preparation time: 10 minutes
Cooking time: 1½–2 hours

INGREDIENTS

1 packet chicken or turkey giblets
700 ml/1¼ pints water
1 onion, left unpeeled, but thickly sliced
1 carrot, peeled and thickly sliced
1 celery stick, sliced
1 tsp dried thyme
1 bay leaf
3 sprigs fresh parsley
salt and pepper

You will need a large, lidded saucepan (about 1.7 litres/
3 pints), a cook's knife, a chopping board, a measuring jug,
a wooden spatula, a slotted spoon, a large bowl and a sieve

METHOD

1 Place the giblets in the saucepan. Add the water, vegetables
and herbs. Season well and bring to the boil over a medium
heat. Skim the surface to remove any scum.

2 Cover the pan, lower the heat and simmer for 1–1½ hours.

3 Remove from the heat, allow to cool a little, then strain into
a large bowl. Discard all the giblets, vegetables and herbs.

4 Cover with clingfilm, chill thoroughly and use as required.
This stock will keep in the refrigerator for up to 1–2 days
before use.

SMOOTH GAZPACHO

This delicious soup is Spanish in origin and is very refreshing served chilled on hot summer days.

Serves 6–8
Preparation time: 20 minutes, plus marinating

INGREDIENTS

10 ripe tomatoes
½ cucumber
1 red pepper
½ white onion, peeled
½ red onion, peeled
2 garlic cloves, peeled
2 slices white bread (crusts removed)
225 ml/8 fl oz tomato juice
1 tbsp balsamic vinegar
2 tbsp wine vinegar
10 fresh basil leaves, torn in half
1 tbsp chopped fresh coriander
pinch of ground cumin
pinch of cayenne pepper
225 ml/8 fl oz olive oil
salt and pepper

To garnish
1 tbsp finely chopped tomato
1 tbsp finely chopped cucumber
fresh sprigs of coriander or chervil

You will need a cook's knife, a chopping board, a glass bowl, a measuring jug, a blender, a sieve and 6–8 serving bowls

1 Dice the tomatoes, cucumber, red pepper, white onion, red onion, garlic, and white bread.

2 Place all the diced ingredients in a glass bowl. Add the tomato juice, vinegars, herbs and spices. Pour in 75 ml/2½ fl oz of the olive oil, cover with clingfilm, and marinate for a few hours, or overnight if possible.

3 After the mixture has marinated, transfer it to a blender and purée to a smooth consistency.

4 Pass the mixture through a sieve. Purée again, then slowly add the remaining olive oil until the mixture is smooth. Season to taste, then cover with clingfilm and chill well for up to 2–3 hours or overnight. Pour the soup into chilled bowls and spoon a little tomato and cucumber on top before serving. Top with sprigs of fresh coriander or chervil.

CARROT AND ORANGE SOUP

Serves 4–6
Preparation time: 15 minutes
Cooking time: 30–35 minutes

INGREDIENTS

6 tbsp butter

2 onions, peeled and finely chopped

900 g/2 lb carrots, peeled and chopped

850 ml/1½ pints vegetable stock

1 bay leaf

juice and grated rind of 3 oranges

salt and pepper

150 ml/5 fl oz crème fraîche, to serve

2 tbsp snipped chives, to garnish

You will need a large, lidded saucepan (about 2.25 litres/
4 pints), a cook's knife, a chopping board, a wooden spatula,
a measuring jug, a blender and 4–6 serving bowls

METHOD

1 Melt the butter in a large saucepan over a medium heat. Add
the chopped vegetables and sauté gently for 3–4 minutes
until soft but not brown. Pour in the stock, add the bay leaf and
grated orange rind and simmer, with the lid on the pan, for 20
minutes or until the vegetables are cooked.

2 Remove from the heat and process the soup in a blender
until smooth. Return to the cleaned pan and stir in the
orange juice. Add salt and pepper to taste.

3 Reheat the stock, then serve in warm bowls with a swirl of
crème fraîche and garnished with chives.

** Suitable for freezing. Prepare up to the end of step 2, allow to cool and
pour into a rigid, lidded container. Freeze for up to 3 months. To use,
allow to thaw at room temperature, then continue from step 3 above.*

SPICY PARSNIP SOUP

Serves 4
Preparation time: 15 minutes
Cooking time: 20–25 minutes

INGREDIENTS

4 tbsp butter

1 medium onion, peeled and chopped

1 medium potato, peeled and chopped

500 g/1 lb 2 oz parsnips, peeled and chopped

½ tsp curry powder

½ tsp ground cumin

½ tsp ground coriander

½ tsp ground cardamom

1.5 litres/2¾ pints chicken stock or vegetable stock made with stock powder

salt and pepper

150 ml/5 fl oz double cream, optional

You will need a large, lidded saucepan (about 2.8 litres/ 5 pints), a cook's knife, a chopping board, a wooden spatula, a measuring jug, a blender and 4 serving bowls

METHOD

1 Melt the butter in the saucepan over a medium heat and cook the onion and potato for 3–4 minutes until softened. Add the parsnips and mix well. Stir in the ground spices and continue to cook for a further minute.

2 Pour in the stock and bring to the boil. Lower the heat, cover the pan, and simmer for 20–25 minutes until the parsnips are soft.

3 Remove from the heat and process the mixture in a blender until smooth. Taste, and season with salt and pepper.

4 Serve hot, with a swirl of cream (if using).

Suitable for freezing. Prepare to the end of step 3, then chill thoroughly and pour into a rigid, lidded container. Freeze for up to 3 months. To use, allow to thaw at room temperature, reheat, and serve as above.

SMOKED HADDOCK CHOWDER

Serves 4 as a starter, or 3 as a main course
Preparation time: 10 minutes
Cooking time: 25–30 minutes

INGREDIENTS

2 tbsp butter

55 g/2 oz lardons or lean, streaky bacon, sliced

1 onion, peeled and finely chopped

350 g/12 oz undyed smoked haddock, skinned

225 g/8 oz small, waxy potatoes

300 ml/10 fl oz milk

425 ml/15 fl oz fish or vegetable stock

4 tbsp single cream

salt and pepper

2 tbsp chopped fresh parsley, to garnish

You will need a large, lidded saucepan (about 2.8 litres/
5 pints), a cook's knife, a chopping board, a small frying pan,
a measuring jug, a wooden spatula, and 4 serving bowls

1 Melt the butter in the frying pan over a medium heat and fry the lardons for 3–4 minutes until they start to brown. Add the onion and continue to cook for 2–3 minutes until soft.

2 Cut the haddock into 2.5 cm/1 inch cubes, place in a bowl, and cover with clingfilm until ready to use.

3 Cut the potatoes into 1 cm/½ inch cubes and place in a large saucepan.

4 Pour over the milk and stock and bring to the boil over a medium heat. Reduce to a gentle simmer and cook for 10–15 minutes until the potatoes are just starting to cook. Add the haddock, lardons and onion, and simmer for a further 5 minutes. Remove from the heat, stir in the cream, season to taste, and serve in warm bowls garnished with parsley.

SQUASH AND ALMOND SOUP

Serves 4–6
Preparation time: 10–15 minutes
Cooking time: 50–55 minutes

INGREDIENTS

900 g/2 lb butternut squash, or any type of pumpkin
1 tbsp olive oil
1 onion, peeled and finely chopped
115 g/4 oz ground almonds
850 ml/1½ pints vegetable stock
juice and grated zest of 1 orange
salt and pepper
55 g/2 oz Parmesan, freshly grated
2 tbsp toasted, flaked almonds, to garnish

You will need a large lidded saucepan (about 2.8 litres/
5 pints), a cook's knife, a chopping board, a roasting tin,
a measuring jug, a blender and 4–6 serving bowls

METHOD

1 Preheat the oven to 200°C/400°F/Gas 6. Cut the squash
into slices and remove the seeds. Place the slices in a
lightly oiled roasting tin and roast in the preheated oven for
30–40 minutes until tender and just starting to brown.

2 Heat the remaining oil in a large saucepan over a medium
heat and cook the onion gently for 2–3 minutes until
softened. Add the almonds and stir well.

3 Remove the squash from the oven. Remove and discard the
rind, then add the cooked pulp to the pan.

4 Pour in the stock, bring to the boil, then simmer over a
gentle heat for 10–15 minutes until the onions are soft.

5 Remove from the heat and purée the soup in a blender until
smooth. Return it to the cleaned pan, then reheat and add
the orange juice and zest. Taste, and season if necessary.

6 Remove from the heat, stir in the Parmesan and then
serve immediately in warm bowls garnished with the
flaked almonds.

*Suitable for freezing. Prepare the soup to the end of step 5, then chill
thoroughly and pour into a rigid, lidded container. Freeze for up to 3
months. To use, allow to thaw at room temperature, reheat and continue
from step 6 above.*

WINTER BEAN AND LENTIL SOUP

Serves 4
Preparation time: 15 minutes
Cooking time: 25–30 minutes

INGREDIENTS

2 tbsp olive oil
1 onion, peeled and finely sliced
350 g/12 oz carrots, peeled and sliced
3 celery sticks, sliced
2 garlic cloves, peeled and chopped
115 g/4 oz Puy lentils, rinsed
1.2 litres/2 pints vegetable stock
1 bay leaf
2 medium leeks, trimmed and sliced
150 g/5½ oz cabbage or spinach, shredded
400 g/14 oz canned borlotti beans, drained
salt and pepper

To garnish
4 tbsp pesto sauce
40 g/1½ oz Parmesan, freshly shaved

You will need a large, lidded saucepan (about 3.5 litres/
6 pints), a cook's knife, a chopping board, a wooden spatula,
a measuring jug, and 4 serving bowls

METHOD

1 Heat the oil in a large saucepan over a medium heat. Add
the onion, carrots, celery and garlic and sauté gently for
3–4 minutes until soft but not brown.

2 Add the lentils and cook for a further 2 minutes.

3 Pour in the stock, add the bay leaf and bring to the boil.
Simmer, covered, for 15 minutes or until the vegetables are
almost tender.

4 Add the leeks, season well and continue to cook for
5 minutes.

5 Finally, add the shredded cabbage or spinach together with
the beans and cook for a further 2–3 minutes.

6 Remove from the heat. Check the seasoning and serve in
warm bowls with a swirl of pesto and the shaved cheese.

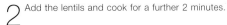

E G G S

Eggs are one of the most versatile and nutritious foods, whether used whole or in their separate — whites and yolks — components. They should be a stock item: you will need large eggs for main recipes and small ones for cooking processes like coating and glazing. You can store them in the refrigerator, but always bring them to room temperature before use.

Make sure you buy your eggs from a reliable supplier and use them as fresh as possible. You can choose between battery, free-range or organic eggs – a matter of preference and price. Shell colour is irrelevant.

We will be concentrating here on hens' eggs. There are others: quails' eggs are increasingly popular, duck eggs are widely available and even ostrich eggs are appearing now.

Choosing and buying eggs

The freshest eggs are the best but it is often impossible to ascertain when the eggs were laid unless you have a local supplier or a friend who keeps hens. In supermarkets we must rely on the date on the carton. This is the 'best before' date and is set at three weeks after the eggs were laid, so look for ones with the date furthest ahead. Always buy from a reliable supplier or from a supermarket where there is a fast turnover.

You can buy eggs in four sizes: very large, large, medium and small. Very large eggs are 70 g/2½ oz or over, large are 60 g/2¼ oz or over, medium are 50 g/1¾ oz or over and small are anything below 50 g/1¾ oz. The eggs used in the recipes in this book are all large but when they are served alone (for example a boiled egg) a very large size would be preferable. Small eggs can be bought for glazing and binding and they are also useful for small children for their boiled eggs and soldiers (toasted fingers of bread).

Check the freshness of an egg by floating it in water: an egg that lies on its side at the bottom of a bowl is fresh, one that stands vertically with the rounded end up is less fresh, and one that floats completely is stale and should not be used.

Storage

There is great debate as to whether you should keep your eggs in the refrigerator or at room temperature. Eggs kept in the refrigerator last longer than those kept at room temperature.

However, eggs are best cooked from room temperature so you will need to get them out of the refrigerator 2–3 hours before they are needed. If you regularly cook for a large number of people, you could keep your eggs in a cool place and not in the refrigerator because you will have a quick turnover, but if you only use eggs now and then they are best kept in the refrigerator. Store them with the pointed ends downwards. It is a good idea to store them in the boxes in which they were bought, rather than in the egg racks in the door of the refrigerator, because this helps to prevent them picking up smells. Separated egg whites can be kept in a lidded container in the refrigerator for up to one week. Egg yolks and beaten whole eggs can be stored in the refrigerator for two days.

Eggs can also be frozen. Separated egg whites will freeze for up to three months if lightly forked and stored in a lidded container. Egg yolks will also freeze satisfactorily, but they should be beaten with a little salt or sugar to prevent them becoming too gelatinous. Label the containers clearly with what they contain and the date they were frozen. Whole eggs may be frozen, lightly beaten and also mixed with a little salt.

Salmonella

Salmonella bacteria in eggs can in some rare cases cause food poisoning. However, thorough cooking will usually prevent this. Undercooked or raw eggs can be the main source of the problem and so recipes that contain raw or lightly cooked eggs should be avoided by vulnerable groups. People in vulnerable groups include the elderly, pregnant and breastfeeding women, small children, sick people and convalescents. This means that foods such as mousses, cold soufflés, mayonnaise, egg custards, home-made ice-creams, and royal icing should be avoided. Luckily some supermarkets are now stocking pasteurised egg so that these dishes can be made without any danger to health.

SEPARATING EGGS

For some recipes it is necessary to separate the white from the yolk of an egg.

1 There are some gadgets available that help to achieve this, but if you have not got a gadget, you can use the shell method described here. You will need a bowl. Crack the egg shell in half on the edge of the bowl.

2 Pass the yolk into one of the shell halves, allowing some of the white to drop into the bowl.

3 Pass the yolk into the other shell half, at the same time allowing more of the egg white to drop into the bowl. Take care not to break the yolk on the sharp edges of the egg shells.

4 Repeat passing the yolk between the egg shells until all the white is in the bowl. Remember that any egg white needed for a meringue should have no trace of yolk in it or it will not whisk up properly.

Note: the fresher the egg, the easier it is to separate because the white is more gelatinous and the yolk firmer. It also helps to chill the egg first before separating.

WHISKING EGG WHITES

Absolutely fresh eggs are not ideal for whisking: those that are 3–5 days old are best. Make sure everything is scrupulously clean and that there is not a trace of fat anywhere on the equipment. Place the separated egg whites in a large bowl and whisk, using a balloon whisk, a hand-held electric mixer or a large, free-standing electric mixer. Depending on whether you are going to incorporate the whites with other ingredients like a soufflé or make a meringue, you must whisk them to the correct consistency. If they are to be mixed, the consistency should be 'soft peaks', that is, the peaks should be firm enough to hold their shape but are still soft and will flop over. 'Firm peaks' are achieved when the mixture is beaten so that it is dry and when the whisk is lifted from the bowl the peaks are firm and stand rigid. Once the whites are whisked, the other ingredients should be folded in very carefully so that the air is retained. Use a plastic spatula or a metal tablespoon for folding in because they cut through the mixture more easily.

COOKING EGGS

It is always advisable to have eggs at room temperature before starting to cook them. They are very sensitive to heat and start to cook (coagulate) at 60°C/140°F. This makes eggs useful in cookery as a binding agent, for thickening sauces, in egg custards and as a food in their own right. However, it is very easy to overcook eggs and end up with some indigestible mass, so gentle and swift cooking is essential.

Baking

A delicious way of serving eggs is to bake them. This is a good way of serving a large number of people without too much trouble. You will need individual ramekin dishes or heatproof tea-cups. Generously butter the dishes and break one egg into each dish, season well and spoon over a tablespoon of single cream into each dish. Place the dishes in a small roasting tin with enough hot water to come halfway up the sides of the dishes. Bake at 190°C/375°F/Gas 5 for 15 minutes for a soft egg and 18–20 minutes for a firmer egg. Other ingredients like fried mushrooms and bacon pieces can be added. This makes a good breakfast dish or a simple starter.

Boiling

You will need a saucepan large enough to hold the eggs you need to boil but not too large to allow the eggs to move around too freely and crack. The water (which should be deep enough to cover the eggs) should be at a gentle simmer. Lower the eggs into the water using a long-handled, metal tablespoon, and simmer for 3–4 minutes for soft-boiled (runny yolk and soft set white), 5–6 minutes for a medium-boiled egg (creamy yolk and firm set white) and 10 minutes for a hard-boiled egg (both yolk and white are firm). If you are serving hard-boiled eggs cold, always run them under cold water immediately to prevent black discoloration (iron sulphide), which results from the reaction of hydrogen sulphide in the white, and iron in the yolk, during cooking.

Poaching

For poaching you really need the freshest of eggs – do not attempt to cook by this method if this cannot be guaranteed because the eggs will break up in the water. You will need a small, shallow pan (a small frying pan is ideal) particularly if you are cooking more than one egg (do not attempt to poach too many in one go). The water needs to be deep enough to just cover the eggs. You can add 1–2 teaspoons of vinegar at this stage if you like, it does help to coagulate the egg white but I don't like the flavour, which always permeates the egg. Break the egg into a cup. If you are more experienced, you could break it directly into the water, but sometimes the egg refuses to break well and I think a cup is an insurance policy. Bring the water to a gentle simmer and carefully pour in the egg – the white should immediately cover the yolk; if not, a gentle help with a slotted spoon works. Allow the egg to cook for 2–3 minutes until the white is set and the yolk still soft, or 4–5 minutes if you like your eggs firmer. You can also baste the top of the egg with the hot water to ensure the egg is completely cooked. Use a slotted spoon to remove it from the water and drain quickly on a piece of kitchen paper. Serve the eggs immediately.

Frying

A fried egg is most delicious when accompanied by bacon for a traditional English breakfast. If you have cooked some bacon, you have the ideal fat in which to cook your egg, but if you just want a fried egg you should heat a tablespoon of oil in a frying pan (a non-stick pan is best for eggs). Set the pan over a medium heat because you need quite a high temperature for frying. Break the egg into a cup and slide the egg into the hot pan. Fry the egg for a few seconds until the white sets, then tip the pan to one side so that the fat accumulates at the edge and you can baste the egg using a tablespoon, making sure the yolk and white are completely cooked on the top but the yolk is still soft in the centre. Use a fish slice or a wooden spatula to remove the egg from the pan. You can rest it for a few seconds

on a piece of kitchen paper in order to absorb any excess oil before serving.

Scrambling

Scrambled eggs need very gentle cooking or you might end up with very rubbery results. Allow 2 eggs per person and break them into a basin. Beat well and season with salt and pepper (you can add a dash of milk if you like). Melt 1 tablespoon of butter in a small, non-stick saucepan over a low heat until foaming. Pour in the beaten eggs and stir well using a wooden spoon. The egg will start to set on the bottom of the pan but just continue to stir, removing the cooked egg from the base of the pan and mixing it well with the runny mixture. When the mixture is starting to be creamy all through, remove from the heat – it will continue to cook in the hot pan. You can, if you wish, add a small knob of butter or a tablespoon of cream at the end for an added treat. Serve at once. Do not try to cook too many eggs at one time: you will have a better result if you cook each portion individually.

Making an omelette

A basic omelette is still one of the quickest meals you can cook without resorting to prepared convenience foods. You really need an omelette pan, which is just a small frying pan kept purely for making omelettes (about 18 cm/7 inches). It should have curved sides and a heavy base, made from aluminium, steel or cast iron – it can also be non-stick.

Begin by breaking two eggs into a basin and beating gently, just enough to break up the eggs. Season well. Heat the pan over a medium heat, add 2 tablespoons of butter and melt until foaming. Pour in the eggs and stir quickly with a wooden spatula or the back of a fork to spread them evenly over the pan. As the egg begins to cook, draw the egg slightly from all round the outside towards the centre of the pan, allowing the liquid egg to run towards the outside. This takes only a few moments. Stop as soon as the egg is almost set but still a little liquid. Remove from the heat and fold half the omelette over the other half. Serve at once on a warm plate. If you want to add a filling, prepare it ahead and add it to the omelette just before folding.

Here are a number of recipes for using eggs and cooking with them. They follow traditional lines but some of the dishes have foreign influences.

COURGETTE AND MUSHROOM FRITTATA

A frittata is the Italian equivalent of a French omelette. It is nearer to the Spanish tortilla because it is thick and firmly cooked. The frittata is also good served cold for a picnic or a packed lunch.

Serves 2
Preparation time: 10 minutes
Cooking time: 15 minutes

INGREDIENTS

1 tbsp butter
1 tbsp olive oil
175 g/6 oz courgettes, sliced
115 g/4 oz chestnut mushrooms, sliced
1 garlic clove, peeled and finely chopped
4 eggs
6 tbsp milk
3 tbsp chopped fresh parsley
salt and pepper

You will need a 23 cm/9 inch non-stick frying pan (with a heatproof handle if possible, but not essential), a wooden spatula, a basin, a balloon whisk, a cook's knife and a chopping board

METHOD

1 Melt the butter with the oil in a frying pan over a low heat.

2 Raise the heat to medium and fry the courgettes for about 5 minutes, turning occasionally, until golden brown.

3 Add the mushrooms and cook for another 2–3 minutes until they are soft. Stir in the garlic.

4 Break the eggs into a basin and beat well using a balloon whisk. Pour in the milk and continue to mix well, then season with salt and pepper.

5 Lower the heat under the pan and pour the egg mixture over the vegetables and sprinkle over the parsley. Stir gently and then leave to cook for about 5–6 minutes or until the mixture is almost set and the base is cooked.

6 To complete the cooking, place the pan under a hot grill for 2 minutes until the top is set (if the handle is not heatproof, or you have not got a grill, turn the frittata onto a plate, slip it back into the pan and cook it on the other side over a low heat for 2 minutes). Serve whilst still warm, cut into wedges.

WINE SUGGESTION
This frittata is delicious with an Italian white Chardonnay or a red Chianti.

TAGLIATELLE CARBONARA

This is a traditional Italian pasta dish. It can be made with any sort of pasta but to be authentic it should always contain bacon pieces and eggs.

Serves 2
Preparation time: 10 minutes
Cooking time: 15 minutes

INGREDIENTS

175 g/6 oz tagliatelle
1 tbsp olive oil
4 bacon rashers, finely sliced
1 garlic clove, peeled and finely chopped
3 eggs
salt and pepper

To garnish
55 g/2 oz Parmesan, freshly grated
1 tbsp chopped fresh parsley

You will need a large saucepan (about 3.5 litres/6 pints), a frying pan, a cook's knife, a chopping board, a basin, a colander and two serving plates

WINE SUGGESTION
Try an oaky New Zealand or Pays d'Oc Chardonnay with this dish.

METHOD

1 Cook the pasta over a medium heat in a large saucepan of salted boiling water, according to the instructions on the packet.

2 Heat the oil in a frying pan and fry the bacon over a high heat for 3–4 minutes until crispy. Add the chopped garlic and mix well.

3 Break the eggs into a bowl and beat well. Add seasoning, but remember that the bacon is salty.

4 When the pasta is cooked, drain it in a colander.

5 Scrape the bacon, garlic and fat from the frying pan into the saucepan and then return to the heat. Add the pasta and stir well.

6 Pour in the eggs and very quickly stir into the pasta so that the eggs start to set. Remove from the heat and serve immediately on hot plates, sprinkled with the Parmesan. Garnish with the parsley.

ONION TART

*You can use this recipe to make six small, individual tarts
instead of one large tart.*

Serves 6–8
Preparation time: 45 minutes, plus chilling
Cooking time: 30 minutes

INGREDIENTS

**225 g/8 oz plain flour, or half wholemeal flour and half
plain flour**
½ tsp salt
115 g/4 oz butter
4 tbsp lard or vegetable shortening
1 egg yolk
cold water, to mix
675 g/1½ lb onions, peeled and thinly sliced
1 tbsp olive oil
salt and pepper
freshly grated nutmeg
3 egg yolks, beaten well
225 ml/8 fl oz double cream

You will need a 25 cm/10 inch flan tin or rectangular baking
dish, a baking sheet, a cook's knife, a bowl and a chopping
board

METHOD

1 Sift the flour and salt into a bowl and gently rub in half of
the butter and all the lard until the mixture resembles
breadcrumbs. Stir in the egg yolk and sprinkle in enough cold
water to form a soft dough. Wrap in clingfilm and allow to rest in
the refrigerator for 1–2 hours.

2 Roll out the dough to form a circle or rectangle, depending
on the shape of your dish; it should be large enough to line
it. Carefully line the dish without stretching the pastry, trim round
the edges and allow to rest in the refrigerator again for 1 hour.

3 Melt the remaining butter with the oil in a large, heavy pan
over a medium heat and add the onions. Stir until they are
well coated and cook, covered, for about 30 minutes until they
are soft and lightly golden. Season well and add a good grating
of nutmeg. Allow to cool a little.

4 Preheat the oven to 200°C/400°F/Gas 6. Stir the egg yolks
and cream into the onion mixture. Pour the filling into the
prepared pastry case and bake in the centre of the preheated
oven, on a heated baking sheet, for 30 minutes.

5 Remove from the oven and serve hot with a green salad
either as a starter or a light lunch.

WINE SUGGESTION

Try serving a medium
French red like Beaujolais or
a Pays D'Oc Syrah with a
touch of oak.

SALAD NIÇOISE

Serves 2
Preparation time: 20 minutes

INGREDIENTS

2 little gem or baby cos lettuces
2 hard-boiled eggs (see page 73–74)
8 baby plum tomatoes
200 g/7 oz canned tuna, drained
55 g/2 oz French beans, blanched for 2 minutes
4 anchovy fillets, sliced
12 black olives, stoned
French bread, to serve

Dressing
4 tbsp extra-virgin olive oil
1 tbsp tarragon vinegar
1 garlic clove, peeled and crushed
salt and pepper
¼ tsp French mustard
2 tbsp chopped fresh tarragon, parsley and chives

You will need a screw-topped jar, a cook's knife, a chopping board, a tin opener and two large salad bowls

METHOD

1 First make the dressing by placing all the ingredients in a jar and shaking well.

2 Cut the lettuces into quarters and arrange in two large bowls. Peel the eggs, cut into quarters and place on top of the lettuce.

3 Slice the tomatoes, flake the tuna and add to the bowls along with the French beans.

4 Scatter the anchovy fillets and olives over the top.

5 Pour over the dressing and serve at once with chunks of French bread.

WINE SUGGESTION
Serve a cold Rosé from Provence or a light Sauvignon with this salad.

MAYONNAISE

Many people are nervous about making mayonnaise, but if you are careful and not in too much of a rush the result will be wonderful. One tip: ensure that the egg yolks and the oil are at the same temperature.

Makes 300 ml/10 fl oz
Preparation time: 10–15 minutes

INGREDIENTS

2 egg yolks
1 tsp Dijon mustard
½ tsp salt
300 ml/10 fl oz light olive oil, or half olive oil and half groundnut oil
2 tsp white wine vinegar
pepper
dash lemon juice, optional

You will need a mixing bowl, an electric hand-mixer or a balloon whisk, and a measuring jug

METHOD

1 Place the egg yolks, mustard and salt in a mixing bowl and whisk until thoroughly mixed.

2 Pour the oil into a measuring jug and then slowly add it drop by drop to the mixture whilst continuing to whisk. It is easier to do with an electric mixer in one hand and the jug in the other. Whisk continuously until the mixture begins to thicken, then you can gradually add the oil in slightly larger quantities but still go slowly. Add the vinegar to thin the mayonnaise and then continue until all the oil is used up.

3 Taste the mayonnaise and add a little pepper and some more salt if needed. If the mayonnaise is too thick you can thin it with a little boiling water, and if it is not sharp enough add a little lemon juice.

4 Store the mayonnaise in a screw-topped jar in the refrigerator for up to one week and use as needed.

Note: if your mayonnaise curdles, start again with one newly whisked egg yolk and add the curdled mayonnaise as if it were the oil, and it will be fine.

CHEESE SOUFFLÉ

Serves 3–4
Preparation time: 20 minutes
Cooking time: 25–30 minutes

INGREDIENTS

1 tbsp butter, melted
1 tbsp finely grated Parmesan
2 tbsp butter
25 g/1 oz plain flour
300 ml/10 fl oz milk
115 g/4 oz Cheddar cheese, finely grated
1 tsp grainy mustard
a good grating of nutmeg
4 large eggs, separated
salt and pepper

You will need a 1.7 litre/3 pint soufflé dish or 3 individual dishes, a medium saucepan, a wooden spoon, an electric hand-held mixer or a balloon whisk, a plastic spatula and a baking sheet

METHOD

1 Preheat the oven to 200ºC/400ºF/Gas 6. Grease the base and sides of the soufflé dish or dishes with the melted butter. Then sprinkle the dish with the Parmesan, turning the dish in your hands so that all the surface is covered with the cheese.

2 Melt the remaining 2 tablespoons of butter in a saucepan (preferably non-stick) over a medium heat. Add the flour, mix well using a wooden spoon, and cook for 1 minute, stirring continuously. Remove from the heat and stir in the milk gradually until you have a smooth consistency.

3 Return the pan to a low heat and continue to stir while the sauce comes to the boil and thickens. Simmer gently, stirring constantly, for about 3 minutes until the sauce is creamy and smooth.

4 Remove from the heat and stir in the cheese, mustard and nutmeg. Taste, then season well. Set aside to cool a little.

5 Whisk the egg whites until soft peaks have formed but are not too dry.

6 Beat the egg yolks into the sauce mixture and then carefully stir in a little of the beaten egg white to slacken the mixture. Then carefully fold in the remaining egg whites.

7 Turn into the prepared dish or dishes. Place on a baking sheet and cook in the preheated oven for 25–30 minutes (or 15–20 minutes for individual dishes) until well risen and golden brown. Serve immediately, perhaps with a light green salad and crusty bread.

WINE SUGGESTION
Serve this with a light white Sauvignon – perhaps Pouilly-Fumé from the Loire.

PANCAKES

You can serve these pancakes with lemon and sugar or with warmed honey or jam. They can also be served with ice cream and chocolate sauce or with stewed fruit. For savoury dishes, use them like cannelloni and stuff them with meat, cheese or vegetable fillings.

Makes 10
Preparation time: 5 minutes
Cooking time: 15–20 minutes

INGREDIENTS

100 g/3½ oz plain flour
pinch of salt
1 egg, beaten
300 ml/10 fl oz milk
10 tsp butter or oil

You will need an 18 cm/7 inch non-stick frying pan, a wooden spatula or palette knife, a mixing bowl, a balloon whisk and a measuring jug

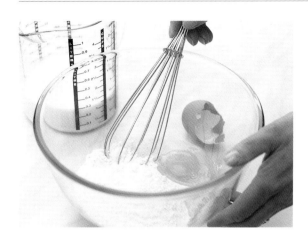

1 Place the flour and salt in a mixing bowl. Make a well in the centre, add the egg and half of the milk. Using a whisk, beat the egg and milk together and gradually incorporate the flour. Continue beating until the mixture is smooth and there are no lumps. Gradually beat in the remaining milk. Pour the batter mixture into a jug.

2 Heat the frying pan over a medium heat and add 1 teaspoon of the butter or oil, depending on what you are going to eat with the pancakes. If you are cooking traditional Shrove Tuesday pancakes to serve with sugar and lemon, then butter is best, but if you are doing something else, for example filling them with grilled vegetables, the oil would be a better choice.

3 Pour in enough batter to just cover the base, then swirl the batter around the pan whilst tilting it so that you have a thin, even layer. Cook for about half a minute, then lift up the edge of the pancake and see if it is brown. Loosen the pancake round the edges and flip it over with a spatula or palette knife. Alternatively, have a go at tossing the pancake by shaking the pan quickly with a deft flick of the wrist and catching the pancake carefully.

4 Cook on the other side for 1 minute until golden brown. Turn out onto a warm plate. Cover with kitchen foil and keep warm. Use all the remaining butter and oil, a teaspoon at a time, until all the pancakes have been cooked. Layer them with baking paper so that you have a separated stack at the end.

Suitable for freezing. Freeze the pancakes interleaved with clingfilm or baking paper, sealed in a plastic bag. To use, thaw at room temperature then reheat, wrapped in foil in a warm oven.

EGGS

ZABAGLIONE

This is a delicious Italian dessert. It is made by beating egg yolks with sugar and Marsala wine until thick.

Serves 4
Preparation time: 5 minutes
Cooking time: 10–15 minutes

INGREDIENTS

4 egg yolks
2 tbsp caster sugar
125 ml/4 fl oz Marsala wine
8 sponge fingers, to serve

You will need a large saucepan, a large, heatproof mixing bowl (make sure it fits snugly on top of the saucepan), a hand-held electric mixer or a balloon whisk, a measuring jug, and 4 glasses for serving

METHOD

1 Whisk the egg yolks and sugar together in a large, heatproof mixing bowl until light and creamy.

2 Place the bowl over a saucepan of hot water over a low heat and continue to whisk until the mixture begins to thicken. Gradually add the Marsala, and continue whisking until the mixture is very thick and frothy and increased in volume. Take care not to overcook it on the base of the bowl.

3 Remove from the stove and lift the bowl off the saucepan. Pour into individual serving dishes and serve at once with sponge fingers.

BLACKCURRANT MOUSSE

Serves 4–6

Preparation time: 30 minutes, plus 2–3 hours chilling

INGREDIENTS

400 g/14 oz fresh blackcurrants, or frozen and defrosted

225 g/8 oz caster sugar

3 eggs, separated

1 tbsp gelatine

3 tbsp cold water

150 ml/5fl oz double cream, lightly whipped

1 tbsp icing sugar

4–6 small mint leaves, to decorate

150 ml/5 fl oz single cream, to serve

You will need a medium saucepan (about 1.7 litres/3 pints), a wooden spatula, a sieve, a large mixing bowl, a hand-held electric mixer, a small saucepan, a heatproof bowl (to fit snugly over the small saucepan), a small basin, a palette knife and a 1 litre/1¾ pint glass serving dish or 4–6 individual serving dishes

METHOD

1 First prepare the blackcurrant purée. Put the blackcurrants and half the caster sugar in a medium saucepan and cook over a low heat for 2–3 minutes until the sugar is dissolved and the berries have formed a rich syrup. Allow to cool, then pour into a sieve over a bowl and press the fruit through to form a purée. You should get about 300 ml/10 fl oz.

2 In a separate bowl, whisk the egg yolks and remaining caster sugar with an electric mixer until thick and light.

3 Soak the gelatine in the 3 tablespoons of water in a heatproof bowl for 1–2 minutes. Place the bowl in a small saucepan with enough hot water to come halfway up the bowl, and heat gently for 2–3 minutes to dissolve the gelatine. When it is warm and clear, stir it into the fruit purée. Fold the fruit purée evenly into the egg mixture and then fold in the cream.

4 Whisk the egg whites until stiff but not too dry and then fold gently into the mixture. Pile the mixture into a serving dish and smooth over the top with a palette knife. Cover with clingfilm and chill for 2–3 hours in the refrigerator until firm.

5 To serve, shake the icing sugar through a sieve over the surface of the mousse and decorate with the mint leaves. Serve accompanied with a little cream poured over the top.

CHOCOLATE AND RASPBERRY PAVLOVA

A pavlova is a meringue cake, but it is not dry like meringue. It has a marshmallow centre, which is made of cornflour, vanilla extract and wine vinegar. It makes a delicious, squidgy dessert.

Serves 8–10
Preparation time: 1 hour 20 minutes
Cooking time: 1 hour

INGREDIENTS

4 egg whites
225 g/8 oz caster sugar
1 tsp cornflour
1 tsp white wine vinegar
1 tsp vanilla extract

To serve
300 ml/10 fl oz double cream
1 tbsp caster sugar
2 tbsp framboise liqueur
175 g/6 oz fresh raspberries
55 g/2 oz dark chocolate, shaved

You will need a large mixing bowl, a hand-held electric mixer, a plastic spatula, a baking sheet with a sheet of baking paper that has a 25 cm/10 inch circle drawn on the underside, and a large serving dish

1 Preheat the oven to 150°C/300°F/Gas 2. In a large mixing bowl, whisk the egg whites until stiff and gradually whisk in 115 g/4 oz of the sugar. In a separate bowl, mix the remaining sugar with the cornflour and then whisk it into the egg white mixture; it should be very shiny and firm.

2 Quickly fold the vinegar and vanilla extract into the egg white mixture.

3 Pile the meringue onto the baking paper on the baking sheet and spread evenly to the edge of the circle; swirl it around on top to make an attractive shape. Bake in the centre of the preheated oven for 1 hour.

4 Remove from the oven, cool slightly then peel off the paper. Place the pavlova on a large serving plate. It will shrink and crack but do not worry about this. It will keep in an airtight container for up to 2 days.

5 One hour before serving, whip together the cream, sugar and liqueur until thick and floppy. Pile on top of the pavlova and decorate with fruit and shaved chocolate. Chill before serving.

DAIRY PRODUCTS

*T*raditional farmhouses remain the main source of this range of rich and natural ingredients. Do not be put off by the fat content. Most dairy products come in a range of fat levels, and cheese is also rich in protein and minerals. The basic raw material is milk, mainly from cows but nowadays also from goats, sheep and even buffalo. It is available in full-fat or reduced-fat forms, as well as powdered and tinned.

Cream is the higher fat form, and is generally used to thicken and enrich soups and savoury dishes, or to enhance desserts. Yoghurt has similar uses, but is generally lower in fat and has healthy properties attributed to it.

Butter, unsalted and salted, contains about 82% fat. It has a huge range of uses in cooking, and is added to sauces, cakes, pastries and biscuits.

Cheese is very versatile and can be served simply as part of a cheeseboard or in sandwiches. The range of cheeses now available opens up many new recipe possibilities – soft cheeses that melt and blue cheeses with very powerful flavours.

MILK

Milk is our most basic food. We all start life drinking milk of some sort: cow's milk is the most complete of all foods, containing nearly all the nutrients important to humans. There is now a wide variety of milk available, and the largest growth area is the organic market.

Pasteurised milk
Most milk is now pasteurised to kill bacteria and enzymes, although some 'green top' – raw milk – is available, often straight from the farm.

Full-fat milk
This is milk just as it comes direct from the cow, with nothing removed or added. It contains 4% fat and is the ideal milk for small children, who need concentrated sources of energy. Above the age of 5 years, children can be given skimmed milk if their diet and weight so dictate. Full-fat milk is used in all these recipes, particularly in desserts, white sauces, batters and soups.

Skimmed and semi-skimmed milk
Skimmed milk contains only 0.1% fat and semi-skimmed milk must by law have between 1.5 and 1.8% fat. The calcium content of these milks is the same as full-fat milk but there is a reduction in vitamins A and D.

Homogenised milk
This milk has had the fat globules mechanically broken up so that the cream is evenly distributed throughout the milk. This means there is no cream layer at the top of the bottle, so no arguments at breakfast! It is good for making sauces.

Longlife/UHT milk
This milk has been subjected to 'ultra-high temperature' of 135°C/275°F for 1–2 seconds. The milk is then cooled rapidly and packed in special containers, and will keep for several months. Once opened, the milk should be treated as fresh. It is a very useful standby in the kitchen for sauces and other recipes, but not so nice in tea or on cereals.

Evaporated milk

This milk has been treated to remove about 60% of its water. It is then sterilised in tins, which gives it its distinctive flavour. It has 9% fat and is used in many recipes, either as it is or diluted, and used instead of full-fat milk.

Condensed milk

This very thick, sweet milk is used in desserts, particularly Banoffee pie. It contains 40–50% sugar. It is a favourite with hikers and mountaineers because it can be used as a sweetener in hot beverages. For sweet tooth fanatics, it is also delicious spread on bread.

Buttermilk

Buttermilk is traditionally made from the whey from butter-making, but is now made from skimmed milk that has been soured with lactic acid. It tastes rather like natural, low-fat yoghurt. Buttermilk is used for baking soda bread and scones. If you cannot find it, you can make your own by adding 1 tablespoon of lemon juice to 225 ml/8 fl oz of full-fat milk.

Powdered milk

This is a fine granule milk made when all the water is removed by evaporation. It is usually low in fat. It is used in recipes by reconstituting it with water. It has a poor flavour but is useful as an emergency item in the cupboard.

Goat's milk

Goat's milk is now widely available. It is useful for people with a lactose intolerance because it is more easily digested by humans than the more difficult to digest cow's milk. The flavour is much stronger than cow's milk, which is why it is so popular with cheese-makers.

Soya milk

This is very popular because more people are now avoiding dairy foods. It is easily available and can be used as ordinary milk, for adding to drinks and in recipes. It is also quite good on cereals, but you might need a little time to adjust to the flavour.

Storage

If you have your milk delivered, always take it indoors as soon as possible; sunlight destroys the vitamin C. Keep it in the refrigerator, always covered to avoid contamination by odours. Make sure you always use a clean jug when serving: do not refill it once used. You can freeze homogenised milk in cartons for an emergency.

Cream is made from the concentrated fatty part of milk. It is delicious and adds flavour, texture and richness to food. Unfortunately, because of its high fat content, cream has a poor reputation but, like all things, it can be enjoyed occasionally as a treat. There are low-fat varieties available, but a half-quantity of the real thing seems a better option.

Half-fat cream
This has the lowest fat content of 12%, rather like the traditional top of the milk. It can be used on fruit, in coffee and hot chocolate and in sauces.

Single cream
This is a pouring cream to be used over desserts. It is not thick enough to whip because it only has a fat content of 18%. Use it in sauces, and garnish soups with a little before serving. It is rather rich for ordinary cereals but delicious on hot porridge. Extra-thick single cream is available for spooning on top of pies and other desserts. It has the same fat content but has been thickened by homogenisation.

Whipping cream
This cream contains 34% fat, allowing it to be whipped to a good consistency. Always use a clean bowl and a hand-held electric mixer or a balloon whisk. The cream should double in bulk and produce a light, airy consistency for piling on desserts, or for piping if desired.

Double cream
This has a minimum fat content of 48% and is exceedingly rich. Use it on special occasions to decorate cakes and desserts. It is good added to sauces because it does not curdle when heated. Take care when whisking it though, because it is so rich it is easy to overbeat and produce a separated butter mixture. Always whisk it cold from the refrigerator. It is used in decadent desserts like crème brûlée and syllabubs. Extra-thick double cream is prepared in the same way as the single variety and produces a thick, spoonable cream, with the same fat content, ready for serving.

Clotted cream
This is the richest cream available; it has a 55–60% fat content. Clotted cream is traditionally made in Devon and Cornwall: it is very thick and can be cut with a knife. Serve it with scones and jam for a cream tea. It can also be served with apple pie or fruit tarts for a really luxurious dessert.

Soured cream
This is a rich, thick cream, thickened by bacterial action, which gives it a richer appearance than its fat content of 18% would suggest. It is used to make sauces, salad dressings and dips. It is also good in soups and in traditional Russian, Polish and Mexican food, such as borsch, stroganoff and tortillas. It has a slightly acidic flavour.

Crème fraîche
This is like soured cream but richer. It has a fat content of between 30–50%, depending on the brand. Check the labels before buying it. Crème fraîche was originally made in France; it has a velvety texture and can be added to hot food without risk of curdling. The low-fat and half-fat varieties seem very acceptable.

Storage
Keep cream in the refrigerator because it deteriorates quickly. Buy it in small quantities and use before the date on the carton. Always keep it well covered to prevent contamination by other flavours in the refrigerator. Crème fraîche has a longer life and will keep for up to 2 weeks, so it is a useful commodity to have to hand.

YOGHURT

Yoghurt is made by fermenting milk with bacteria, which thickens it and also gives it its unique flavour. It has similar uses to cream but is generally lower in fat and has healthy properties attributed to it. Use it for breakfast, on cereal or with fruit. You can thicken soups and sauces with it or use it in a marinade.

There are many varieties available: Greek-style yoghurt is probably the thickest and is useful in recipes such as ice-cream or yoghurt ambrosia (see page 101). Low-fat varieties are particularly useful for serving with fruit and desserts. Beware of some of the fruit-flavoured varieties: they have a high proportion of sugar and are often artificially thickened with modified starches. They also contain artificial colourings, which can trigger allergic reactions in sensitive people, so check labels before purchasing. Organic varieties are now widely available and are becoming very popular.

Storage

Buy yoghurt little and often and store it in the refrigerator. Cover any open cartons with clingfilm and use by the date on the pack.

BUTTER

Butter is made from cream, which is churned until it separates into butter and buttermilk. Salted and unsalted varieties are available. Butter contains not less than 80% milk fat, and 1–2% of salt in the salted varieties. Many people prefer the tang of salt on their bread, others prefer the bland flavour of unsalted butter so that they can taste the bread. For desserts and cakes, unsalted butter is often preferred. Choose salted or unsalted according to your taste. Cost is a factor, as is the country of origin; try a new one from time to time. There are new 'spreadable' butters, which will stay soft in the refrigerator and spread directly without bringing them to room temperature. These are convenient but are a blend of butter with other oils. Always read the label on the packet before buying. Small, half-sized packets are useful for people who do not eat much butter.

Storage

Keep butter in the refrigerator, and keep it well wrapped to avoid tainting it with other flavours. Check the label for the 'use by' date. Butter freezes well and can be stored in the freezer for up to 5–6 months.

There are thousands of cheeses throughout the world. Here we will concentrate on those that are readily available and which we use regularly both for eating raw and for cooking.

Cheese is formed when milk is separated into curds and whey. The curds are cut and drained and then can be pressed and left to mature, as in our familiar hard cheeses. Soft, fresh cheeses are produced by beating the curds to a smooth paste and then adding seasonings.

BRITISH CHEESE

Cheese-making in Britain has been a long-standing tradition. Many British cheeses are known world-wide and are often served in Britain as a ploughman's lunch, in sandwiches, grilled on toast and in sauces for vegetables and pasta. They are also served as a cheeseboard at the end of a meal instead of, before, or after a dessert.

Cheddar

This is the best-known British cheese and has been imitated many times. The original Cheddar comes from Cheddar in Somerset and is at its best when prepared on the farm from unpasteurised milk. It has a yellow colour and a very creamy texture with a nutty flavour. The flavour varies in strength, which makes it an excellent all-purpose cheese. It is wonderful on a cheeseboard served with some good crusty bread and some mustard or chutney. Mild Cheddar is good for grating and scattering over au gratin dishes or for incorporating into a sauce.

Stilton

This is known as the king of cheeses. It has a very strong, tangy flavour, which comes from its distinctive blue-green mould. This mould gives the cheese its attractive veining. The best Stiltons are very expensive but have a wonderful flavour. In Britain, this cheese is traditionally eaten at Christmas with walnuts and a glass of port. It is also very good in sauces, soufflés, and in soups, where its strong flavour enhances blander ingredients.

Lancashire

This is a pale-coloured cheese with a crumbly texture. It has a mild, sharp flavour. Lancashire cheese is good on a cheeseboard served with celery and pickle. It is also good in cooking because it crumbles and melts well.

Double Gloucester

This cheese resembles Cheddar but has a rich orange colour. It has a mellow flavour and a smooth, firm texture. Eat it on its own or in sandwiches. Double Gloucester can also be used in cooking wherever Cheddar is required.

Wensleydale

Another white, crumbly cheese with a milk flavour. This cheese comes from Yorkshire, where it is served to accompany apple pie. It is good for cooking too.

FRENCH CHEESE

Brie

A large, round, mild, soft cheese, which is one of the world's greatest favourites. It is perfect for ending a meal with a few grapes or as part of a summer's lunch. Try to buy it cut from the whole cheese and eat it within 1–2 days before it dries out. Unpasteurised brie made on the farm is the best.

Camembert

Another famous French cheese, from Normandy. It is stronger and made in smaller rounds, which can be bought whole or halved. Allow it to ripen (it should be soft inside) before eating it with a crisp baguette.

Roquefort

A famous sheep's-milk cheese with green veining. Roquefort is a very salty cheese with a very pungent flavour. It is France's king of cheeses.

ITALIAN CHEESE

Many delicious Italian cheeses are now widely available, from hard cheeses such as Parmesan and pecorino, to soft cheeses such as mascarpone.

Parmesan

This hard cheese is widely used both for eating and for cooking. It has a good, strong, sweet flavour. Parmigiano Reggiano is the original and still the best you can buy. Buy a large piece and keep it handy for slicing off a piece to have with some fruit at the end of a meal, or grate some ready to serve with pasta or to sprinkle on baked au gratin dishes. Shaved Parmesan, prepared with a potato peeler, is a popular way to serve it scattered over salad leaves. Never buy ready-grated powder in little plastic bags – it has an inferior taste and consistency.

Mozzarella

This is a soft, white, slightly rubbery cheese, which is best when made from buffalo milk. It often comes in small, white plastic bags to keep it moist. You can also buy it from cheese shops, where it is often kept in large bowls. Mozzarella is traditionally used on pizzas, but it is equally delicious in a tomato salad with fresh basil leaves.

Cheddar

Blue Stilton

Lancashire

Wensleydale

Brie

Camembert

Roquefort

Gorgonzola

A soft, blue-veined cheese with a strong flavour. Use it to end a meal or to serve with fruit and salad leaves as a starter.

Dolcelatte

This cheese is similar to Gorgonzola but is made in a factory. It is slightly blander, has a creamy, moist texture and keeps well. Torte de dolcelatte is layered with cream cheese and tastes heavenly.

Pecorino

This is a cheese made from sheep's milk. It is a hard, grainy cheese and can be used in the same way as Parmesan.

Mascarpone

A very rich cream cheese, which is whisked to give it a creamy texture. Mascarpone forms the basis of the dessert Tiramisù. It can also be used in baked pasta dishes.

Ricotta

This is a rich version of British cottage cheese. It has quite a grainy texture and can be found on delicatessen counters in its traditional pyramid shape. It is also available in small cartons in supermarkets. Use it in sweet and savoury dishes.

SWISS CHEESE

Gruyère

A hard, pressed cheese, which has an oily texture. It has holes throughout the cheese and a good flavour and can be used for cooking and as a dessert cheese.

Emmenthal

This is similar to Gruyère but with larger holes. Its nutty flavour goes well with fruit as a dessert, and it can also be used for cooking. Emmenthal and Gruyère are both good melting cheeses and form the foundation of the heated cheese dish known as a 'fondue'.

GREEK CHEESE

Feta

A soft, white cheese, which is very salty. It has a hard, crumbly texture and quite an acidic flavour. It is best served with olives and tomatoes, as in a Greek salad.

Halloumi

This is a sheep's milk cheese. It is firm and has a salty flavour, and can be sliced and grilled before serving with salad.

Parmesan

Dolcelatte

Ricotta

Mozzarella

Gorgonzola

Mascarpone

FRESH, SOFT CHEESES

More and more soft cheeses are arriving in our shops. They are gaining popularity and can be used in a variety of ways.

Cream cheese

This is made from single or double cream. It is a very creamy cheese and is often used in desserts and cheesecakes. It has a fairly high fat content.

Cottage cheese

This is made from skimmed milk. It has a low fat content and a lumpy texture. It is rather bland and needs to be mixed with flavourings to make it palatable. However, many people find it acceptable and eat it as part of a weight loss programme.

Curd cheese

A smooth cheese, which is blended with salt. It has a slightly acidic flavour and is lower in fat content than cream cheese. Use it for spreading on bread or biscuits or in recipes requiring a cream cheese.

Fromage frais

This cheese originally came from France. It is made from skimmed milk but can be mixed with cream to give a range of richness from almost fat-free to a high fat content. You can use fromage frais in the same way as cream or add it to dips and salad dressings.

Storage

A refrigerator is really too cold to store cheese. An ideal temperature is 10°C/50°F, but not many homes have a larder or a cold room so the refrigerator is the only place. Make sure the cheese is loosely wrapped in waxed paper or a plastic bag, not the wrapper it was bought in because this is too tight and will make the cheese sweat. Remove any cheese at least 2 hours before serving in order for it to come to room temperature. Hard cheeses can be grated ready for use and stored in the refrigerator for up to one week. Grated cheese also freezes well but is only suitable for cooking, not for salads. Fresh cream cheeses should be bought when needed and used before the 'best before' date on the carton.

Cottage cheese

Cream cheese

Emmenthal

Gruyère

Curd cheese

CHEESE AND POTATO GRATIN

Serves 4
Preparation time: 20–30 minutes
Cooking time: 30–35 minutes

INGREDIENTS

1 tbsp butter

1 tbsp olive oil

1 onion, peeled and chopped

1 garlic clove, peeled and finely chopped

115 g/4 oz ham slices, chopped

2 eggs

300 ml/10 fl oz milk

85 g/3 oz Gruyère cheese, grated

2 tbsp freshly grated Parmesan

whole nutmeg, for grating

450 g/1 lb potatoes, peeled

1 tbsp chopped fresh parsley

salt and pepper

You will need an oval gratin dish (about 1.2 litre/2 pint capacity), a baking sheet, a frying pan, a wooden spatula, a large basin, a balloon whisk, a measuring jug and a grater or food processor

WINE SUGGESTION

Try a Californian wine – an oaky white Chardonnay, or a soft red Pinot Noir.

METHOD

1 Use a little butter to grease the gratin dish. Melt the remaining butter with the oil in a frying pan over a low heat. Add the onion and garlic and soften for about 10 minutes. Add the ham and keep it warm on top of the stove.

2 Preheat the oven to 190ºC/375ºF/Gas 5. In a separate basin, beat the eggs then add the milk. Stir in three-quarters of the cheese and season. Grate about a quarter of the nutmeg into the mixture.

3 Grate the potatoes using a grater or a food processor if you have one. Squeeze them between your hands to extract as much water as possible. Add them to the egg mixture along with the ham and onion and the parsley and mix well.

4 Pour into the prepared dish, scatter the remaining cheese on top, place on a baking sheet and bake at the top of the preheated oven for about 30 minutes until golden brown.

5 Serve warm for lunch or supper with a tomato salad.

SAVOURY CHEESE BAKE

Serves 4
Preparation time: 15 minutes
Cooking time: 20–30 minutes

INGREDIENTS

6 thick slices day-old white bread

4 tbsp butter, softened

1 tbsp olive oil

3 large eggs

300 ml/10 fl oz milk

150 ml/5 fl oz Greek yoghurt

1 garlic clove, peeled and left whole

175 g/6 oz Cheddar or Double Gloucester, grated

4–8 spring onions, finely sliced

1 tbsp chopped fresh parsley or mint

2 tbsp grated Parmesan

salt and pepper

You will need a bread knife, a cook's knife, a chopping board, a basin, a pastry brush, a large baking sheet, a measuring jug, a grater and a 25 x 20 cm/10 x 8 inch deep baking dish

METHOD

1 Preheat the oven to 160°C/325°F/Gas 3. Spread the bread slices with butter on one side only. Brush a large baking sheet with a little of the olive oil and lay out the bread on it. Bake in the preheated oven for 5–10 minutes until the bread is nearly dry and slightly brown. Remove the bread from the oven but leave the oven switched on.

2 In a separate basin, beat the eggs and add the milk and yoghurt. Season generously with salt and pepper.

3 Use the remaining oil to brush the baking dish. Cut the crisp bread into thick fingers and rub over with the garlic clove. Lay half the pieces in the dish and sprinkle over the cheese, spring onions to taste, and chopped parsley or mint.

4 Cover with the remaining bread and pour over the egg mixture. Let the dish stand for about 15 minutes to absorb the liquid.

5 Sprinkle over the Parmesan and bake in the preheated oven for 20–30 minutes until almost set and golden brown. Serve warm for lunch or supper with a green salad.

WINE SUGGESTION

Try a sturdy Australian red Cabernet Sauvignon or an oaky Australian Chardonnay from the same area.

HOT GOAT'S CHEESE SALAD

This salad makes a good lunch or light supper dish.

Serves 2
Preparation time: 5 minutes
Cooking time: 25 minutes

INGREDIENTS

225 g/8 oz cherry vine tomatoes
4 garlic cloves, unpeeled
1 tbsp olive oil
200 g/7 oz soft rind goat's cheese, such as Capricorn
55 g/2 oz wild rocket
2 tbsp balsamic vinegar
salt and pepper
a few fresh basil leaves, to garnish

You will need a small roasting tin, a sharp knife, a chopping board, a heatproof dish and 2 serving plates

METHOD

1 Preheat the oven to 180°C/350°F/Gas 4. Put the tomatoes and garlic in a small roasting dish. Sprinkle over the oil and season well. Cook them at the top of the preheated oven for 20 minutes.

2 Remove the top and bottom rinds from the goat's cheese and cut in half horizontally. If you are using two smaller cheeses, cut them both in half horizontally.

3 Place the cheese pieces on a heatproof dish and cook under a hot grill for 3–4 minutes until they begin to melt and turn golden.

4 Arrange the rocket on two plates. Remove the tomatoes and garlic from the oven. Use a slotted spoon to remove them, and reserve the roasting juices. Arrange the tomatoes and garlic around the plates and put the cheese in the centre.

5 Add the balsamic vinegar to the juices in the roasting dish and mix well to make a dressing. Drizzle the dressing over the cheese and salad and serve garnished with the basil leaves.

WINE SUGGESTION

A fruity and unoaked white New Zealand Sauvignon, or a South African Chenin.

PENNE WITH MUSHROOMS AND DOLCELATTE

This is a delicious pasta dish, which uses penne (tube pasta) and rich Italian blue dolcelatte cheese.

Serves 4
Preparation time: 5 minutes
Cooking time: 15 minutes

INGREDIENTS

400 g/14 oz penne (tube pasta)
1 tbsp olive oil
250 g/9 oz chestnut mushrooms, sliced
225 g/8 oz dolcelatte, crumbled
200 g/7 oz half-fat crème fraîche
150 g/5½ oz rocket leaves or spinach
salt and pepper
55 g/2 oz Parmesan, freshly shaved, to garnish

You will need a large saucepan (about 3.5 litres/6 pints), a colander, a frying pan, a wooden spatula, a cook's knife, a chopping board and 4 serving bowls

WINE SUGGESTION
Try a fresh red Châteauneuf-du-Pâpe or a simpler Côtes de Ventoux with this cheesy pasta dish.

METHOD

1 Cook the pasta over a medium heat in a large saucepan of salted boiling water, according to the instructions on the packet.

2 Heat the oil in a frying pan over a low heat and gently sauté the mushrooms for 3–4 minutes until they start to soften.

3 Stir in the dolcelatte and allow it to melt, then add the crème fraîche.

4 Add the rocket or spinach and heat for 1–2 minutes until just wilted. Taste, and add salt and pepper.

5 Drain the cooked pasta in a colander and serve in hot bowls with the sauce poured over the top. Serve immediately garnished with the Parmesan shavings.

PANNA COTTA

This is a delicious, creamy, rich Italian dessert, which is lightly set with gelatine.

Serves 6
Preparation time: 15 minutes, plus chilling

INGREDIENTS

1 tbsp vegetable oil
1 vanilla pod
600 ml/1 pint double cream
4 tbsp caster sugar
2 tsp powdered gelatine
3 tbsp cold water

To decorate
6 sprigs fresh mint
about 18 strawberries, sliced

You will need a small saucepan (preferably non-stick), a small, heatproof bowl that fits snugly over the saucepan, a sharp knife, a wooden spoon, six 125 ml/4 fl oz dariole moulds or ramekins, a pastry brush and 6 small serving plates

METHOD

1 Use the oil to grease the moulds well. Split the vanilla pod with a sharp knife and scrape out all the seeds. Put the pod and the seeds in a saucepan with the cream and sugar and stir well over a low heat. Carefully bring to simmering point and simmer gently for 2–3 minutes. Remove from the heat and leave to cool a little.

2 Soak the gelatine in 3 tablespoons of cold water in a small, heatproof bowl. Place the bowl over a saucepan of hot water and heat gently until the gelatine is dissolved and clear.

3 Remove the vanilla pod from the cream and stir in the gelatine. Pour the mixture into the prepared moulds, cover with clingfilm and chill for at least 3 hours, or overnight, until set.

4 To serve, dip the moulds up to the rim (do not immerse completely) in hot water for 2 seconds and then turn out onto serving plates. Serve decorated with the mint sprigs and fresh berries.

YOGHURT AMBROSIA

This sweet, creamy dessert is very simple to make but it tastes absolutely heavenly.

Serves 6
Preparation time: 10 minutes, plus chilling overnight

INGREDIENTS

300 ml/10 fl oz double cream
300 ml/10 fl oz thick Greek yoghurt
6 tbsp dark muscovado sugar

You will need a large basin, a balloon whisk, and a large, shallow serving bowl (about 20 cm/8 inches in diameter) or 6 small ramekins

METHOD

1 In a large basin, use a balloon whisk to beat the cream until thick. Add the yoghurt and mix together well. Pour into the serving dish or ramekins.

2 Sprinkle the sugar over the surface of the mixture in quite a thick layer. Cover with clingfilm and chill in the refrigerator overnight. The sugar will dissolve, leaving a luscious toffee layer.

APRICOT BREAD AND BUTTER PUDDING

Serves 4

**Preparation time: 10 minutes, plus
15 minutes standing**

Cooking time: 30–40 minutes

INGREDIENTS

6 tbsp unsalted butter, softened

6 slices thick, white bread

2 tbsp apricot jam

55 g/2 oz ready-to-eat dried apricots, chopped

3 large eggs

150 ml/5 fl oz double cream

300 ml/10 fl oz milk

85 g/3 oz caster sugar

grated rind of 1 orange

1 tbsp demerara sugar

125 ml/4 fl oz single cream, to serve

You will need a 25 x 20 cm/10 x 8 inch baking dish, a
baking sheet, a bread knife, a chopping board, a measuring jug,
a bowl and a balloon whisk

1 Use a little of the butter to grease the baking dish and butter the slices of bread. Butter three slices on one side only and three on both sides.

2 Spoon the apricot jam onto the three slices of bread that have been buttered on one side only. Put a slice of double buttered bread on top of each one to make three sandwiches.

3 Cut the sandwiches into quarters and arrange them, overlapping, in the dish. Scatter the chopped dried apricots over the bread.

4 Whisk the eggs well and mix in the double cream, milk, sugar and orange rind. Pour the mixture over the pudding and leave to stand for 15 minutes to allow the bread to soak up some of the egg mixture. Sprinkle over the demerara sugar.

5 Preheat the oven to 180°C/350°F/Gas 4. Place the pudding on the baking sheet. Bake at the top of the preheated oven for 30–40 minutes until just set and golden brown.

6 Remove the pudding from the oven and serve immediately with single cream.

FISH AND SHELLFISH

Thank heavens eating fish is regaining popularity. The days of only eating it as a penance on Fridays are long past, and recipes are no longer limited to just steaming or deep-fat frying. We do not have to worry about filleting or gutting fish anymore either: fishmongers and supermarkets have taken the pain out of preparation.

Nowadays we recognise the health benefits of fish. They are a good source of protein and are rich in healthy oils. TV programmes and foreign travel have also made them popular.

The range of fish now available is much wider too. Times have changed since oysters were a cheap staple and salmon was expensive. Now we have white flat fish, such as plaice, or round fish, such as cod. There are healthy oily fish such as herrings, mackerel and tuna, and pink freshwater fish such as salmon and trout. We can also buy smoked fish, a delicious range of shellfish, and new more exotic types of fish such as shark, red mullet and monkfish. Now is the time to experiment with this abundance of healthy flavours and textures.

Buying fish

There is no need to worry about buying and cooking fish nowadays. Fishmongers and the fish counters in our supermarkets are very reliable and have a good turnover of fish, so we are able to buy it really fresh. Preparation need not be a problem either. We do not expect to butcher our own meat, and likewise we should not have to worry about gutting our own fish. Experts at the task do a better job than we can, so it is best to let them do it. The supermarket counter staff are well trained and will do any job asked of them.

Always buy fish that is in season to get the best flavour and value. Cod and haddock are always on sale but they may have been frozen and come from Australia. The best cod and haddock come from fishing grounds in the colder waters around the British coast and from the North Atlantic, and have the finest flavour and the best texture. The season is from May/June to February. Due to air freight, it is possible to get most fish fresh all the year round, but it is still good to wait for our own season before buying shellfish, especially oysters and mussels.

Storage

Always buy your fish at the end of your shopping trip so that you can take it home immediately. Ask the fishmonger to wrap it in some ice to ensure it stays cool on the journey. In hot weather I keep a cool box in the boot of my car to carry home any fresh fish and frozen foods. When you get it home, remove the fish from its wrapping and wipe it over with some kitchen paper. Then place it in a dish, cover with clingfilm and place in the refrigerator before using the same day.

Smoked fish is often bought vacuum-packed: store it in the refrigerator and use by the date shown on the pack. Fresh smoked fish should be well wrapped and refrigerated for as short a time as possible to avoid contamination with other foods.

Frozen fish is very good and can be stored in the freezer for up to 6 months without deterioration. It is a good idea to buy small fillets or steaks and freeze them individually so that you can have a quick meal at any time. Frozen fish should be thawed in the refrigerator; this helps to retain the flavour and texture. Thaw the fish for at least 8 hours or overnight. Small fillets can be cooked from frozen, but they might need a little longer cooking time.

WHITE FISH

These are divided into round and flat fish. The most familiar round fish is cod and its relatives are haddock, hake, whiting and coley. They can all be bought as fillets, steaks or cutlets. Flat fish include sole, plaice, turbot and halibut.

Cod

This can be as large as 6.5 kg/14 lb. It has a firm, flaky flesh, which is soft and white when cooked. It can be baked, grilled, poached, pan-fried, or deep-fried in batter or breadcrumbs.

FILLETING A FISH

There is no need to fillet your own fish nowadays – your local fishmonger can do it for you. If you prefer to fillet your own, however, here is an example.

1 Wash the fish under cold running water, then place it on a clean work surface. Remove any scales first.

2 Using a pair of kitchen scissors, cut off the tough fins: this Dover sole has a few small ones on top on either side, whereas salmon and sharks only have one fin.

3 To take the fillet off, slide the knife across the top of the bone, from the neck end right down to the tail.

4 Turn the fish over and, once again, take the fillet off by sliding the knife across the top of the bone, from the neck end right down to the tail. The head and tail will come off automatically.

D epending on its size, a flat fish can yield two or four fillets. Always make sure you trim and scale the fish before you start filleting.

Haddock

This is usually smaller than cod and has a finer texture. It can be used in the same way as cod.

Hake

This is a thinner version of the cod family, so the steaks tend to be smaller. You can bake or steam it; it is also useful in soups and stews.

Whiting

This is a succulent fish and can be fried or baked.

Coley

This has grey-looking flesh and is rather unappealing when raw; also, it does not have a good flavour. However, it is useful in fish cakes, fish pies and well-flavoured recipes such as curry.

Sole

There are two varieties of sole: Dover and lemon. Dover sole has the better flavour. It comes in different weights, from 225g/8 oz to 900 g/2 lb. The smaller ones are ideal for cooking whole, either by pan-frying or grilling. The larger ones are filleted and can be grilled, fried, baked or poached. Since the flavour is so fine, a little seasoning and a squeeze of lemon are all that is required. Lemon sole has not got the flavour of its Dover sole relation, but it is good when the fillets are used in recipes with stuffings or other flavourings. Lemon sole can also be made into goujons (small pieces of white fish, usually crumbed and fried).

Plaice

This is very similar to sole but it does not have the fine flavour. If you are buying fillets, buy the white underside ones because the skin is very tender and can be eaten, whereas the black skin of the upperside needs removing. Plaice can be baked, poached, grilled, or pan-fried and made into goujons. A sauce accompaniment, such as tartare, is often served with plaice to pep up the flavour.

Turbot

This fish can weigh up to 6.5kg/14lb; the larger the fish, the better the eating. Turbot has a firm, moist flesh with a delicious, sweet flavour. The steaks are large and, because of their dense state, can be grilled without damaging the texture of the flesh. Turbot is a very expensive fish but is worth it for its excellent flavour.

Halibut

This is the largest flat fish and can measure up to 2 m/6½ ft long and 1 m/3¼ ft wide. This fish is expensive but has a good flavour and texture. It can be used in the same way as turbot. It can also be cut into cubes and made into kebabs.

FROM TOP Brown trout, Dover sole, herring, mackerel, and red mullet

OILY FISH

These fish are rich in omega-3 fatty acids, which are believed to help reduce cholesterol in our blood and prevent heart disease. They are a healthy food and have a delicious flavour due to their fat content. Oily fish need to be absolutely fresh.

Herring family

This consists of herrings, sprats, sardines and whitebait. They all have a similar texture and unfortunately lots of small bones. They are best grilled or pan-fried (or barbecued) so that the skin crisps and the flesh stays moist. Ask your fishmonger to remove all the innards and as many bones as possible. Whitebait are the very young fish of the family, so they can be tiny herrings or small sprats or sardines. They should be washed thoroughly, then tossed in seasoned flour and deep-fried whole. Drain well and serve immediately.

Mackerel

Mackerel have a wonderful silver-grey skin, with shadows of blue and green. They are delicious but must be eaten on the day they are caught, so eat them while you are on holiday or use a reliable supplier. They have a good flavour and are at their best when simply grilled. They can be oven-baked with a piquant stuffing. Traditionally, they are served with gooseberry sauce.

Tuna

Tuna is now widely available and very popular. Its solid steaks are cooked simply by grilling or pan-frying. Tuna is a 'meaty' fish, so it is acceptable to people who normally avoid fish. It has a good flavour but do not overcook it or it will dry out. Cook for 2–3 minutes on each side, depending on thickness. For the best flavour, it should be a little underdone in the centre.

Salmon

This is probably the most popular fish. Farming methods keep it cheap and it is available all year round. If you can ever get wild salmon (in season from February to October), then do so because it is quite a different fish. Salmon can be cooked whole, in fillets, in steaks and cutlets, and by many methods including poaching, grilling, pan-frying, steaming and 'en papillote' (baked inside a parcel of baking paper). It is very versatile and can be served with butter, in sauces, or in more complex recipes, from soups and starters to main courses. Do not overcook the salmon or the result will be dry.

Trout

The wild brown trout is hardly ever seen now, but the farmed rainbow trout is easily available. An average whole trout makes a perfect meal for one person – poach, grill, pan-fry or bake it in the oven. Make sure the fishmonger guts the fish and removes the head for you first.

SMOKED FISH

Smoking imparts a wonderful flavour, and with some fish the process of hot-smoking actually cooks the fish too so that we can eat it cold, for example as smoked salmon, trout or mackerel. Other fish, such as haddock and cod, are cold-smoked to avoid cooking the fish. These then need to be cooked before they can be eaten. Sometimes these fish have been dyed to give them a stronger yellow colour. However, there is now a return to undyed, naturally smoked fish. All these fish are usually available in the shops.

Smoked salmon

This is a traditional delicacy, usually served cold with some brown bread and butter. A scattering of freshly milled pepper and some lemon wedges are usually offered, but you should try really good smoked salmon as it is to appreciate the delicate flavour. Buy a whole side if possible, and cut it as you need it. Pre-sliced smoked salmon tends to dry out, so eat it soon after purchase.

Smoked trout

Delicately flavoured smoked trout is available whole (minus the head). Serve it simply with lemon wedges and some horseradish sauce mixed with a little crème fraîche.

Smoked mackerel

This is rather rich and oily, and needs a sharp sauce to accompany it. A dill and mustard sauce, or horseradish sauce mixed with a little crème fraîche, would be a good choice. Smoked mackerel can also be used to make a quick smoked fish pâté with lots of lemon juice and grated lemon zest and a little butter.

Smoked haddock

This is the best-known smoked fish. It is delicious simply poached and then served with a poached egg on top. It is also good with buttered spinach or lentils. It forms the basis of kedgeree (a popular breakfast dish consisting of rice, lentils, onions, smoked fish, hard-boiled eggs and a rich cream sauce).

Smoked cod

This is similar to smoked haddock but quite often is thicker with chunkier flakes. It makes a fine fish pie and can be used in fish cakes.

Kippers

These are smoked herrings, which can be reheated by quickly grilling or poaching them. A traditional method is to put the kippers in a tall jug, fill the jug with boiling water and leave them for 5 minutes. They are usually served for breakfast but they also make a good supper dish.

NEWER VARIETIES OF FISH

We have more varieties of fish available than ever before and some are gaining in popularity. The following are the most popular of the newer types of fish.

Monkfish

Just the tail of this fish is used. It has a very fine texture and a reasonably sweet flavour. It is very firm and can be cooked on skewers; it is also good grilled. Monkfish has no bones, which is a great attraction. The fishmonger will remove the skin and divide the tail into two fillets for you, ready for cooking.

Red mullet

This fish is easily recognised on the fish counter. It is a vivid red and is wonderful grilled, particularly on a barbecue. It can also be pan-fried. It has a firm texture with a mild flavour.

Other newcomers are sea bass, bream, red snapper, red gurnard, shark and swordfish. All are worth trying.

SHELLFISH

We are very lucky that there is such a wide variety of shellfish available, both fresh and frozen, in the shops today. Extra care should be taken with shellfish because they can cause food poisoning. Always order direct from your supplier to ensure you get what you require, then use them on the day of purchase. If you are collecting them, get them home as quickly as possible and keep them in the refrigerator.

Prawns

These can be bought frozen, raw or cooked, and in different sizes. Ordinary prawns are sold cooked, either shelled or unshelled. The shelled variety are available frozen. It is a good idea to have a packet of shelled, cooked prawns in the freezer because a handful can be added to rice dishes or other fish dishes to add interest. They are also useful as a garnish. Large freshwater prawns are the next in size and they are usually sold uncooked and headless. Tiger prawns are warm-water prawns and can be bought cooked or uncooked, with or without their heads. They are round and fat and have a good flavour. Whole prawns, with their shells on, are useful for a garnish and to eat simply as a starter with a bowl of mayonnaise.

Scallops

These are now becoming very popular. They are expensive, but their delicate flavour and texture make them a worthwhile special purchase. They need the lightest of cooking and are best pan-fried for 1–2 minutes on each side.

Mussels

These are still relatively cheap and they have a great flavour. Buy them only when in season (October to March) and eat on the day of purchase. Before using, make sure all the shells are closed; if not, discard them along with any broken shells. Scrub to remove any deposits and pull away the 'beards'. Wash them well in two or three changes of water, then leave in clean, cold water until you are ready to cook them. After cooking, check the shells again and if any have not opened, discard them.

Oysters

Oysters are usually eaten raw. They are farmed in carefully monitored water conditions. They can also be cooked in many ways, by steaming or grilling or adding to fish soups and stews. Serve them well chilled with a little lemon or vinegar on the side. Some finely chopped shallots can also be added.

You need a special oyster knife to open them. Hold the oyster in a cloth to protect the hand. The flatter shell should be on top. Put the blade of the knife in between the shells at the narrowest point. Work the knife backwards and forwards to break the hinge. Twist the knife and remove the top shell.

Squid

Squid looks more like a little octopus, but it is a mollusc, like mussels and oysters. You can buy it already prepared, and even cut into rings. However, it is best to buy it whole and cut it to size yourself, to preserve the tentacles and give a less uniform appearance. Squid has a good flavour but a bad reputation for being rubbery – that is because people overcook it. It should be sautéed quickly for only 2–3 minutes and served immediately.

Crab

Crab is usually cooked before buying, but it is difficult to remove the meat from the shell and claws. If you practise you will be able to master it eventually. The easiest way to eat it is to buy it ready prepared. Sometimes you can even buy the white meat separated from the brown, but usually you have a mixture. Crab has a very delicate flavour and is often served simply, on its own with some brown bread and butter. If it is to be mixed with other foods, they need to be subtle so the flavour is not overpowered. Pasta, savoury tarts and salads are good with crab. Crab cakes are also in fashion at the moment.

Lobster

This is a real extravagance but it is the ultimate of all shellfish. The flavour is unsurpassable and the experience one to be remembered. You can find prepared lobsters in shops but they are not as good as those you will find by the sea where they are caught. If you want to buy a lobster, go to a good fishmonger and order a live one for him to cook specially for you – this way it will be at its best.

Scallops

Prawns

Squid

Mussels

Lobster

Oysters

Crab

HERB CRUSTED COD

Serves 4
Preparation time: 10 minutes
Cooking time: 15–20 minutes

INGREDIENTS

4 thick pieces of skinless cod, about 175 g/6 oz each
2 tbsp olive oil
115g/4 oz fresh breadcrumbs (white or wholemeal)
1 garlic clove, peeled and chopped
2 tbsp chopped fresh parsley
grated zest of 1 lemon
salt and pepper
cooked whole green beans, to serve

You will need a shallow, ovenproof dish (lightly brushed with a little of the oil), a mixing bowl, a blender, a cook's knife, a chopping board, and a grater or lemon zester

METHOD

1 Preheat the oven to 190°C/375°F/Gas 5. Arrange the cod pieces in the dish, brush with oil and season well.

2 In a separate bowl, mix together the breadcrumbs, garlic, parsley and lemon zest and season well.

3 Pile the breadcrumb mixture carefully on top of the fish pieces and press down well.

4 Place the dish in the centre of the preheated oven and bake for 15–20 minutes until the fish is cooked and the crust is crisp and golden brown. Serve on a bed of freshly cooked green beans.

WINE SUGGESTION

A white Rioja or an Australian white Semillon will go well with this herbed fish dish.

TARTARE SAUCE

Tartare sauce is based on mayonnaise (see page 80), but for this recipe you can use a good branded mayonnaise instead. It is traditionally served with fish.

Makes 225 ml/8 fl oz
Preparation time: 20 minutes

INGREDIENTS

225 ml/8 fl oz mayonnaise
1 tbsp chopped capers
1 tbsp chopped gherkins
1 tbsp chopped fresh parsley
1 tsp chopped chives
1 tbsp lemon juice
salt and pepper

You will need a basin and a plastic spatula

METHOD

1 Place the mayonnaise in the bowl and fold in the other ingredients. Check the seasoning and adjust if necessary.

2 Cover the basin with clingfilm and chill in the refrigerator for at least 30 minutes. This sauce will keep in a screw-top jar in the refrigerator for up to one week.

BAKED TROUT

Trout makes an ideal quick supper. It can be grilled or pan-fried in just 10 minutes. For more than two people, oven baking is best and it also avoids frying odours. Serve one trout per person.

Serves 4

Preparation time: 20 minutes
Cooking time: 12–15 minutes

INGREDIENTS

2 shallots, peeled and finely chopped

2 tbsp butter, melted

1 garlic clove, peeled and finely chopped

1 tbsp finely chopped root ginger

1 stick lemon grass, crushed and finely chopped

55 g/2 oz baby spinach

pinch crushed dried chilli, optional

4 fresh trout, about 350 g/12 oz each, cleaned and fins removed

1 tbsp light soy sauce

salt and pepper

To serve
2 spring onions, finely chopped

1 tbsp butter, melted

125 ml/4 fl oz white wine

2 tbsp fish sauce

½ tbsp chopped fresh coriander

½ tbsp chopped fresh basil

1 lime, quartered, to garnish

You will need a shallow, ovenproof baking sheet covered with foil, a cook's knife, a chopping board, a medium saucepan, a wooden spatula, a small saucepan and 4 serving plates

WINE SUGGESTION

This dish suits the juicy flavours of a New Zealand Semillon or Semillon Chardonnay blend.

METHOD

1 Put the shallots and the 2 tablespoons of melted butter in a medium saucepan and soften over a medium heat for 2–3 minutes. Add the garlic, ginger and lemon grass. Cook for a further 2 minutes, then add the spinach. Cook it for 2–3 minutes then add the chilli (if using). Season well. Remove from the heat and allow to cool. Drain if necessary.

2 Preheat the oven to 220ºC/425ºF/Gas 7. Wipe the trout carefully with kitchen paper and, using a sharp knife, slash the skin of each fish diagonally on both sides about five times – this allows the fish to cook quickly. Season well inside and out, and rub with the soy sauce.

3 Fill the trout with the spinach stuffing, then re-shape them as neatly as you can.

4 Lift the trout carefully onto the prepared baking sheet. Cook at the top of the preheated oven for 12–15 minutes, until the skin is crispy and golden.

5 In a small saucepan, soften the spring onions in the melted butter over a low heat for 1–2 minutes and add the wine and the fish sauce. Season to taste. Raise the heat and cook rapidly for 1 minute to produce a slightly thickened sauce. Add the herbs and stir well.

6 Serve the trout on warmed serving plates with the sauce poured over. Serve immediately, garnished with the lime quarters.

FISH CAKES

This recipe makes 4 large fish cakes. You can make 8 smaller cakes if you prefer, but they are more fiddly.

Serves 4
Preparation time: 30 minutes
Cooking time: 10 minutes

INGREDIENTS

450 g/1 lb potatoes, peeled
450 g/1 lb mixed fish fillets, such as cod, haddock and salmon, skinned
2 tbsp chopped fresh parsley or tarragon
grated zest of 1 lemon
1 tbsp plain flour
1 egg, beaten
115 g/4 oz white or wholemeal breadcrumbs, made from one-day-old bread
4 tbsp vegetable oil, for frying
salt and pepper

You will need a large saucepan, a potato peeler, a cook's knife, a chopping board, a colander, a potato masher, a frying pan, a mixing bowl, a baking sheet, and a palette knife or fish slice

METHOD

1 Cut the potatoes into chunks and cook in a large saucepan of boiling, salted water for 15 minutes. Drain well and mash with a potato masher until smooth.

2 Place the fish in a frying pan and just cover with water. Bring to the boil over a medium heat, then cover and simmer gently for 5 minutes until just cooked. Remove from the heat and drain the fish onto a plate. When cool enough to handle, flake the fish and ensure that there are no bones.

3 Mix the potatoes with the fish, herbs and lemon zest in a bowl. Season well and shape into four round, flat cakes.

4 Dust the cakes with flour, dip them into the beaten egg, then coat thoroughly in the breadcrumbs. Place on a baking sheet and allow to chill for at least half an hour.

5 Heat the oil in the frying pan and fry the cakes over medium heat for 5 minutes on each side. Use a palette knife or fish slice to turn them carefully.

*Suitable for freezing. Complete to the end of step 4 and open freeze on a baking sheet. When frozen, remove the baking tray and wrap the fish cakes in freezer bags. Seal well. Store in the freezer for up to 3 months. To use, allow them to thaw in the refrigerator overnight and then continue to cook from step 5 above.

FRIED SQUID AND COURGETTES

Serves 2
Preparation time: 15 minutes
Cooking time: 8–10 minutes

WINE SUGGESTION

A New World Sauvignon has the guts to match the spicy flavouring of this recipe.

INGREDIENTS

2 tbsp olive oil

3 courgettes, trimmed and cut into 1 cm/½ inch cubes

400 g/14 oz prepared squid, cut into rings

4 plum tomatoes, deseeded and chopped

1 red chilli, deseeded and very finely chopped

1 garlic clove, peeled and finely chopped

2 tbsp white wine

salt and pepper

2 tbsp chopped fresh coriander, to garnish

You will need a cook's knife, a chopping board, a heavy frying pan, a wooden spatula, a slotted spoon and a heated serving dish

METHOD

1 Heat the oil in the pan over a high heat and fry the courgettes quickly for 3–4 minutes until they are dark golden brown. Remove the courgettes from the pan using a slotted spoon and place in a hot dish to keep warm.

2 Add the squid to the pan and fry over a high heat for 2 minutes.

3 Reduce the heat, add the tomatoes, chilli and garlic and continue to cook for another minute. Pour in the white wine and let the mixture bubble for a few seconds.

4 Remove from the heat and pour on top of the courgettes. Sprinkle over the coriander and serve immediately with lots of warm crusty bread.

GOUJONS OF PLAICE

Serves 2
Preparation time: 20 minutes
Cooking time: 5–6 minutes

INGREDIENTS

2 plaice fillets, about 175 g/6 oz each, skinned

2 tbsp plain flour

1 egg, beaten

115 g/4 oz white or wholemeal breadcrumbs, made from one-day-old bread

1 tbsp finely chopped fresh parsley

1 garlic clove, peeled and crushed (optional)

225 ml/8 fl oz vegetable oil, for frying

salt and pepper

1 lemon, halved, to serve

You will need a cook's knife, a chopping board, a basin, a shallow dish, a plastic bag, a frying pan and a slotted spoon

METHOD

1 Cut the fillets across diagonally into thin strips, about 1 cm/ ½ inch wide.

2 Season the flour well and put onto a plate. Roll the strips of fish in the flour until well covered.

3 Place the beaten egg in a shallow dish and then dip the fish into it.

4 Mix the breadcrumbs with the parsley, and garlic if using, and season well. Put the mixture into a plastic bag, add the goujons and toss to coat thoroughly. Chill in the refrigerator for at least half an hour.

5 Heat the oil in a frying pan and fry half the goujons over a medium heat for 2–3 minutes, turning them with a slotted spoon. Remove from the pan and drain on kitchen paper. Keep warm. Repeat using the remaining fish.

6 Serve at once with a half lemon per portion to squeeze over the goujons.

Suitable for freezing. Complete to the end of step 5, allow to cool, then cover with clingfilm and chill quickly. Open freeze on a baking sheet, then store in the freezer in a lidded, rigid container. To use, reheat from frozen: place on a baking sheet in an oven preheated to 200°C/400°F/Gas 6 until hot, cooked through and crispy.

MEDITERRANEAN FISH CASSEROLE

Serves 6
Preparation time: 25 minutes
Cooking time: 30 minutes

INGREDIENTS

2 tbsp olive oil

1 red onion, peeled and sliced

2 garlic cloves, peeled and chopped

2 red peppers

400 g/14 oz canned chopped tomatoes

1 tsp chopped fresh oregano or marjoram

a few saffron strands soaked in 1 tbsp warm water for 2 minutes

450 g/1 lb white fish (cod, haddock or hake), skinned and boned

450 g/1 lb prepared squid, cut into rings

300 ml/10 fl oz fish or vegetable stock

115 g/4 oz cooked shelled prawns

salt and pepper

chunky bread, to serve

To garnish
6 cooked whole prawns in their shells

2 tbsp chopped fresh parsley

You will need a 2 litre /3½ pint ovenproof lidded casserole dish, a frying pan, a wooden spatula, a cook's knife and a chopping board, a measuring jug and 6 bowls

METHOD

1 Heat the oil in a frying pan and fry the onion and garlic over a medium heat for 2–3 minutes until beginning to soften.

2 Deseed and thinly slice the peppers and add to the pan. Continue to cook over a low heat for a further 5 minutes. Add the tomatoes with the herbs and saffron and stir well.

3 Preheat the oven to 200°C/400°F/Gas 6. Cut the white fish into 3 cm/1¼ inch pieces and place with the squid in the casserole dish. Pour in the fried vegetable mixture and the stock, stir well and season to taste.

4 Cover and cook in the centre of the preheated oven for about 30 minutes, until the fish is tender and cooked. Add the prawns at the last minute and just heat through.

5 Serve in hot bowls garnished with the whole prawns and the parsley. Provide lots of chunky bread to mop up the casserole juices.

WINE SUGGESTION

Try a light white Pinot Grigio, or a Tokay d'Alsace for more bite.

117

POACHED SALMON

A whole salmon can often be bought in supermarkets and it makes a good centrepiece for a buffet or large party. It can be served hot or cold.

KETTLE METHOD

A fish kettle is necessary for larger fish. If you haven't got one in your household, you can usually hire one from your local supermarket or fishmonger.

Serves 12
Preparation time: 10 minutes
Cooking time: 20 minutes, plus cooling (if serving cold), or 45 minutes (if serving hot)

INGREDIENTS

1 whole salmon (head on), about 2.7 kg/6 lb to 3.6 kg/8 lb prepared weight
3 tbsp salt
3 bay leaves
10 peppercorns
1 onion, peeled and sliced
1 lemon, sliced

You will need a large fish kettle (with a two-handled rack), a cook's knife, a chopping board and a pair of scissors

METHOD

1 Wipe the salmon thoroughly inside and out with kitchen paper, then use the back of a cook's knife to remove any scales that might still be on the skin. Remove the fins with a pair of scissors and trim the tail. Some people prefer to cut off the head but it is traditionally served with it on.

2 Place the salmon on the two-handled rack and place in the kettle. Fill the kettle with enough cold water to cover the salmon adequately. Sprinkle over the salt, bay leaves and peppercorns and scatter in the onion and lemon slices.

3 Place on the heat, over two low burners, and bring just to the boil very slowly.

4 Put on the lid and simmer very gently. To serve cold, simmer for 2 minutes only, remove from the heat and allow to cool in the liquor for about 2 hours with the lid on. To serve hot, simmer for 6–8 minutes and allow to stand in the hot water for 15 minutes before removing.

WINE SUGGESTION
Ideally you should choose a French white Sauvignon, preferably Sancerre.

OVEN METHOD

This method is suitable for fish under 2.25 kg/5 lb in weight.

Serves 8
Preparation time: 10 minutes
Cooking time: 40 minutes, plus cooling (if serving cold), or 1 hour (if serving hot)

INGREDIENTS

1.8 kg/4 lb fresh whole salmon, prepared weight
2 tbsp butter, melted
1 lemon, sliced
a few sprigs fresh parsley
125 ml/4 fl oz white wine or water
salt and pepper

You will need a sharp knife, a chopping board, a pair of scissors, a large roasting tin, a measuring jug, a pastry brush and kitchen foil

METHOD

1 Preheat the oven to 180°C/350°F/Gas 4. Wipe the salmon thoroughly inside and out, removing any scales that might still be on the skin. Remove the fins with a pair of scissors and trim the tail.

2 Line the roasting tin with a double layer of foil and brush with the melted butter. Season the salmon with salt and pepper both inside and out.

3 Lay the salmon in the foil and place the lemon and parsley in the body cavity. Pour over the wine or water and gather up the foil to make a fairly loose parcel.

4 Bake in the preheated oven for about 30–40 minutes. When cooked, test with the point of a knife; if the fish is cooked thoroughly, the flesh should flake. To serve hot, leave for 15 minutes before removing from the foil. To serve cold, leave for 1–2 hours until lukewarm.

PACIFIC PIE

Serves 6
Preparation time: 30 minutes
Cooking time: 45 minutes

INGREDIENTS

675 g/1½ lb small potatoes, unpeeled

1 tbsp olive oil

250 g/9 oz small leeks, trimmed and finely sliced

115 g/4 oz small mushrooms, sliced

450 g/1 lb white fish fillets, such as cod or haddock, skinned

600 ml/1 pint milk

4 tbsp butter

175 g/6 oz cooked peeled prawns and/or mussels, optional

1 tbsp chopped fresh parsley or tarragon

3 tbsp plain flour

200 g/7 oz Cheddar cheese, grated

salt and pepper

You will need a cook's knife, a chopping board, a medium saucepan, a frying pan, a wooden spatula, a colander, a 1.7 litre/ 3 pint ovenproof dish and a baking sheet

METHOD

1 Slice the potatoes into thick slices. Cook in a large saucepan of boiling, salted water for 5 minutes, then drain well.

2 Put the oil and the leeks in a frying pan and cook gently over a low heat for 2–3 minutes until soft. Add the mushrooms and cook for about 2 minutes.

3 Place the fish in the rinsed saucepan and just cover with a little milk. Over a gentle heat, bring to a simmer and poach for 5 minutes until tender. Drain, and reserve the poaching milk.

4 Use a little of the butter to grease the baking dish. Flake the fish and place in the dish with the leeks, mushrooms, and prawns (if using). Scatter over the parsley or tarragon.

5 Preheat the oven to 200ºC/400ºF/Gas 6. In the same saucepan, make a white sauce. Melt the remaining butter in the saucepan and add the flour. Stir well and cook over a low heat for 2–3 minutes. Remove from the heat and gradually stir in the remaining milk, beating well after each addition. When all the milk has been added and the sauce is smooth, return the saucepan to the heat. Cook over a low heat, stirring continuously, until thickened. Cook for a further 2–3 minutes, then add 100 g/3½ oz of the cheese. Season to taste.

6 Pour half the sauce over the fish, arrange the potato slices on top and cover with the remaining sauce.

7 Sprinkle over the remaining cheese and cook on a baking sheet, in the centre of the preheated oven, for 45 minutes until golden brown.

WINE SUGGESTION

A chilled white Viognier would be delicious with this fish pie.

SEARED TUNA

Serves 4
Preparation time: 15 minutes, plus marinating
Cooking time: 6 minutes

INGREDIENTS

four 140 g/5 oz tuna steaks
2 tbsp soy sauce
zest and juice of 1 lime
1 tbsp olive oil

To serve
2 spring onions, trimmed and finely chopped
4 plum tomatoes, deseeded and chopped
pinch chilli flakes
1 tbsp shredded fresh basil leaves
2 tbsp olive oil, plus extra for brushing
1 tbsp balsamic vinegar
4 bagels or burger buns, to serve (optional)

You will need a griddle pan or heavy frying pan, a cook's knife, a chopping board, a small bowl, a shallow, non-metallic dish, a pastry brush, a palette knife or fish slice and 4 plates

WINE SUGGESTION

A full-bodied red, such as a Chilean Merlot or Australian Shiraz, would be perfect with this dish.

METHOD

1 Put the tuna in a shallow, non-metallic dish. Add the soy sauce and the lime juice and zest, and leave to marinate for 1–2 hours, or overnight if possible.

2 Make the salsa by mixing together the spring onions, tomatoes, chilli, basil, oil and vinegar in a small bowl. Season well. Put to one side for 15–30 minutes to allow the flavours to mix.

3 Preheat the pan over a high heat for 2–3 minutes until very hot. Brush the fish with oil, and then place on the hot pan for 2–3 minutes; do not move it until the time is up, so that the tuna can brown. Then brush the other side of the fish with oil and turn carefully. Cook for a further 2–3 minutes without moving it. The tuna should be just pink in the centre.

4 Transfer the fish to warm plates and serve with the salsa, in buns if desired, or with a simple green salad.

MEAT

Meat has had a bad press recently, with its fat content linked to heart disease and the publicity given to BSE and associated diseases. But do not let that put you off. Meat is rich in protein, vitamins and minerals and lean cuts are low in calories. Surplus fat can always be trimmed off before cooking or drained off after cooking.

The wide variety of cuts of beef, lamb and pork that are available can be confusing but are easily divided up. Large, tender joints are ideal for roasting, and cheaper, tougher cuts are suitable for casseroling.

Smaller and leaner cuts are quicker to cook and have less fat, such as lamb or pork fillet, or chops and beef steaks. They are delicious grilled in the winter or barbecued in the summer. They are also useful thinly sliced and stir-fried quickly with lots of vegetables – a modern healthy alternative to traditional cooking. Do not forget the many uses of lean mince – beef, pork or lamb – to make quick meals with herbs and spices.

Here are the different sorts of meats available and the best ways to cook them. Some of the recipes that follow are traditional, and one or two newer ideas reflect more contemporary eating.

Choosing Meat
Red meats should look fresh and moist but not too red. If the meat is bright red, it will not have been hung long enough to develop a good flavour. A ruby/burgundy colour is better. The fat should be creamy rather than white. Do not worry too much about the amount of fat round a joint, because it will keep the meat moist and will naturally protect the flesh during the cooking process. You can remove it after cooking if you feel there is too much for your taste. Flesh that has a marbling of fat will be richer and moister when cooked than that which has no fat. Braising steak with a good marbling is

best because this melts during the long, slow cooking and gives a tender, well-flavoured result.

Pork flesh should be smooth and moist and a pale pink colour. There should be a reasonable amount of fat covering it. Organic pork will have a higher percentage of fat than factory pork and will certainly have a better flavour. The rind should be clean and hairless and joints should be of an even thickness to allow even cooking.

Always use a reliable supplier, either your supermarket counter or your local butcher. Farmers' markets can also be a good source of locally produced meat.

For roasting, buy about 175g/6 oz to 225 g/8 oz per person for a boneless joint and about 350 g/12 oz per person if the meat is on the bone. For casseroling, allow the same amount as a boneless joint and for steaks allow individual appetites to dictate.

Storage
Ensure that you take home fresh meat as soon as possible after buying. Unwrap the meat and place it in a clean dish, cover with clingfilm or foil and store in the refrigerator. Use minced and cut meat on the day of purchase; joints can be stored for up to 3 days and chops for 2 days. If you buy prepacked meat, make sure you read the label and use by the date stated on the pack; do not unwrap these packs because they have been prepared under controlled atmospheric conditions to preserve the meat longer. Always allow the meat to return to room temperature before cooking.

Beef

Lamb

Pork

Not only has beef suffered from health scares over the last few years, it has also suffered from intensive agricultural methods, poor hanging times and poor butchery. However, if you want to eat beef as it used to be, with a wonderful flavour and texture, you can buy it organically reared. This will cost more but it will be worthwhile. And if you buy it in smaller quantities, it will be more economical and you will be satisfying the health lobby not to eat too much red meat.

CUTS FOR ROASTING

Sirloin
This is the tenderest cut from the back of the loin. It can be a large joint on the bone but more usually it is boned and rolled so you can choose the size you need.

Ribs
Fore-rib, wing-rib and prime-rib are all excellent roasting joints, and are best roasted on the bone. They have a good layer of fat, which cooks out during the roasting, producing a well-flavoured joint. It can be boned and rolled to give smaller joints.

Topside
This cut is often sold for roasting but it is better if pot-roasted or braised.

Silverside
This is similar to topside, from the hind leg. It has a good flavour but can be tough. It can be slow-roasted but pot-roasting or braising is recommended.

Roasting times and temperatures
Start by roasting at 230°C/450°F/Gas 8 for 15 minutes, then cook for :
- 15 minutes per 450 g/1 lb plus 15 minutes at 190°C/375°F/Gas 5 for rare
- 20 minutes per 450 g/1 lb plus 20 minutes at 190°C/375°F/Gas 5 for medium
- 25 minutes per 450 g/1 lb plus 25 minutes at 190°C/375°F/Gas 5 for well done

Allow the roasted meat to stand for 20 minutes, in a warm place, before carving.

CUTS FOR CASSEROLING
These cuts of meat require long, slow cooking to become really tender.

Blade and chuck steak
Both of these cuts come from the shoulder area of the animal and are quite lean. They are sold either sliced or diced and are often labelled 'braising steak'.

Leg or shin meat
Both of these cuts come from the leg. Shin is very gristly and should only be used for stock, but leg meat can be stewed for 6–8 hours to soften the connective tissue. This is rather heavy on fuel, but if you have an Aga or similar cooker it might be worth buying, because an Aga is permanently on and the meat can be cooked slowly overnight.

FRYING AND GRILLING
Only the very best tender meat is suitable and requires very little cooking.

Fillet steak
This is the finest cut of beef: it is lean and boneless. It comes from below the sirloin and is the most expensive. It can be roasted whole, but it is usually sold in steaks cut into sizes dictated by appetite and wallet – anything from 115 g/4 oz to 280 g/10 oz.

Entrecôte steak
This is the lean and tender eye muscle of the sirloin. It is also boneless, and can be cut into even-sized steaks, about 3–4 cm/1¼–1½ inches thick. It can also be used cut into thin strips for stir-frying.

Rump steak
This comes from the hind quarter of the animal. It has a good layer of fat, which melts quite a bit on cooking. It is thought to have the best flavour of all the steaks and can be cut into any size, the usual being from 225 g/8 oz to 350 g/12 oz.

Below: Always use separate utensils for cutting and preparing raw and cooked meats. Wash utensils well after use, and keep raw and cooked meats away from each other.

The sweet flavour of lamb and its tender flesh make it the most delicious of all meats and my favourite. We have home-reared lamb from the West Country and Wales quite early in the year, about April, then later from the Lake District and Scotland. In the winter we have lamb imported from New Zealand. There is not much need to buy organic lamb because most have lived healthy outdoor lives, but it is there if you want to be assured of its provenance.

CUTS FOR ROASTING

Leg
This tender and lean joint is probably the most popular cut for roasting.

Shoulder
This is more economical than leg and in my opinion has the sweeter flavour. It has more fat than leg but that cooks out whilst roasting and can be poured off after cooking. It is a difficult joint to carve, but you can get your butcher to bone it first and then it is simple.

Rack of lamb
This is a very small joint, cut from the top end of the loin. It has very tender meat and looks like a row of cutlets. It is easy to carve by cutting down between the bones to serve as individual cutlets. It is a very useful joint if you are cooking for only two people.

Saddle
This is the largest joint, consisting of a whole pair of loins. It is excellent for a large gathering of people.

Roasting times and temperatures
Start by roasting at 230°C/450°F/Gas 8 for 20 minutes, then cook for:
- 25 minutes per 450 g/1 lb at 180°C/350°F/Gas 4 for medium
- 30 minutes per 450 g/1 lb at 180°C/350°F/Gas 4 for well done

Shoulders will need a little more cooking than legs, about 5 minutes per pound. Cook a rack for only 10 minutes at the higher temperature. Allow to stand for 15 minutes, in a warm place, before carving.

CUTS FOR CASSEROLING

Leg
When boned and cut into cubes, leg joints make extremely good casseroles. The joint is quite expensive but the cooking time is shorter and therefore more economical.

Shoulder
This can be boned and cut into cubes and used for casseroles. It has more fat so it needs to be well trimmed before using.

Lamb shanks
Braised lamb shanks are often on the menu at top restaurants. They are convenient because you can allow one per person, but they do take a long time to cook – at least 3 hours. However, they have a lovely flavour and the meat is very tender.

FRYING AND GRILLING

Gigot of lamb
These are also known as Gigot chops. The top end of the leg is sliced into large, round steaks with the bone going through the centre. They are delicious marinated in red wine with garlic and rosemary, and can be barbecued. Serve one per person (but the size can vary with the thickness of the cut).

Loin chops
These are chops cut from the loin. They have a T-shaped bone and are best grilled to reduce the fat content.

Chump chops
These are smaller chops with a central bone. They can be grilled or pan-fried.

Best end of neck cutlets
These are very small chops, cut from the best end of neck, with tender sweet meat and long, thin bones. Serve 2–3 per person.

Neck fillet
This is a boneless strip of meat, cut from the middle neck. It is good cubed and made into kebabs with onions and bay leaves. It can also be cut up into strips and stir-fried.

Below: Lamb cut into cubes is ideal for casseroling. Make sure that you trim off all the excess fat first.

Pigs are now bred to have less fat than in the past, because it was thought that the consumer wanted it that way. Unfortunately, these newer breeds do not have as much flavour as their predecessors and it is quite difficult to get a crispy crackling. Luckily, organic farmers are now producing pork with higher fat content, because as the pigs live outdoors they have to build up their own insulation. This is an improvement for the people who want to enjoy well-flavoured pork with crackling.

CUTS FOR ROASTING

Leg
This is sold whole or divided into fillet end and knuckle. The knuckle is cheaper because it has a larger bone content.

Loin
This is the best choice for roasting. The hind loin, from the back of the animal, is superior to the fore loin from the rib end. These joints can be cut by the butcher to the size of your choice. They are available on the bone or can be boned and rolled. Loin on the bone gives the best crackling.

Fillet
This is also known as tenderloin. It can be roasted but, because it is so lean, it is best used for other methods of cooking. If it is roasted, however, it is usually wrapped in bacon or Parma ham to give it some fat; it is also often stuffed to add moisture to the meat.

Roasting times and temperatures
Start by roasting at 230°C/450°F/Gas 8 for 20 minutes, then cook for:
• 25 minutes per 450 g/1 lb at 180°C/350°F/Gas 4 for loin
• 35 minutes per 450g/1 lb at 180°C/350°F/Gas 4 for leg
Allow the roasted meat to stand for 15 minutes, in a warm place, before carving.

CUTS FOR CASSEROLING

Shoulder
This is often called 'hand and spring' when sold whole. It can be roasted but it is best cut into cubes for casseroles. It produces a delicious, tender meat when cooked in a long, slow, moist way.

Leg
This can be cut into cubes, and is also ideal for casseroles.

Spare ribs
These are cut from the thick end of belly of pork. They are cooked in the oven but not roasted as such because they are usually cooked in a spicy sauce, slowly, for 2–2½ hours.

FRYING AND GRILLING

Fillet
This can be thinly sliced and pan-fried quickly. A sauce is often added before serving. It can also be cut into thin strips for stir-frying, which are usually marinated before cooking. It can also be cubed and made into kebabs.

Loin chops
These are large, lean chops with a good edge of fat. Trim off the rind to prevent the chops curling when cooked. They are best cooked under a hot grill or on a barbecue.

Chump chops
These come from the hind loin. Cook them in the same way as loin chops.

Below: To make crispy crackling, spread plenty of salt over the rind of the joint, then use a sharp knife to score lines over it before roasting in the oven.

Lamb and Mint

Pork and Sage

Beef

Vegetarian

HAM

Ham also comes from the pig: it is the hind leg, which is removed before processing. Gammon comes from the same part but is processed by curing it in brine, whilst it is still part of the carcass.

Cooking

Ham and gammon joints are cooked in a pan of just simmering water for about 20 minutes per 450 g/1 lb. If they are being served cold, let them cool in the water. Alternatively, remove the skin and glaze before finishing off in an oven preheated to 200°C/400°F/Gas 6 for 15–20 minutes. Whole hams need only 15 minutes of oven time per 450 g/1 lb.

SAUSAGES

No longer are we restricted to pork or beef sausages. We have specific 'sausage shops', which sell about 80 different flavours, including vegetarian, chicken and game. Sausages are an ideal quick food as long as you buy good-quality ones. Always check the label for meat content and only buy those that contain at least 80% meat. Cheap sausages contain all sorts of things we would not choose to eat, so only buy the best. If you buy from your butcher or a special shop, always use the sausages on the day of purchase. Pre-packed sausages will contain preservative and can therefore be stored in the refrigerator for a few days. Check the label before storing. If the sausages are particularly spicy, make sure you keep them well wrapped to avoid the flavours spoiling other foods.

Cook them by grilling, baking or frying at not too hot a temperature to stop the casings splitting, but make sure they are cooked through. Try experimenting with different flavours.

MINCED MEAT

This is available as beef, lamb, pork, veal and poultry. Mince can be a very useful commodity but it needs to be chosen with care. There are some awful examples of 'economy' mince, which should be avoided because they are high in fat and contain unpleasant gristly bits. The source of the meat can also be questionable. The meat and fat content of minced meat is regulated by Government regulations and states that the fat content of minced beef should not exceed 20%, lamb 25%, and pork 30%. Lean mince should contain less than 7% fat. Supermarkets have their own system and the fat content should be clearly labelled on the packaging.

Minced meat can be used to make meatballs, burgers, shepherd's pie, cottage pie, spaghetti bolognese, chilli con carne, and to stuff vegetables.

BEEF IN GUINNESS

A casserole benefits from being made the day before and then being reheated before serving. If you do this, cool the casserole as quickly as possible and store it in the refrigerator or a cool larder overnight.

Serves 6
Preparation time: 20–25 minutes
Cooking time: 2½–3 hours

INGREDIENTS

3 tbsp olive oil
2 onions, peeled and finely sliced
2 garlic cloves, peeled and chopped
1 kg/2 lb 4 oz stewing steak
2 tbsp plain flour
300 ml/10 fl oz Guinness
bouquet garni (see page 50)
150 ml/5 fl oz beef stock or vegetable stock, or water
salt and pepper
1 tbsp chopped fresh parsley, to garnish

To serve
mashed potato
a cooked green vegetable, such as cabbage or spinach

You will need a casserole dish (about 1.7 litre/3 pint capacity), a large frying pan, a wooden spatula, a slotted spoon, a measuring jug, a cook's knife and a chopping board

METHOD

1 Preheat the oven to 150°C/300°F/Gas 2. Heat 1 tablespoon of the oil in a large frying pan and fry the onions and garlic over a medium heat for 4–5 minutes until soft and brown. Remove the onions and garlic from the pan using a slotted spoon, then place them in the casserole dish.

2 Cut the meat into thick strips. Using the remaining oil, fry the meat over a high heat for about 5 minutes, stirring well until it is brown all over. Sprinkle in the flour and stir well to prevent lumps. Season well.

3 Lower the heat to medium, pour in the Guinness, and continue to heat, stirring constantly, until boiling.

4 Remove from the heat, and carefully turn the contents of the frying pan into the casserole. Add the bouquet garni and the stock. Cover the dish and cook gently in the centre of the preheated oven for 2½–3 hours.

5 Remove from the oven, discard the bouquet garni and check the seasoning. Garnish with parsley and serve immediately with mashed potato and a cooked green vegetable such as cabbage or spinach.

*Suitable for freezing. Follow the recipe to the end of step 6, cool quickly and turn into a rigid lidded container. Freeze for up to 3 months. To use, allow to thaw overnight in the refrigerator, then reheat either on top of the stove or in the oven at 180°C/350°F/Gas 4 for 30–40 minutes before serving.

WINE SUGGESTION

This dish should be served with a classic red Cabernet Sauvignon, perhaps from Australia – try a Barossa or a Coonawarra.

ROAST LOIN OF PORK

The best joints of pork for roasting are the leg and the loin. The leg is best for larger numbers of people. The loin can be bought in smaller sizes and is the best for crackling.

Serves 4
Preparation time: 20 minutes
Cooking time: 1 hour 20 minutes

INGREDIENTS

1 kg/2 lb 4 oz piece of pork loin, chined (backbone removed) and the rind scored by the butcher
1 tbsp flour
300 ml/10 fl oz dry cider, apple juice, chicken stock or vegetable stock
roast potatoes and cooked vegetables, to serve

Stuffing
1 tbsp melted butter
½ onion, peeled and finely chopped
1 garlic clove, peeled and finely chopped
1 cm/½ inch root ginger, peeled and finely chopped
1 pear, cored and chopped
6 fresh sage leaves, chopped
55 g/2 oz fresh breadcrumbs, white or wholemeal
salt and pepper

You will need a good, solid roasting tin, a small saucepan, a wooden spatula, some string, aluminium foil, a skewer, a balloon whisk, a measuring jug, a cook's knife and a chopping board

METHOD

1 Preheat the oven to 220°C/425°F/Gas 7. Make the stuffing by heating the butter in a small saucepan and frying the onion and garlic over a medium heat for 3 minutes until soft. Add the ginger and pear, mix well and cook for a further minute.

2 Remove from the heat and stir in the sage and breadcrumbs, and season well.

3 Put the stuffing in the joint along the middle of the loin, then roll it up and tie with string; you will need 4–5 pieces to hold the joint in shape. You can cover the stuffing on the ends with small pieces of foil to stop it burning.

4 Season well, and in particular use a lot of salt on the rind to make a crisp crackling. Place the joint in a roasting tin and roast in the centre of the preheated oven for 20 minutes.

5 Reduce the heat to 180°C/350°F/Gas 4 and cook for an hour until the skin is crispy and the juices run clear when the joint is pierced with a skewer.

6 Remove from the oven, lift out the meat and place on a hot serving plate. Cover with foil and leave in a warm place.

7 Pour off most of the fat from the roasting tin, leaving the meat juices and sediments behind. Sprinkle in the flour and whisk well. Cook the paste for a couple of minutes, then add the cider, apple juice or stock a little at a time until you have a smooth gravy. Boil for 2–3 minutes until the gravy is the required consistency. Season well and pour into a hot serving jug.

8 Cut the string from the joint and remove the crackling by cutting into the fat. Carve the stuffed pork into slices and serve on hot plates with pieces of crackling and the gravy. Serve with roast potatoes and cooked vegetables in season.

WINE SUGGESTION
Try an Italian Sangiovese red, such as Chianti, with this dish.

GREEK LAMB CASSEROLE

Serves 6
Preparation time: 25 minutes
Cooking time: 1–1½ hours

INGREDIENTS

3–4 tbsp olive oil

1 small aubergine (about 225 g/8 oz), sliced

2 onions, peeled and chopped

1 garlic clove, peeled and chopped

900 g/2 lb lamb (either leg or shoulder), cubed

1 tsp ground coriander

whole nutmeg, for grating

400 g/14 oz canned chopped tomatoes

2 tbsp tomato purée

300 ml/10 fl oz vegetable stock (fresh, or made using stock powder)

400 g/14 oz canned apricot halves in juice

3 bay leaves

salt and pepper

1 quantity Fruit and Nut Pilaf (see page 190), to serve

To garnish
1 tbsp chopped fresh coriander

grated rind of 1 orange

You will need a casserole dish (about 1.7 litre /3 pint capacity), a frying pan, a wooden spatula, a cook's knife, a canelle knife, a chopping board, a grater, a bowl, a measuring jug, and a large, deep serving dish

METHOD

1 Heat 3 tablespoons of the oil in a large frying pan and fry the aubergine over a high heat for 3 minutes each side until browned. Remove from the pan and drain on kitchen paper.

2 Fry the onions and garlic in the frying pan (adding another tablespoon of oil if necessary), over a medium heat for 3–4 minutes until transparent.

3 Add the meat and continue to cook over a high heat until it has a good dark brown colour. Stir in the ground coriander and grate in a good quarter of the nutmeg. Season well.

4 Preheat the oven to 180°C/350°F/Gas 4. Pour the tomatoes into the frying pan and stir in the tomato purée. Add the stock and the juice from the drained apricots, keeping the fruit for a garnish.

5 Add the bay leaves and bring to the boil. Transfer the lamb mixture and the fried aubergines to a casserole dish. Cover, and cook in the centre of the preheated oven for 1–1½ hours until the lamb is cooked (depending on which cut is used – see page 125).

6 Ten minutes before the end of cooking, pour the apricot halves into a dish, cover with foil and heat in the oven at the same temperature for 10 minutes.

7 Prepare the orange rind by using a canelle knife or a zester so that you have long strips of rind to use as a garnish.

8 Serve the lamb casserole in a deep serving dish. Arrange the warm apricot halves around the lamb, scatter over the coriander and top with the orange rind.

9 Serve hot with a tasty pilaf.

WINE SUGGESTION

Full-bodied reds are needed here – try a rich Chilean Malbec or a powerful Spanish Rioja.

PORK ESCALOPES WITH APPLES AND CRÈME FRAÎCHE

Serves 4
Preparation time: 25 minutes
Cooking time: 25–30 minutes

INGREDIENTS

550 g/1 lb 4 oz pork fillet

2 tbsp olive oil

2 tbsp butter, melted

1 small onion, peeled and finely chopped

1 garlic clove, peeled and finely chopped

2 dessert apples, cored and diced into 1 cm/½ inch cubes

1 tbsp soft brown sugar

225 ml/8 fl oz medium cider

125 ml/4 fl oz cider vinegar

2 tbsp crème fraîche

salt and pepper

1 tbsp chopped fresh parsley, to garnish

mashed potato, to serve

You will need a cook's knife, a chopping board, a large frying pan, a rolling pin, a measuring jug, some clingfilm and a heated serving dish.

WINE SUGGESTION

Try a traditional cider with this apple dish, or a Gewürztraminer.

METHOD

1 Cut the pork fillet into slices 1 cm/½ inch thick. Place each piece between two pieces of clingfilm or inside a plastic food bag and, using any part of a rolling pin, beat out the meat until it is very thin and twice the size. Season the meat well.

2 Heat half the oil and butter in a frying pan and cook the pork escalopes on a high heat for 2–3 minutes on both sides. You may need to do this in two or three batches. Remove from the pan and keep warm in a hot serving dish.

3 Heat the remaining oil and butter in the pan over a medium heat and then fry the onion and garlic for about 5 minutes until soft.

4 Add the apples and sugar to the pan and fry over a high heat for about 4–5 minutes until they are caramelised and turning golden brown.

5 Lower the heat, add the cider and the vinegar and then gently simmer for about 5 minutes until the mixture is thick and glossy.

6 Return the pork escalopes to the pan and mix well. Taste, and adjust the seasoning if necessary. Stir in the crème fraîche. Serve the pork escalopes on warmed plates with the apple and onion sauce spooned over. Garnish with the parsley and serve some creamy mashed potatoes alongside.

GLAZED GAMMON

There is great debate as to whether the best way to cook a ham or gammon joint is to boil it or roast it. A compromise of doing both seems to be the best answer, resulting in a moist and well-flavoured meat.

Serves 6
Preparation time: allow time for soaking (see step 1), plus 10 minutes for glazing
Cooking time: 1 hour 20 minutes

INGREDIENTS

1.3 kg/3 lb boneless gammon

2 tbsp Dijon mustard

85 g/3 oz demerara sugar

½ tsp ground cinnamon

½ tsp ground ginger

18 whole cloves

1 quantity Apricot Sauce (see page 139), to serve

You will need a roasting tin, a large lidded saucepan, a plate, a cook's knife and a chopping board

---

WINE SUGGESTION

Try a French Tavel Rosé or a Riesling from Alsace with this dish.

1 Check with your butcher or on the wrapper to see the supplier's instructions regarding soaking the gammon. Some gammons are presoaked and some are not. Place the joint in a large saucepan, cover with cold water and slowly bring to the boil over a gentle heat. Discard the water and cover with fresh water (this removes all the scum). Bring to the boil again, then cover and simmer very gently for 1 hour.

2 Remove the gammon from the pan and drain. Remove the rind from the gammon and use a sharp knife to score the fat into a diamond-shaped pattern.

3 Preheat the oven to 200°C/400°F/Gas 6. Spread the mustard over the fat. On a plate, mix together the sugar, cinnamon and ginger, then roll the gammon in it, pressing down well so that there is an even coating all over.

4 Stud the diamond shapes with the cloves and then place the gammon in a roasting tin. Roast in the centre of the preheated oven for 20 minutes until the glaze is a rich golden colour. To serve hot, allow to stand for 20 minutes before carving. Serve with hot apricot sauce. If the gammon is to be served cold, it can be cooked the day before and stored, covered with clingfilm, in the refrigerator before using.

STUFFED SHOULDER OF LAMB

This joint can be difficult to carve, so get your butcher to bone the lamb for you first and you will then have no trouble carving this delicious meat.

Serves 6–8
Preparation time: 20 minutes
Cooking time: 1½ hours

WINE SUGGESTION

Try a robust red wine for this robust dish, such as Cahors, from the Dordogne area of France.

INGREDIENTS

1.8 kg/4 lb shoulder of lamb, boned
salt and pepper

Stuffing
1 tbsp butter, melted
1 onion, peeled and finely chopped
1 garlic clove, peeled and finely chopped
115 g/4 oz minced veal or pork
115 g/4 oz fresh breadcrumbs, white or wholemeal
grated zest and juice of 1 lemon
1 tbsp chopped fresh parsley
1 tbsp chopped fresh rosemary
1 tbsp olive oil
225 ml/8 fl oz red wine

To serve
flageolet beans, cooked with a crushed clove of garlic and 1 tbsp chopped fresh parsley (see step 6)

You will need a trussing needle and some fine string, a roasting tin, a small saucepan, a large bowl, a measuring jug and a wooden spatula

1 Preheat the oven to 200ºC/400ºF/Gas 6. Wipe the lamb with kitchen paper and season well inside and out. To make the stuffing, melt the butter in a small saucepan and fry the onion and garlic over a medium heat for about 3 minutes until soft and transparent. Transfer to a large bowl and mix with the veal, breadcrumbs, lemon juice and zest, and herbs.

2 Season the mixture well. Using your hands, carefully put the stuffing into the shoulder.

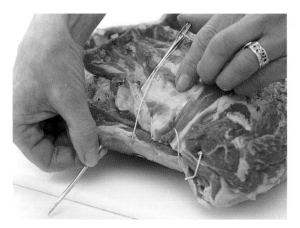

3 Sew up the pocket to form a good shape (do not worry about the stitches – they will be removed – but try to use only one piece of string).

4 Place the lamb in a roasting tin and rub over with the oil. Season with salt and pepper, and roast in the centre of the preheated oven for 1½ hours, basting from time to time.

5 Remove the tin from the oven, then lift out the meat and place on a warm serving plate. Remove all the string, cover the meat with foil and keep it warm.

6 Pour off the excess fat from the tin and make a simple gravy with the remaining juices. Add the red wine, scrape all the sediment off the bottom of the tin and boil vigorously for 2–3 minutes until well reduced. Pour the gravy into a warm jug. Serve the lamb thickly sliced with flageolet beans, simply heated with a crushed clove of garlic and a tablespoon of chopped parsley.

STIR-FRIED BEEF

This is a substantial dish, but if you prefer you can serve some Chinese noodles or rice to accompany the dish.

Serves 4
Preparation time: 35 minutes, including marinating
Cooking time: 15–20 minutes

INGREDIENTS

450 g/1 lb steak (rump or entrecôte)
2 tbsp light soy sauce
2 tbsp rice wine or dry sherry
2 tbsp tomato purée
pinch of Chinese five-spice powder
1 garlic clove, peeled and finely chopped
2 small pak choi, shredded
1 red pepper, cut into matchsticks
2 carrots, cut into matchsticks
2 courgettes, cut into matchsticks
4 spring onions, sliced diagonally
100 g/3½ oz beansprouts
2 tbsp vegetable oil
3 tbsp sesame seed oil
2 tbsp toasted sesame seeds
salt and pepper
cooked Chinese noodles or rice, to serve (optional)

You will need a wok or a large, deep frying pan, a shallow bowl, aluminium foil, a cook's knife and a chopping board, a serving dish and 4 plates

METHOD

1 Cut the steak into very thin slices, about 5 cm/2 inches long and 1 cm/½ inch thick.

2 Place the beef in a shallow bowl and mix in the soy sauce, rice wine, tomato purée and five-spice powder. Allow to marinate for half an hour.

3 While the meat is marinating, prepare the vegetables.

4 Heat the vegetable oil the pan until it is very hot, swirl it around and then add the steak. Stir-fry over a high heat for about 3 minutes. Use a slotted spoon to remove the beef from the pan, and keep warm in a hot serving dish covered with aluminium foil.

5 Heat 2 tablespoons of sesame oil in the pan and fry the garlic, pak choi, red pepper, carrots, courgettes and spring onions over a high heat for about 1 minute – they should still be crisp. Add the beansprouts last and allow them just to heat through. Season the vegetables well and spoon onto 4 serving plates. Arrange the steak on top and pour over any remaining sauce from the pan.

6 Drizzle over the remaining sesame oil and garnish with the toasted sesame seeds.

WINE SUGGESTION

A Barossa Shiraz from Australia or Syrah (it's the same) from the French Pays D'Oc would be good with this stir-fry.

ROAST BEEF

Roast beef is the most difficult roast to get right. Unlike the other meats, you need to cook it so that it is still pink in the centre, so careful timing is important. The best beef is a rib cooked on the bone, but this must be a good size. For a smaller number of people a sirloin, boned and rolled, is a good alternative.

Serves 8
Preparation time: 5 minutes
Cooking time: 2 hours 35 minutes

INGREDIENTS

2.7 kg/6 lb prime rib of beef
2 tsp dry English mustard
3 tbsp flour
600 ml/1 pint beef stock, or red wine or cider
2 tsp Worcestershire sauce, optional
salt and pepper

To serve
a selection of accompaniments such as roast potatoes (see page 173), Yorkshire puddings (see page 138), and cooked carrots and cauliflower

You will need a good, solid roasting tin, a wooden spatula, a measuring jug, some aluminium foil and a carving knife

METHOD

1 Preheat the oven to 230°C/450°F/Gas 8. Season the meat and rub in the mustard and 1 tablespoon of the flour. Place the meat in a roasting tin large enough to hold it comfortably.

2 Roast the meat in the preheated oven for 15 minutes, then reduce the heat to 190°C/375°F/Gas 5 and cook for 15 minutes per 450 g/1 lb, plus 15 minutes (1 hour 45 minutes for rare beef), or 20 minutes per 450 g/1 lb plus 20 minutes (2 hours 20 minutes for medium beef).

3 Baste the meat from time to time to ensure a moist result. If the tin becomes too dry, add a few tablespoons of stock or red wine.

4 Remove the tin from the oven, lift out the meat and place on a hot serving plate. Cover with foil and leave in a warm place.

5 Pour off most of the fat from the roasting tin, leaving behind the meat juices and the sediment. Return the tin to the top of the stove over a medium heat and scrape all the sediments from the base of the tin. Sprinkle in the remaining flour and quickly mix it into the tin juices. A small whisk can be used for this. When you have a smooth paste, gradually add the remaining stock, wine or cider, whisking all the time. Adjust the seasoning, and add a little Worcestershire sauce if using. Bring to the boil, and stir until thickened and smooth.

6 When ready to serve, carve the meat into medium slices and serve on hot plates with the chosen accompaniments.

7 Pour the gravy into a warm jug and pass round separately.

WINE SUGGESTION

The greatest dish deserves the greatest wine – a good red Claret from Bordeaux. Try a St. Emilion.

YORKSHIRE PUDDINGS

Makes 12
Preparation time: 5 minutes
Cooking time: 25–30 minutes

INGREDIENTS

100 g/3½ oz plain flour
1 egg, beaten
300 ml/10 fl oz milk and water mixed (half milk, half water)
3 tbsp roast beef dripping, goose fat or olive oil
salt and pepper

You will need a mixing bowl, a hand-held electric mixer or a balloon whisk, a measuring jug, a bun tray with 12 deep moulds and a ladle

METHOD

1 Preheat the oven to 220°C/425°F/Gas 7. Place the flour and a pinch of salt in a mixing bowl. Make a well in the centre, add the egg and half the liquid. Using a whisk, beat the egg and milk together and gradually incorporate the flour. Continue beating until the mixture is smooth and there are no lumps. Gradually beat in the remaining liquid. Season with the pepper.

2 Put a little dripping or oil into each mould of the bun tray. Heat at the top of the preheated oven for 3–4 minutes until very hot. Remove the hot tray very carefully, use a ladle to pour the batter into each mould, then return the tray to the oven.

3 Bake for 20–25 minutes until the Yorkshire puddings are well puffed up and golden brown.

4 Serve immediately with roast beef (see page 137) or any other meat you wish.

APRICOT SAUCE

Serves 6
Preparation time: 5 minutes
Cooking time: 2–3 minutes

INGREDIENTS

400 g/14 oz canned apricot halves in syrup
150 ml/5 fl oz vegetable stock (made from powder)
125 ml/4 fl oz Marsala wine
½ tsp ground ginger
½ tsp ground cinnamon
salt and pepper

You will need a small saucepan, a wooden spoon, a measuring jug and a blender

METHOD

1 Put the canned apricots and syrup into a blender and blend until smooth.

2 Pour the pureé into a saucepan, add the other ingredients and mix well. Heat the sauce gently over a low heat for about 4–5 minutes until warm. Season to taste.

3 Remove from the heat and pour into a serving jug. This sauce goes well with gammon.

QUICK HORSERADISH SAUCE

Horseradish sauce is made using freshly grated horseradish, but this is difficult to find. An alternative can be made with commercial horseradish sauce mixed with crème fraîche.

Serves 6–8
Preparation time: 2 minutes

INGREDIENTS

6 tbsp creamed horseradish sauce
6 tbsp crème fraîche

METHOD

1 In a small serving bowl, mix the horseradish and crème fraîche together. Serve the sauce with roast beef, or smoked fish such as trout or mackerel.

MINT SAUCE

Serves 6–8
Preparation time: 10 minutes, plus 30 minutes standing

INGREDIENTS

small bunch fresh mint leaves
2 tsp caster sugar
2 tbsp boiling water
2 tbsp white wine vinegar

You will need a cook's knife, a chopping board and a small bowl

METHOD

1 Make sure the mint is clean and tear the leaves from their stems. If the mint is dirty, wash it gently and dry thoroughly before tearing.

2 Place the leaves on the chopping board and sprinkle with the sugar. Chop the leaves finely (the sugar helps the chopping process) and place in a small bowl. Pour over the boiling water and stir to dissolve the sugar.

3 Add the vinegar and leave to stand for 30 minutes. This sauce goes particularly well with roast lamb.

POULTRY AND GAME

Poultry and game represent one of the healthiest sources of protein. They are mostly low in fat but rich in essential vitamins and minerals. If your butcher or supermarket has done the preparation for you, poultry and game offer a good variety of reasonably quick and easy-to-prepare dishes, particularly roasts and casseroles.

We think of chicken as the main variety of poultry. It comes fresh or frozen, corn fed or free range. You can eat all the meat – roasted whole, casseroled in quarters, or grilled breasts and legs – then make a stock with the carcass. There is also turkey, which is traditional at Christmas, though some people prefer goose. And of course duck – available whole or in breasts – as well as guinea fowl or quail.

On the game side we have pheasant and partridge, pigeon, wild duck and grouse. All can be cooked like chicken. However, since it is impossible to know their age, it is generally best to casserole them. Rabbit and venison are also traditional game dishes.

All of these birds and animals are discussed below, along with how to choose, prepare and cook them. There is also a selection of recipes using poultry and game, both for everyday use and for special occasions. Traditional accompaniments are also included.

CHICKEN

Chicken is the most popular protein food. It is eaten in great quantities all over the world. Chickens are sold, oven-ready, either fresh or frozen, and can be reared in a variety of ways. The standard British chicken, for example, is kept in chicken houses and has no chance to run around. Free-range chicken categories are now governed by law.

Free-range chickens
These birds are allowed to roam in open air runs for half their average life (56 days). They must be fed at least 70% cereal.

Traditional free-range chickens
These are similar to the free-range chickens above but they have more space (only 4,888 birds allowed in each house!). They are from slow-growing breeds and have daytime access

to open-air runs. Their average life is 81 days and their diet must be 70% cereal.

Free-range total freedom chickens
These chickens have free access to pasture land without any fenced runs.

Organic chickens
These chickens live in less crowded conditions, usually between 100–500 in a group. They have permanent access to pasture land. Their feed is at least 80% organic and the use of preventative antibiotics is banned.

Corn-fed chickens
These chickens can be reared in the standard or free-range system. The difference is that their feed must contain 50% corn, hence the deep corn colour of the birds.

Choosing chicken
Always buy from a reputable supplier, such as a good butcher or poulterer, or buy from the supermarket where you are sure of a quick turnover. Choose fresh birds for roasting, but frozen chickens and cut pieces are useful for casseroles. Fresh birds should look soft, plump and creamy pink, they should not be scrawny, discoloured or bruised. If you want chicken joints, it is often cheaper to buy a whole chicken and get the butcher to joint it for you; that way you also get a variety of meat rather than all legs or breasts. If you prefer to joint it yourself, see opposite. Buy reputable frozen brands and do not store for too long: check the 'use by' date on the packaging. Never buy frozen chicken that has damaged packaging.

Chicken pieces are easily available in all types and sizes: legs, drumsticks, thighs and breasts whole, part-boned, boned and skinned. Stir-fry strips and minced chicken are also available, and are economical and quick to cook.

STUFFING A CHICKEN

1 Use your hands or a spoon to place the stuffing in the neck end of the bird. Do not pack the stuffing in too tightly or the bird will not cook all the way through – this could encourage harmful bacteria to develop. Pull the skin over and secure with a poultry pin. Twist the wing tips up and over; tie the wings and legs with string.

JOINTING A CHICKEN

1 Put the bird breast-side up on a chopping board. Using a sharp knife, cut one leg away from the bird. Repeat with the other leg, then cut off both wings.

2 Use poultry shears or kitchen scissors to cut the breast in half from tail to neck. Turn the bird over and cut out the backbone. Remove the two breast pieces.

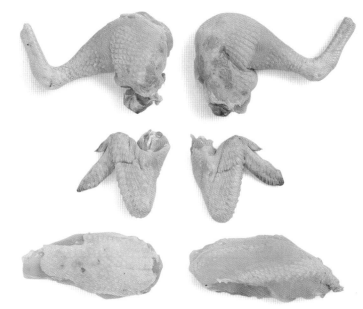

Sizes

Poussins are the smallest chickens (4–6 weeks old). They weigh up to 450 g/1 lb and are ideal as a single portion. Larger ones (6–10 weeks old) are called double poussins and are ideal for barbecuing, especially when spatchcocked (cut up the backbone and then flattened out). You can buy them ready prepared in the supermarket.

Roasting chickens are available from 1.3 kg/3 lb up to 2.7 kg/6 lb, and even larger ones are available sometimes. These birds are suitable for roasting and also for casseroling.

Storage

Take the chicken home as soon as possible after buying it. Unwrap and store it, lightly covered with clingfilm, in the refrigerator. If your chicken has giblets, remove them from the body at once, and use them within 24 hours. Use the chicken within 1–2 days. If you buy a packet of chicken joints and you do not need them all at once, put the remainder individually in freezer bags, seal well and freeze for up to 3 months. They are very useful for when you need a meal for just one. Frozen chicken should be placed in the freezer at once until you want to use it, then it is best to defrost it the refrigerator overnight. Always make sure the chicken is thoroughly defrosted before use. Do not refreeze it once it has been defrosted.

COOKING CHICKEN

Roasting times and weights (including stuffing)
- 25 minutes per 450 g/1 lb at 190°C/375°F/Gas 5 for a chicken weighing 900 g/2 lb to 1.3 kg/3 lb
- 20 minutes per 450 g/1 lb plus 20 minutes at 190°C/375°F/Gas 5 for a chicken weighing 1.3 kg/3 lb to 1.8 kg/4 lb
- 20 minutes per 450 g/1 lb at 190°C/375°F/Gas 5 for a chicken weighing 1.8 kg/4 lb to 2.7 kg/6 lb

If the bird is getting too brown, cover it with foil towards the end of cooking. Baste well every half an hour and check that it is cooked by piercing the thickest part of the leg with a sharp knife; if it is cooked thoroughly the juices will run clear. You can also tug the leg to see if it comes away from the body easily. Never eat under-cooked chicken – it can cause food poisoning.

Frying and grilling
Chicken legs and breasts are most suitable for these types of cooking. For grilling, brush the breasts with oil or melted butter to ensure they stay moist. The legs have enough fat in them not to need this. Season well before cooking. For frying, use a mixture of olive oil and a little butter, to give the chicken colour and flavour.

All chicken is suitable for barbecuing. The breasts are best if left on the bone because they will stay more moist. It is a good idea to marinate chicken pieces before cooking, because this helps the meat to stay moist through a fierce cooking process. It also adds additional flavours to the meat.

TURKEY

Whole turkeys are usually only available fresh at Christmas time, but they are widely available frozen all the year round. Turkey is a very healthy meat, and contains less than half the fat of chicken. It can be bought in many sizes, from tiny to massive. The most popular size range is between 2.7 kg/6 lb to 7.2 kg/16 lb. Turkey is extremely good hot or cold, so it makes an ideal meat for over the holiday period.

Like chickens, most turkeys are reared under intensive conditions, but there are now more free-range and organically reared free-range turkeys available. If you want a well-flavoured bird, do consider these alternatives. The traditional breeds, which are more moist, such as the Cambridge bronze turkey, are making a come-back; they are reared specially for

their flavour and are allowed to hang for some time in order to develop it even further.

Choosing turkey
As with chicken, use a reliable supplier and buy according to your needs. If you are buying a frozen turkey, make sure you buy a reliable brand and allow to thaw thoroughly before cooking – check on the label for times but allow at least 10–12 hours in the refrigerator per 1 kg/2 lb 4 oz. At room temperature, allow 4–6 hours for the same weight, but as room temperatures vary it is impossible to give exact guidance. Personally, I think thawing slowly in a refrigerator seems to be the safest method.

Turkey portions are available throughout the year. Thighs, drumsticks, breasts, escalopes, stir-fry strips and turkey mince – all make a good, economical alternative to red meat.

Storage
Always store turkey in the refrigerator as soon as possible after buying. There may be a space problem at Christmas if your refrigerator is full to bursting, so collect it as late as possible from your supplier and, if the weather is cold, you can keep it in the boot of the car overnight. Make sure you remove the giblets before storing in the car and keep the turkey well covered with clingfilm or foil. Frozen turkeys should always be kept in the freezer until required to defrost. Turkey pieces should be treated like chicken, see above. Allow both types to come to room temperature before cooking.

COOKING TURKEY
It is difficult to give absolute times for roasting a turkey: it will depend on the breed, how it has been reared, how old it is, and the size. Start it off at a high temperature to get the fat running and the skin starting to crisp and colour.

Roasting times and temperatures
Start by roasting at 220°C/425°F/Gas 7 for 30 minutes, then cover with foil. Then cook for 15 minutes per 450 g/1 lb, plus 15 minutes at 180°C/350°F/Gas 4.

You may need to add 15–30 minutes extra if you are stuffing the body cavity. Baste every half an hour to ensure a moist bird.

Remove the foil 30 minutes before the end of cooking to allow final browning. Test the bird is cooked by piercing a leg with a skewer: if the juices run clear, the bird is cooked.

Cover lightly with foil and leave for 30 minutes in a warm place to rest before carving.

Frying and grilling
Use turkey breast strips in stir-fries – turkey can replace chicken in any stir-fry recipe. Turkey mince can be used to make meatballs or turkey burgers.

Quail

Corn-fed chicken

Guinea fowl

Barbary duck

DUCK

This is a much fattier bird. You need to allow about 700 g/1 lb 9 oz per person when buying a whole duckling or duck. Ducks are readily available in the shops and can be bought all the year round. If you want to serve more than four people, it is probably best to buy two smaller ducklings because the meat will be more tender. Ducks' breast and legs are also available, ready to cook.

Choosing duck

Again, a good supplier is the answer. A fresh duck is preferable but a frozen one will suffice. Make sure it is well thawed out and thoroughly dry before cooking. Most of the ducks sold in Britain come from Lincolnshire but we are getting more French ducks like Barbary, which are superior when bought as ducks' breasts.

Storage

You should store duck in the same way as you would store chicken (see page 141).

COOKING DUCK

Duck is very fatty and requires a high temperature to give it a crisp, golden finish. Cook it on a trivet or wire rack in a roasting tin so that the fat runs off and the base of the duck is crispy. Before cooking, use a skewer to prick the skin of the duck all over. Season well and start by roasting at 220°C/425°F/Gas 7 for 15 minutes. Reduce the temperature to 180°C/350°F/Gas 4 and cook for 30 minutes per 450 g/1 lb. Pour excess fat off from time to time; keep it in a screw-top jar in the refrigerator for roasting potatoes at a later date. It will keep for one month.

The duck should be really golden and crunchy but, if you feel it is getting too crisp, cover it with foil. Drain well and use kitchen scissors to 'carve' the duck into quarters. Alternatively, you can use a knife to carve slices and smaller pieces but, since there is only a small amount of meat, it is a time-consuming task. Serve it with an orange sauce, or apricot sauce (see page 139).

Duck breasts are good grilled or barbecued, but the legs are rather tough and need pre-cooking (simmering in stock) before roasting. They are also good cooked in casseroles.

Below: Use a carving fork or a skewer to prick the skin of the duck all over before roasting it. This allows the fat to run out. It is best not to stuff duck because it is too fatty. However, you could use a little chopped onion or apple to give it some flavour.

Below: Cooking the duck on a trivet or a wire rack allows the fat to run off and keeps the base of the bird crispy.

GOOSE

Goose has even more fat than duck, but it has delicious dark meat. You need at least 675 g/1½ lb raw weight per person. Fresh geese are only available near to Christmas, although city suppliers will probably be able to get some at other times. They tend to be raised on smaller farms and are often free-range. My own butcher raises his own geese annually. The way to tell a young goose is by its feet – they are soft and yellow; the older birds have drier, firmer feet. Frozen geese are available throughout the year and are a good substitute for fresh because they freeze well. Do make sure you thaw it properly and dry it well before cooking.

COOKING A GOOSE

Like duck, this bird is best cooked on a trivet and benefits from being cooked upside down first so that the base becomes crisp; then turn it over to cook the breast. It is best not to stuff it because so much fat is naturally given off during cooking that the stuffing can become very fatty, but you can place a cut apple and onion inside the cavity instead to give it some flavour. Prick the skin all over and roast the bird at 220°C/425°F/Gas 7 for about 30 minutes. Turn the bird over and drain off the fat, which will have collected in the roasting tin. Keep the fat in a screw-top jar for making the best roast potatoes you will ever have. It will keep for one month in the refrigerator. Roast for a further 15 minutes and then turn the oven down to 180°C/350°F/Gas 4 and collect the fat again. Store the fat in a screw-top jar in the refrigerator. Continue to roast for 15 minutes per 450 g/1 lb until the bird is really crisp. Cover with foil towards the end of cooking if you feel that the goose is getting too brown. Carve the goose carefully and serve it with some cooked purple sprouting broccoli and red cabbage casserole (see page 168).

GAME

This is the term given to wild animals and birds that are hunted, but nowadays they are often bred specially for the table. Game meat has become very popular because it is less fatty and healthier than meat from other species. Game only used to be available from specialist game dealers, but it is now to be found in most supermarkets, fresh when in season or frozen. Take care, when eating any game, to look for any lead shot that might still be in the flesh – biting on it can be an unpleasant experience.

Pheasant

These are intensively reared for shooting – the season in Britain is from 1 October – 1 February. If you buy from a supermarket they will not have been hung for long, so they will have a milder flavour than those you might buy from a game dealer. The female is tenderer than the male and tends to be slightly fatter. Pheasant can be roasted but, since the age will be unknown, it is best to casserole it.

Grouse

These birds are in season in Britain from 12 August until 10 December. They are small birds, and weigh about 750 g/1lb 10oz, so one is suitable for one person. The meat is very dark. Roast at 190°C/375°F/Gas 5 for 30–35 minutes. It is a good idea to wrap them in bacon to keep them moist. Older birds can be casseroled according to any game or chicken recipes.

Rabbit

These are usually bred for the table but sometimes wild rabbit is available, which has a stronger flavour. Farmed rabbit is a bit like chicken. It is best cooked in a casserole because the meat can be very dry. Boned rabbit is available in some supermarkets and would be a good way to try this meat for the first time.

Venison

This is the meat from hunted wild deer, but it is now also available farmed all year round. It is a good, red meat and can be used in many ways like beef. It is a healthier meat, lower in cholesterol, and is becoming very popular. The best meat comes from a male deer under the age of 2 years. It can be bought as roasting joints (leg and saddle) and as prepared meat for braising and casseroles (shoulder and neck). Due to the dry nature of venison, casseroling is the best way to enjoy the meat's flavour and texture. However, if you live somewhere where you have access to freshly hunted venison, a roast saddle would be a great treat.

ROAST CHICKEN

Chicken is an ever-popular favourite. Simply roasted, with lots of thyme and garlic, chicken produces a succulent gastronomic feast for many occasions. You can make a thicker gravy with giblet stock (see page 61), using the method for roast turkey (see pages 152–3).

Serves 6
Preparation time: 15 minutes
Cooking time: 2¼ hours

INGREDIENTS

2.25 kg/5 lb free-range chicken
4 tbsp butter
2 tbsp chopped fresh thyme (lemon thyme if possible)
3 garlic cloves, peeled and crushed
1 lemon, cut into quarters
125 ml/4 fl oz white wine
salt and pepper
6 sprigs fresh thyme, to garnish

To serve
1 quantity bread sauce (see page 157)
cooked new potatoes
green salad leaves

You will need a small roasting tin, a cook's knife, a chopping board, a bowl, a measuring jug, a fork and a wooden spatula

METHOD

1 Preheat the oven to 220°C/425°F/Gas 7. Make sure the chicken is clean: wipe it inside and out using kitchen paper and place it in the roasting tin.

2 In a bowl, soften the butter with a fork, mix in the thyme and garlic and season well.

3 Butter the chicken all over with the herb butter, inside and out, and place the lemon quarters inside the body cavity.

4 Roast in the centre of the preheated oven for 20 minutes. Reduce the temperature to 190°C/375°F/Gas 5, add half of the wine and continue to roast for another 1¼ hours, basting frequently. If the tin dries out too much, add 2–3 tablespoons of wine or water.

5 Test that the chicken is cooked by piercing the thickest part of the leg with a sharp knife or skewer and make sure the juices run clear. Remove from the oven.

6 Lift out the chicken from the roasting tin, place it on a warm serving plate, cover with foil, and leave to rest for 10 minutes before carving.

7 Return the roasting tin to the top of the stove, add the remaining wine and simmer gently over a low heat for 2–3 minutes until the pan juices have reduced and are thick and glossy. Taste and adjust the seasoning.

8 Scatter over the thyme sprigs, then serve the chicken with the pan juices along with some bread sauce, new potatoes and salad leaves.

WINE SUGGESTION
A medium red Burgundy, such as Nuits St. Georges, goes well with this chicken.

CHICKEN DAUPHINOISE

Serves 4
Preparation time: 25 minutes
Cooking time: 1–1½ hours

INGREDIENTS

675 g/1 lb 8 oz trimmed leeks
280 g/10 oz small, waxy potatoes
1 tbsp olive oil
1 garlic clove, peeled and chopped
200 g/7 oz soft cheese with garlic and herbs
125 ml/4 fl oz white wine
175 ml/6 fl oz chicken stock
2 tsp cornflour
4 chicken breasts, skinned and boned
2 tbsp butter, melted
salt and pepper
2 tbsp chopped fresh parsley, to garnish

You will need a large, shallow baking dish (about 1.7 litre/
3 pint capacity), a frying pan, a cook's knife, a measuring jug,
a chopping board and a blender

WINE SUGGESTION
This dish really needs a rich
New Zealand Chardonnay,
but if a red is preferred, try
a cool red Beaujolais.

METHOD

1 Preheat the oven to 180°C/350°F/Gas 4. Clean and thickly slice the leeks.

2 Slice the potatoes as thinly as possible.

3 Heat the olive oil in a frying pan over a medium heat and cook the leeks and garlic for 3–4 minutes until beginning to soften. Remove from the heat and put the leeks in the baking dish.

4 Place the cheese, wine, stock and cornflour in a blender and process until smooth.

5 Arrange the chicken pieces on top of the leeks, season well and pour over the sauce.

6 Layer the potatoes on top, season, and brush very thoroughly with the melted butter.

7 Cook in the preheated oven for about 1–1½ hours until the potatoes are well cooked and brown. Serve at once with the parsley scattered over.

ROAST GOOSE

Goose has become unfashionable in recent times due to its high fat content and the fact that you get little meat in proportion to the carcass; you need to buy 675 g/1½ lb dressed weight per person. It is best not to stuff it because so much fat is naturally given off during cooking that the stuffing can become very fatty. It is best to place flavourings such as onions and lemons inside the body and cook the stuffing separately.

Serves 6
Preparation time: 15 minutes
Cooking time: 2¼–2½ hours

INGREDIENTS

4 kg/8 lb 8 oz goose
1 onion, peeled and coarsely chopped
1 apple, coarsely chopped
1 lemon, quartered
2 sprigs fresh sage
1 tbsp plain flour
350 ml/12 fl oz giblet stock (see page 61)
salt and pepper

To serve
sage and onion stuffing (see page 159)
apple sauce
roast potatoes (see page 173)
red cabbage casserole (see page 168)
cooked vegetable such as purple sprouting broccoli

You will need a large, solid roasting tin with a trivet, a cook's knife, a chopping board, some aluminium foil, a wooden spatula or a small whisk

METHOD

1 Preheat the oven to 200°C/400°F/Gas 6. Make sure the goose is clean: wipe it inside and out using kitchen paper. Remove any excess fat from inside the body cavity. Season well, rubbing the salt into the skin. Place the onion, apple, lemon and sage inside the body cavity.

2 Place the bird, upside down, on a rack in a roasting tin, and use a skewer to prick the skin all over to allow the fat to run out during cooking.

3 Roast in the preheated oven for 15 minutes until the skin is starting to crisp, then turn over and roast for a further 15 minutes. Pour off the excess fat and retain. Baste, and reduce the temperature to 180°C/350°F/Gas 4 and continue to roast for another 2 hours, basting frequently. Carefully pour off the excess fat each time, and keep it for roasting potatoes – it is delicious. If the goose is getting too brown, cover it with foil.

4 Test that the goose is cooked by piercing the thickest part of the leg with a sharp knife or skewer: the juices should run clear if it is cooked thoroughly.

5 Lift out the goose from the roasting tin and place on a warm serving plate, cover with foil and leave to rest whilst you complete the meal.

6 Carefully drain the excess fat from the tin, leave 2 tablespoons in the tin and return to a low heat on top of the stove. Sprinkle in the flour and stir well using a small whisk or wooden spatula. Scrape all the crusty bits off the bottom of the tin and cook for 1 minute. Pour in the giblet stock, a little at a time, whisking constantly until smooth. Simmer over a medium heat for 3–4 minutes until the gravy is the correct consistency and has reduced a little. Taste, and adjust the seasoning.

7 Carefully pour the gravy into a warmed serving jug and serve.

WINE SUGGESTION

An Italian red Barolo or Merlot will go well with roast goose.

DUCK BREAST SALAD

Serves 4
Preparation time: 10 minutes
Cooking time: 15–20 minutes

INGREDIENTS

4 duck breast fillets, about 175 g/6 oz each
1 cm/½ inch piece root ginger, peeled and finely chopped
2 tbsp soy sauce
2 tbsp runny honey
2 tbsp lemon juice
115 g/4 oz mixed salad leaves, including rocket and watercress
115 g/4 oz sugar snap peas, blanched for 1 minute
salt and pepper

You will need a sharp knife, a heavy-based frying pan with a heatproof handle that will go into the oven or an ordinary frying pan, a roasting tin and a large serving plate

METHOD

1 Preheat the oven to 230ºC/450º/Gas 8. Use a sharp knife to score the skin on the duck breasts diagonally, about 1 cm/½ inch apart. Repeat in the other direction to make a diamond pattern. This allows the fat to run and the skin to become crisp.

2 Heat the dry frying pan over a high heat and place the duck breasts in the pan, skin side down, and fry for 4–5 minutes until golden. Turn over the breasts and place the pan in the oven or transfer the duck to a roasting tin.

3 Cook at the top of the preheated oven for 10–15 minutes, depending how rare you like your duck.

4 Remove the duck from the pan, cover with foil, and allow to rest on a warm serving plate in a warm place whilst you make the sauce.

5 If there is excess fat in the pan, spoon out all but 2 tablespoons. Return the pan to the top of the stove and add the ginger. Stir well and scrape all the sediment from the pan. Spoon in the soy sauce, honey and lemon juice and mix well. Bubble for a minute until thick, then season to taste.

6 Slice the duck thinly and lay on a large serving plate. Arrange the salad leaves alongside and pour the sauce over the duck. You can also serve the duck and leaves on individual serving plates.

7 Scatter over the peas and serve just warm.

WINE SUGGESTION
A Californian Zinfandel or an Australian red blend would go well with this salad.

COQ AU VIN

A delicious chicken casserole, cooked in red wine with baby onions and mushrooms. Like all casseroles, this benefits from being made the day before. Cool it quickly and then reheat it when needed.

Serves 8
Preparation time: 40 minutes
Cooking time: 1½ hours

INGREDIENTS

2 tbsp plain flour

1.8 kg/4 lb fresh chicken, jointed into 8 pieces (ask your butcher to do this or use 8 chicken joints)

2 tbsp olive oil

2 tbsp butter

225 g/8 oz lardons or streaky bacon, cut into strips

450 g/1 lb button onions, peeled

750 ml/1½ pints red wine

2 garlic cloves, peeled and crushed

1 bouquet garni (see page 50)

350 g/12 oz button mushrooms

2 tbsp chopped fresh parsley

salt and pepper

You will need a large, flameproof casserole dish (about 3.5 litre/6 pint capacity), a large polythene bag, a cook's knife, a chopping board, a measuring jug, a slotted spoon and a serving dish

WINE SUGGESTION

A spicy red Burgundy would be good with this dish – try a Côte de Beaume.

1 Preheat the oven to 180°C/350°F/Gas 4. Season the flour and put it into a large polythene bag. Add the chicken and shake well to coat it evenly. Heat the oil and butter in the casserole dish. Fry the chicken over a high heat for 5–6 minutes until browned. You will need to do this in two batches. Lift it out of the pan and keep warm. Fry the bacon in the casserole for 3–4 minutes until crisp and well coloured. Lift it out and keep it warm.

2 Fry the onions over a high heat for 4–5 minutes until they begin to brown. Pour in the wine and stir well to remove any sediment from the base of the casserole dish.

3 Return the bacon and chicken to the casserole dish and add the garlic and bouquet garni. Bring to the boil, cover, then cook in the centre of the preheated oven for 1¼ hours.

4 Add the mushrooms and cook for a further 15 minutes. Discard the bouquet garni and use a slotted spoon to lift out the chicken joints, bacon, onion and mushrooms. Put them in a serving dish and keep them warm.

5 Return the casserole and its juices to a low heat and check for seasoning. Boil rapidly until the sauce is thick and glossy. Pour the sauce over the dish and serve at once garnished with the parsley.

Suitable for freezing. Prepare up the end of step 5. Place the chicken in a rigid, lidded container, pour over the sauce, cool and freeze for up to 3 months. To use, allow to thaw and reheat on the stove or in the oven at 180°C/350°F/Gas 4 for 40–45 minutes.

CLASSIC ROAST TURKEY

Traditional roast turkey cannot be beaten. It is a seasonal favourite that many people enjoy. There is much discussion as to whether it is good to stuff the bird; here we use a light celery and walnut stuffing for the body, which is not too dense and also keeps the bird moist, and a traditional chestnut stuffing for the neck. Stuffing should not be packed too tightly because it prevents the bird cooking properly. There are also recipes for bread sauce and cranberry sauce (see page 157).

Serves 10

WINE SUGGESTION

Try a Riesling if you prefer white, but a lighter Bordeaux claret would be good – Mèdoc for example.

Preparation time: 20 minutes

Cooking time: 3½–4 hours

INGREDIENTS

4.5 kg/10 lb turkey

1 quantity celery and walnut stuffing (see page 158)

1 quantity chestnut stuffing (see page 158)

115 g/4 oz butter, softened

10 rashers streaky bacon

2 tbsp plain flour

1 litre/1¾ pints giblet stock (see page 61)

125 ml/4 fl oz red wine

salt and pepper

You will need a large, solid roasting tin, a wooden spatula, a measuring jug, metal skewers, string, some aluminium foil, and a large serving plate

1 Preheat the oven to 220°C/425°F/Gas 7. Make sure the turkey is clean – use kitchen paper to wipe it inside and out. Season inside and out. Stuff the body cavity with the celery and walnut stuffing and the neck with the chestnut stuffing. Secure the neck skin with metal skewers and the legs with string.

2 Butter the bird all over and squeeze some under the breast skin. Use a little to grease the roasting tin. Place the bird in the tin, season again and cover the breast with the bacon rashers. Cover the bird with aluminium foil and roast in the preheated oven for 30 minutes. Reduce the temperature to 180°C/350°F/Gas 4 and continue to cook for 2½–3 hours.

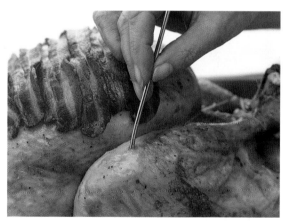

3 Baste the turkey with the pan juices every half an hour. Forty-five minutes before the end of the cooking time, remove the foil and let the turkey brown, basting from time to time. Remove the bacon when crispy and keep it warm.

4 Test that the turkey is cooked by piercing the thickest part of the leg with a skewer: the juices should run clear. Also, pull a leg away from the body: it should feel loose. Lift the turkey from the tin, put it on a warm serving plate, cover with foil and leave to rest for up to one hour.

5 Drain the fat from the tin; return the tin to a low heat on the stove. Sprinkle in the flour and stir to a smooth paste. Cook for 1 minute. Pour in the giblet stock a little at a time, whisking constantly until smooth. Add the wine and cook for 3–4 minutes until the gravy is the correct consistency and has reduced a little.

6 Taste, and adjust the seasoning. During the carving of the turkey there will be some meat juices escaping – add these to the tin. Carefully pour the gravy into a warmed serving jug and serve.

VENISON CASSEROLE

This casserole benefits from being made the day before to allow the flavours to develop. Reheat gently before serving, on top of the stove or in the oven at 180°C/350°F/Gas 4 for 35–40 minutes. Ensure you cool the casserole as quickly as possible and store, covered, in the refrigerator or a cool larder overnight.

Serves 6
Preparation time: 30 minutes
Cooking time: 2½ hours

INGREDIENTS

3 tbsp olive oil
1 kg/2 lb 4 oz casserole venison, cut into 3 cm/
1¼ inch cubes
2 onions, peeled and finely sliced
2 garlic cloves, peeled and chopped
350 ml/12 fl oz beef or vegetable stock
2 tbsp plain flour
125 ml/4 fl oz port or red wine
2 tbsp redcurrant jelly
6 juniper berries, crushed
4 cloves, crushed
pinch of cinnamon
small grating of nutmeg
salt and pepper
baked or mashed potatoes, to serve

You will need a casserole dish (about 1.7 litre/3 pint capacity), a cook's knife, a chopping board, a frying pan, a measuring jug, a wooden spatula and a slotted spoon

METHOD

1 Preheat the oven to 180°C/350°F/Gas 4. Heat the oil in a large frying pan and cook the cubes of venison over a high heat for 2–3 minutes until brown. You may need to fry the meat in two or three batches – do not overcrowd the pan. Remove the venison from the pan using a slotted spoon and place in the casserole dish.

2 Add the onion and garlic to the pan and fry over a medium heat for about 3 minutes until a good golden colour, then lift out and add to the meat.

3 Gradually add the stock to the frying pan, stir well and scrape up the sediment, then bring to the boil.

4 Sprinkle the meat in the casserole dish with the flour and turn to coat evenly.

5 Add the hot stock to the casserole and stir well, ensuring that the meat is just covered.

6 Add the wine, redcurrant jelly and the spices.

7 Season well, cover and cook gently in the centre of the preheated oven for 2–2½ hours.

8 Remove from the oven, check the seasoning and adjust if necessary. Serve immediately piping hot with baked or mashed potatoes.

* Suitable for freezing. Complete up the end of step 7, then cool and pour into a rigid, lidded container. Freeze for up to 3 months. To use, allow to thaw at room temperature for 5–6 hours or overnight and reheat gently when needed.

WINE SUGGESTION
Try a full-bodied claret, such as Pomerol or an Australian Shiraz, with this dish.

MUSTARD RABBIT

This casserole also benefits from being made the day before to allow the flavours to develop. Ensure you cool the casserole as quickly as possible and store, covered, in the refrigerator or a cool larder overnight. Reheat gently for 35–40 minutes before serving.

Serves 4

Preparation time: 20 minutes

Cooking time: 1½ hours

INGREDIENTS

2 tbsp plain flour

1 oven-ready rabbit (about 900 g/2 lb), jointed

1 tbsp olive oil

1 tbsp butter

100 g/3½ oz lardons or streaky bacon, cut into strips

4 shallots, peeled and chopped

1 garlic clove, peeled and chopped

150 ml/5 fl oz dry white wine

225 ml/8 fl oz chicken or vegetable stock

3 tbsp wholegrain mustard

115 g/4 oz button mushrooms, finely sliced

125 ml/4 fl oz double cream

salt and pepper

2 tbsp chopped fresh parsley, to garnish

You will need a casserole dish (about 2 litre/3½ pint capacity), a cook's knife, a chopping board, a large frying pan, a measuring jug, a wooden spatula, a slotted spoon, a large polythene bag and a large serving dish

METHOD

1 Season the flour well, put it into a large polythene bag, and add the rabbit pieces. Shake well to coat the joints evenly.

2 Heat the oil and butter in the frying pan. Cook the rabbit over a high heat for 4–5 minutes until brown. Use a slotted spoon to lift the joints from the pan and put in the casserole dish.

3 Preheat the oven to 160°C/325°F/Gas 3. Add the bacon to the pan and cook over a medium heat for 3–4 minutes until crisp and golden, then transfer to the casserole dish.

4 Add the shallots and garlic to the pan and sauté for 2–3 minutes until soft and brown.

5 Pour in the wine and scrape all the sediment from the bottom of the pan. Add the stock and bring to the boil, then simmer for 2 minutes.

6 Stir in the mustard and then pour the contents of the frying pan over the rabbit in the casserole dish.

7 Season well, cover, and cook in the centre of the preheated oven for 2–2½ hours until the rabbit is tender.

8 Add the mushrooms 15 minutes before the end of the cooking time and stir well. Remove from the oven. Transfer the rabbit, using a slotted spoon, to a warm serving plate.

9 Place the casserole on top of the stove and simmer to the desired consistency. Adjust the seasoning if necessary.

10 Stir in the cream, then pour over the rabbit in the serving dish. Serve immediately garnished with the chopped parsley.

* Suitable for freezing. Make up to the end of step 8. Cool, then freeze in a rigid, lidded container for up to 3 months. To use, thaw overnight in the refrigerator then reheat in the oven at 170°C/325°F/Gas 3 for 35–40 minutes before adding the cream and garnish.

WINE SUGGESTION

Try a full-bodied Italian red Montalcino with this dish.

PHEASANT AND CHESTNUT CASSEROLE

This casserole benefits from being made the day before. Cool it as quickly as possible, cover, and store in the refrigerator or a cool larder overnight. Reheat gently on the stove or in the oven at 180°C/350°F/Gas 4 for 30–35 minutes.

Serves 4
Preparation time: 30 minutes
Cooking time: 1½–2 hours

INGREDIENTS

1 tbsp olive oil

2 tbsp butter

1 large, prepared pheasant, jointed

175 g/6 oz lardons or streaky bacon, cut into strips

225 g/8 oz vacuum-packed chestnuts

2 onions, peeled and finely sliced

1 garlic clove, peeled and chopped

2 tbsp plain flour

425 ml/15 fl oz game or vegetable stock

150 ml/5 fl oz red wine

zest and juice of 1 orange

2 tbsp redcurrant jelly

salt and pepper

To garnish
1 whole orange, sliced
small bunch fresh watercress

You will need a casserole dish (about 2 litre/3½ pint capacity), a cook's knife, a chopping board, a measuring jug, kitchen tongs, a slotted spoon and a large frying pan

METHOD

1 Melt the oil and butter in a large frying pan. Add the pheasant joints and cook over a high heat for 4–5 minutes until brown. Use a slotted spoon to remove the pheasant from the pan and place in the casserole dish.

2 Add the bacon to the pan and cook over a medium heat for 2–3 minutes until crisp and golden, then transfer to the casserole dish.

3 Preheat the oven to 180°C/350°F/Gas 4. Gently fry the chestnuts over a low heat for 3–4 minutes until lightly browned, then transfer to the casserole.

4 Add the onions and garlic to the pan and sauté over a medium heat for 2–3 minutes until soft and brown.

5 Stir in the flour and mix well to prevent any lumps. Add the stock, a little at a time, and gradually mix with the onions, scrape up the sediment and bring to the boil. Pour in the wine.

6 Pour the contents of the frying pan over the pheasant in the casserole dish.

7 Add the orange zest and juice and the redcurrant jelly. Season well, cover and cook in the centre of the preheated oven for 1½–2 hours until the pheasant is tender. Turn the joints in the sauce halfway through.

8 Remove from the oven, then check the seasoning and adjust if necessary.

9 Serve garnished with the slices of orange and a little fresh watercress.

* Suitable for freezing. Complete up the end of step 8. Cool, then pour into a rigid, lidded container. Freeze for up to 3 months. To use, allow to thaw at room temperature overnight and reheat gently when needed.

WINE SUGGESTION
Try a powerful red Californian Pinot Noir or a white Australian Riesling with this casserole.

BREAD SAUCE

This is a traditional accompaniment to turkey for Christmas, but it is also very useful for serving with cold meats, such as chicken and ham.

Serves 6–8
Preparation time: 10 minutes
Cooking time: 1 hour 20 minutes

INGREDIENTS

1 onion
12 cloves
1 bay leaf
6 black peppercorns
600 ml/1 pint milk
115 g/4 oz fresh white breadcrumbs
2 tbsp butter
whole nutmeg, for grating
2 tbsp double cream, optional
salt and pepper

You will need a saucepan (preferably non-stick), a wooden spoon, a small knife and a grater

METHOD

1 Make small holes in the onion using the point of a sharp knife or a skewer, and stick the cloves in them.

2 Put the onion, bay leaf and peppercorns in a saucepan and pour in the milk. Bring to the boil, then remove from the heat, cover, and leave to infuse for 1 hour.

3 To make the sauce, discard the onion and bay leaf, and sieve the milk to remove the peppercorns. Return the milk to the cleaned saucepan and add the breadcrumbs.

4 Cook the sauce over a very low heat for 4–5 minutes, until the breadcrumbs have swollen and the sauce is thick.

5 Beat in the butter and season well with the salt and pepper, and a good grating of nutmeg. Stir in the cream just before serving, if using.

CRANBERRY SAUCE

Serves 6–8
Preparation time: 2 minutes
Cooking time: 10 minutes

INGREDIENTS

225 g/8 oz fresh cranberries
85 g/3 oz soft brown sugar
150 ml/5 fl oz orange juice
½ tsp ground cinnamon
½ tsp grated nutmeg

You will need a saucepan and a wooden spoon

METHOD

1 Place the cranberries, sugar, orange juice and spices in a saucepan and stir well.

2 Cover the saucepan and bring slowly to the boil over a gentle heat.

3 Simmer for 8–10 minutes until the cranberries have burst. Take care because they may splash.

4 Put the sauce in a serving bowl and cover until needed. Serve warm or cold.

CELERY AND WALNUT STUFFING

This is a delicious stuffing for turkey, but it is also good with chicken and duck. If you are using it to stuff a chicken, you will need only half the quantity.

Makes enough for a large turkey about 5.5 kg/12 lb
Preparation time: 15 minutes
Cooking time: 10 minutes, plus extra for the bird

INGREDIENTS

2 onions, peeled and finely chopped
2 tbsp butter
115 g/4 oz fresh wholemeal breadcrumbs
4 sticks celery, trimmed and chopped
2 Cox's apples, cored and roughly chopped
115 g/4 oz dried ready-to-eat apricots, chopped
115 g/4 oz walnuts, chopped
2 tbsp chopped fresh parsley
salt and pepper

You will need a cook's knife, a chopping board, a small saucepan, a mixing bowl and a wooden spatula

METHOD

1 Put the onions and butter in a saucepan and cook gently over a low heat for 2–3 minutes until soft but not coloured.

2 In a bowl, mix together the breadcrumbs, celery, apples, apricots and walnuts. Add the cooked onions and season to taste.

3 Stir in the parsley and use to stuff a turkey. If you have a small turkey, then you might have some stuffing left over. If you have, cook this in a baking dish in the oven at 180°C/350°F/Gas 4 for 30–40 minutes. Alternatively, cover with clingfilm and store in the refrigerator for 3–4 days.

CHESTNUT STUFFING

This recipe makes a classic stuffing for turkey.

Makes enough for a turkey of about 5.5 kg/12 lb
Preparation time: 15 minutes
Cooking time: 10 minutes

INGREDIENTS

115 g/4 oz lardons or streaky bacon, cut into strips
1 onion, peeled and finely chopped
2 tbsp butter
115 g/4 oz button mushrooms, sliced
225g/8 oz chestnut purée
50 g/1¾ oz fresh wholemeal breadcrumbs
2 tbsp chopped fresh parsley
grated rind of 2 lemons
salt and pepper

You will need a cook's knife, a chopping board, a frying pan, a mixing bowl, a wooden spatula, a grater and a fork

METHOD

1 In the frying pan, gently fry the bacon and onion in the butter over a low heat for 2–3 minutes until soft and just beginning to colour.

2 Add the mushrooms and cook for 1–2 minutes, then remove from the heat.

3 In a mixing bowl, fork over the chestnut purée and break it up. Mix with the breadcrumbs, parsley and lemon rind.

4 Add the contents of the frying pan and mix well. Season to taste.

5 Cool before using to stuff the neck end of the turkey.

SAGE AND ONION STUFFING

Sage and onion stuffing is underrated. Sage is a wonderful herb if used carefully and when fresh. It goes really well with fattier meats like duck, goose and pork, but it can also be used with chicken.

Makes enough for a chicken or small joint of pork
Preparation time: 10 minutes
Cooking time: 10 minutes

INGREDIENTS

2 tbsp butter
2 onions, peeled and finely chopped
115 g/4 oz fresh white breadcrumbs
1 tbsp chopped fresh sage leaves
salt and pepper

You will need a saucepan, a mixing bowl, a cook's knife, a chopping board and a wooden spatula

METHOD

1 Melt the butter over a low heat in a saucepan. Add the onions and cook gently over a low heat for 2–3 minutes until soft but not coloured.

2 In a separate bowl, mix together the breadcrumbs and sage. Add the cooked onions and season to taste.

3 You can use the mixture to stuff a chicken or a joint of pork. If you want to serve this stuffing with goose or duck, place it in an ovenproof dish and bake at 180°C/350°F/Gas 4 for 30–45 minutes.

VEGETABLES AND SALADS

*U*nder *this heading we have the widest range of food varieties, with different ones available at different times of the year. Buy them fresh when they are in season to get the best quality of flavours and textures.*

Root vegetables, such as parsnips, carrots and swedes, are at their best in winter; use them in thick soups or roasts. Potatoes, the best known of the root vegetables, are wonderful roast, baked or mashed, or simply boiled when new in the summer.

Brassicas, such as broccoli, cabbage, cauliflowers and sprouts, are generally best in the winter too. They are usually served with roasts but can make wonderful dishes on their own. Pods – the various forms of peas and beans – are equally good with meat, fish, game or in compilation dishes such as risottos.

Greens are even more versatile: spinach is good cooked or raw in salads, as are the range of lettuces and the new range of leaves including rocket, pak choi and mizuma, which now make summer salads so tasty.

There is a whole range of tomatoes too – for cooking or salads, in sauces and in purées – as well as mushrooms, garlic, peppers and chillies, all of which add flavours to hot and cold dishes. Onions and leeks also add flavour in summer and winter.

Most vegetables used to be boiled before serving, but roasting and grilling brings out the flavours and conserves their nutritional value much better. Remember: eat vegetables raw as much as you can for the healthiest eating of all.

Organic vegetables are making an increasing appearance now and need to be bought to taste the real vegetable flavours. How often you buy them is up to your preference and budget.

ROOTS

Botanically speaking, we should call some of these tubers, but we will stick to roots and include all the vegetables grown below the ground.

Potatoes

Potatoes come in all shapes and sizes. New potatoes mean exactly that and come in different varieties; the most sought after are Jersey Royals. Simply boil them unpeeled with a little mint and serve with butter. Older potatoes can be used in different ways – for boiling, mashing, baking, roasting and frying. There are many types of potato, varying from waxy to floury. Use the small, waxy varieties such as Pink Fir Apple for salads and choose floury ones such as King Edwards or Maris Piper for jackets and mashed potatoes. A good all-rounder, such as Cara or Desirée, is good for chips and bakes. Buy and use new potatoes as needed, but you can store main crop potatoes in a cool, dark place for some weeks.

Carrots

Buy baby carrots when in season and main crop all year round. Eat them raw, whole or grated, boiled, steamed and roasted.

Parsnips

These are best in winter; buy medium-sized roots with a smooth skin. Parboil and then roast them. Parsnips also make a good purée and are good in soups.

Swedes and turnips

Large turnips and swedes need to be peeled thickly and are best boiled and mashed. Baby turnips are delicious plainly boiled and served with butter; they also roast well.

Celeriac

A very knobbly looking vegetable with a thick skin. Peel it thickly, boil and then mash it – it has a delicious celery flavour.

Beetroot

Buy small to medium-sized beetroots. Peel and grate them raw for salads, or boil, bake or roast in their skins and serve hot.

Jerusalem artichokes

These are knobbly but there are rearing varieties, which are easier to peel. They are delicious roasted and are good in soup.

Radish

This is the smallest root vegetable. Use it in salads and as a nibble with drinks. Slice larger radishes for use as a garnish.

White sante potato

Maris bard potatoes

Red salad potatoes

Baby new potatoes

Carrots

Parsnips

Radishes

Beetroots

French onion

Shallots

Spring onions

Leek

Red onion

Fresh garlic

BULBS

This category includes all the onions and leeks (see page 161). Buy bulbs that are firm and crisp, and reject any that have discoloured skin or that are sprouting. Bulbs can be stored in a dark, airy place.

Onions

Onions are available in yellow, white and red. The ordinary yellow onion is the one normally used for cooking – fried before adding to sauces and casseroles, sliced and cooked slowly for onion tart, chopped and used in stuffings, and baked whole. White and red onions are sold for their colour and flavour. Red onions have a sweet, mild flavour and are good eaten raw in salads or grilled. White onions have a stronger flavour.

Shallots

These small onions divide into cloves when peeled. They have a very mild flavour and are used in dishes when a gentle onion taste is required. Shallots are also good roasted whole with other vegetables.

Pickling onions

These are the smallest onions and are grown specifically for pickling. They are useful for dishes such as coq au vin, where small, whole onions are required. They are also handy for kebabs, where they can be cooked with pieces of meat or skewered and grilled as part of a vegetable kebab.

Leeks

Buy leeks in small to medium sizes because large ones tend to be tough. Clean them thoroughly before use. Leeks are good simply sliced and boiled as an accompaniment or they can be used in place of onions in some dishes where a milder flavour is required. Leeks can also be served with a cheese sauce as a dish on their own, or wrapped in ham.

Spring onions

These young onions are usually eaten raw in salads. They look attractive when sliced and are often used as a garnish. Spring onions can also be stir-fried as part of a dish and are a useful addition to soups. Buy them frequently and use within 2–3 days for maximum freshness.

Garlic

Buy whole heads of garlic that are plump and firm. Garlic is an indispensable ingredient in many dishes; use it in any dish that needs its pungent aroma and flavour. Garlic is usually chopped and fried as part of a recipe, but it can also be crushed and added to salad dressings and stuffings, or roasted whole with other vegetables.

GREENS

Cabbages

Buy cabbages that feel firm and crisp and heavy in the hand. Avoid any with blemishes or discolourings. For years cabbage had been an unpopular vegetable due to overcooking. However, it is delicious and also healthy when finely shredded, steamed, boiled or stir-fried quickly, with a little spice added. Some cabbage can be eaten raw in salads. Red, green and white varieties are available.

Brussels sprouts

These are available in the winter around Christmas time. Take care not to overcook them or their flavour and texture will be ruined. They are also good shredded in salads or shredded and added to stir-fries.

Cauliflower

Cauliflowers are not really 'green' but they fit into this category. Buy really white heads without any blemishes. Divide them into florets and steam or boil gently. They can be eaten raw in salads. They are often served with a cheese sauce as a supper dish, and are good mixed with broccoli. They can be used in stir-fries and as part of a vegetable curry to add colour and texture, or to make soup.

Broccoli

Purple sprouting broccoli is the original broccoli and is only available for a short period. Steam or boil it gently, and serve it with butter and a grating of nutmeg; it is absolutely delicious. Calabrese (a variety of green sprouting broccoli) is readily available all the year round. Buy it when the colour is a rich, dark blue-green; avoid any that is turning yellow. Simply divide it into florets and then steam, boil or stir-fry it. It also makes good soup.

Spinach

Spinach is rich in iron and is therefore very nutritious. You should buy it on the day you want to use it, to ensure maximum freshness. Baby spinach is wonderful raw in salads. Buy fresh leaves without any sign of yellowing. Wash the leaves well in lots of cold running water first, and then quickly stir-fry them or reduce them in a hot saucepan until just wilted. Season well and serve with butter and nutmeg. Spinach soup is very good.

Chinese leaves

These are available all the year round. They are a versatile vegetable because they can be used as a cabbage and as a lettuce. Make sure the leaves are fresh and crisp when buying; they will keep for 3–4 days in the refrigerator. Slice finely to serve in salads; steam or stir-fry to serve hot.

Savoy cabbage

Brussels sprouts

Broccoli

Spinach leaves

Celery

Chinese leaves

Cauliflower

Butterhead lettuce

Round lettuce

3

VEGETABLES AND SALADS

Pak choi

This is sometimes called 'bok choy'. Pak choi is another Chinese vegetable that is readily available all the year round. Slice it thickly and stir-fry.

Celery

Celery is available all year round. Choose stems that are very firm and rigid. Celery is good raw in salads but can also be chopped and used in soups and casseroles. Celery hearts can also be braised.

Lettuce

Buy lettuce when it is fresh and has a good colour. It is normally used in salads but lettuce hearts such as Little Gem may be quickly grilled or fried. Varieties include round butterhead, cos, iceberg, oak leaf, lollo rosso, and Webb's wonder. Store it in a plastic bag in the refrigerator. Some varieties will keep for 1–2 days.

Salad leaves

These are very popular and can be found in most supermarket chill cabinets. Use them on the day of purchase for the best texture and flavour. Varieties include Swiss chard, mustard greens, mizuma, sorrel, lamb's lettuce, rocket and endive.

PEAS, BEANS AND PODS

Peas

Peas are the most popular green vegetable. Garden peas and petit pois (small peas) are available fresh in pods during the summer, and frozen all year round. Fresh garden peas take some beating and are a real treat: serve them simply with some butter. Choose firm, rigid pods when buying. For the best flavour, pod the peas just before cooking. Frozen peas are very good and can be served alone or as part of a dish. They also make good soups.

Mangetouts and sugar snap peas

Both of these peas are eaten with the pod. Mangetouts are softer and need very little cooking. Sugar snaps are much crispier and are good added to stir-fries – both have a delicate, sweet flavour.

Broad beans

Buy the smaller pods because the beans will be more tender. Broad beans can be stored for up to a week, but they are best used when freshly bought. They are good as a vegetable, in risottos, added to soups and as a purée. Frozen broad beans are available all year round and are very good.

Green beans

Buy firm beans with a good colour and a smooth skin; they can be stored in the refrigerator for 2–3 days. Varieties include runner beans (slice them before cooking – they have a very good flavour and texture, but a short season), and French beans (small, thin beans, which have a delicate flavour – cook them whole). Frozen beans are not as good as fresh.

Sweetcorn

Sweetcorn is included here as a pod; the husk is removed before the kernels can be used. Buy it fresh to eat whole on the cob, boiled and served with butter. For kernels, it is easier to buy them frozen or tinned. Use sweetcorn in salads, soups and casseroles. Baby corn is also available and should be boiled quickly and served whole, or eaten raw.

SQUASHES

This group includes courgettes and cucumbers as well as squashes and pumpkins.

Courgettes

These are summer vegetables, and people who grow them always have a glut. Buy smaller ones because they have the better flavour. They should be firm and have a good colour (they come in yellow as well as green). Eat them raw, sliced or grated in salads. They are delicious stir-fried, fried or grilled until golden brown. Marrows are large courgettes, and need peeling before cooking.

Pumpkins

Pumpkins are available in various sizes. We have only started using pumpkins in cooking recently, rather than making masks from them. They are rather difficult to peel, but they can be sliced and baked before removing the skin. They are available in the autumn – use them in soups and casseroles, or simply roast them.

Squashes

Acorn and butternut squashes are the most easily available. They have a delicious flavour and can be cooked like pumpkins. They are also delicious in soups.

Cucumber

Cucumbers are always available, and they can be stored in the refrigerator for up to a week. They are normally used in salads, but are also used to garnish cold salmon and are the traditional filling in cucumber sandwiches. When cut into chunks, cucumber can also be stir-fried quickly.

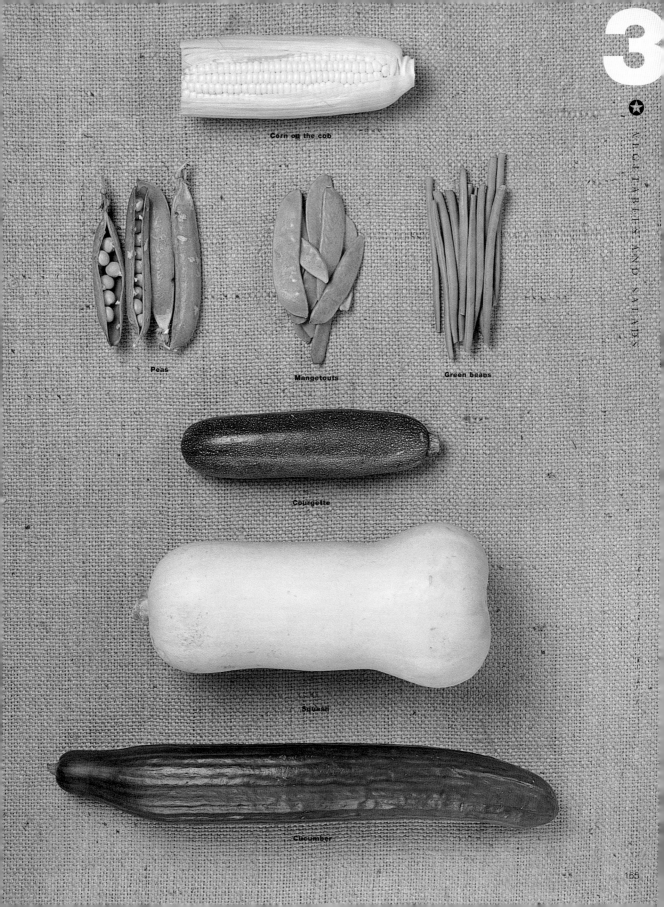

Corn on the cob

Peas

Mangetouts

Green beans

Courgette

Squash

Cucumber

Plum tomato

Cherry vine tomatoes

Salad tomato

Beefsteak tomato

Aubergine

Avocado

Sweet peppers

Chillies

Field (or Portobello)
mushroom

Chestnut mushrooms

White closed-cup
mushrooms

Shiitake mushrooms

VEGETABLE FRUITS

This category covers all the vegetables that are really fruits.

Tomatoes

These are available all the year round and come in all shapes and sizes. They are usually eaten raw but are also delicious when cooked – pan-fried, halved and grilled, baked whole, stuffed and baked, or made into sauces and soups.

Buy tomatoes in season if possible and from a good supplier; they should be of a good, even colour and still firm to the touch. Leave soft tomatoes in the shop. Eat them soon after buying in order to enjoy their fullest flavour.

Cherry tomatoes

These are the smallest and sweetest tomatoes. Eat them like grapes for a snack, in a salad, or use them as a garnish.

Vine tomatoes

These tomatoes are sold still on the vine. They are more expensive but the flavour is considerably better than others.

Salad tomatoes

These are the most common tomatoes, and they vary in terms of quality. If you are able to buy local produce from a grower or from a farmers' market, they will be wonderful; there is nothing like a home-grown tomato. But so often we are offered imported tomatoes, which have not been allowed to ripen properly, and their flavour and texture are poor.

Plum tomatoes

These tomatoes can be recognised by their shape. They have a good flavour and, because they have fewer seeds, they are good to use in cooking.

Beefsteak tomatoes

These are the largest tomatoes. Sometimes they have a good flavour but they can be watery. They are good stuffed and baked.

Aubergines

Buy them in small to medium sizes with a smooth, glossy skin. Slice or dice them before cooking. Aubergines cannot be eaten raw. Their flavour is mild but they can absorb flavours so they are used in dishes mixed with other strongly flavoured ingredients, such as onions and garlic, spices and chillies.

Avocados

These are probably the most difficult vegetable to buy at the right degree of ripeness. Unripe avocados are inedible and so are overripe ones. You have to buy them a couple of days before you want to eat them and allow them to ripen on a warm windowsill. A good greengrocer will always help with your choice. Never buy any with bruises because they will quickly blacken once cut open. Serve them halved with vinaigrette or sliced in salads (brush with lemon juice to prevent discoloration). They can also be puréed to make a dip.

Sweet peppers

These are available in yellow, orange, red and green. I find the green variety too bitter and do not use it; the red pepper is in fact the ripened green one and has a much better flavour. Buy peppers that are smooth and firm to the touch. Store them in a plastic bag in the refrigerator for a few days. They can be eaten raw in salads, or stuffed and grilled.

Chillies

These are from the same family as peppers, but they are very hot. Usually the smaller the chilli, the hotter the flavour. They are available in green or red. Use rubber gloves when preparing, because any contact with eyes or delicate skin can give a burning sensation, which will last some time. Remove all seeds before use unless you like a really hot dish.

Mushrooms

Mushrooms are not really vegetables but edible fungi. They are eaten as vegetables, however, and that is why they are included here. There are two types: cultivated and wild. Wild mushrooms have a better flavour. The most commonly available cultivated mushrooms are white or button mushrooms, followed by chestnut mushrooms, which are darker in colour and slightly larger. Shiitake mushrooms have a silky texture when cooked and have a fine flavour – they are used in Asian recipes. The field mushroom is found in the wild – it is larger and has black gills and a good, strong flavour. The flat mushroom is the cultivated equivalent.

Ceps, morels and chanterelles are other wild mushrooms (although cultivation of some of these is now underway). They are rare to find and very expensive (buy them on holiday in France or Italy if you see them in markets there). These are often available dried, which are still expensive, but keep a small packet in the cupboard and add a few to dishes containing cultivated mushrooms and the flavour will be greatly enhanced.

Buy mushrooms fresh: they should be dry on the outside and have a fresh smell. Keep them in a paper bag in the refrigerator and use within 1–2 days of purchase. It is unnecessary to wash them: just wipe them carefully with a soft cloth or a soft brush to remove dirt.

Mushrooms are good cooked whole or sliced in casseroles, pies, soups, pasta and rice dishes, or simply fried and served on toast for supper. Button mushrooms may be sliced and served raw in salads. Large field mushrooms may be stuffed and grilled, baked, or cooked on a barbecue. Mushroom sauce can be made to accompany steak. Rehydrate dried mushrooms in a little warm water for 30 minutes before cooking.

RED CABBAGE CASSEROLE

If you are not cooking for a large group of people, it is still worth making this casserole for eight people because it will keep for 2–3 days in the refrigerator and can be served with sausages for a quick supper dish.

Serves 8
Preparation time: 20 minutes
Cooking time: 2½ hours

INGREDIENTS

1 red cabbage, about 750 g/1 lb 10 oz
2 onions, peeled and finely sliced
1 garlic clove, peeled and chopped
2 small cooking apples, peeled, cored and sliced
2 tbsp muscovado sugar
½ tsp ground cinnamon
whole nutmeg, for grating
2 tbsp red wine vinegar
zest and juice of 1 orange
2 tbsp redcurrant jelly
salt and pepper

You will need a casserole dish (about 2.8 litres/5 pints), a sharp knife, a chopping board and a grater

METHOD

1 Preheat the oven to 150°C/300°F/Gas 2. Cut the cabbage into quarters and remove the centre stalk. Shred finely.

2 In the casserole dish, layer up the red cabbage, onions, garlic and apples. Sprinkle over the sugar and cinnamon and grate a quarter of the nutmeg over the top.

3 Pour over the wine vinegar and orange juice and scatter over the orange zest.

4 Stir well and season. The dish will be quite full but the volume of the cabbage will reduce during cooking.

5 Cook in the centre of the preheated oven for 1–1½ hours, stirring from time to time. If you prefer, you can cook it more quickly in a flameproof casserole dish on the top of the stove over a medium heat for 8–10 minutes until the cabbage is just tender. The stove way leaves the cabbage more crunchy.

6 Stir in the redcurrant jelly, and adjust the seasoning if necessary. Serve hot with any meat or game.

BAKED POTATOES

Baked potatoes make a delicious, nutritious snack or meal at any time. To be successful, you need to buy large, floury potatoes like King Edwards, Cara or Desirée.

Serves 4
Preparation time: 2 minutes
Cooking time: 1½ hours

INGREDIENTS

4 potatoes, about 200 g/7 oz each
salt and pepper
4 knobs of butter, about 2 tsp each, to serve

You will need a pointed knife, a fine skewer and an oven glove

METHOD

1 Preheat the oven to 200°C/400°F/Gas 6. Wash and wipe the potatoes thoroughly. Prick them all over using the point of a knife or a skewer to prevent the skin splitting (you can insert a large metal skewer into each potato to ensure the centre is cooked if wished).

2 Bake the potatoes near the top of the preheated oven for 1–1½ hours, until they are soft inside and the skin is crisp. Test by pushing a fine skewer into the centre of a potato.

3 Cut a large cross in the top of each potato and, using a clean, thick cloth or oven gloves, squeeze the potato so that the soft filling starts to push out of the skin. Alternatively, cut each potato in half if preferred.

4 Season well and add a knob of butter before serving.

Variations

You can also try some of the following fillings. Each of these makes enough to fill one potato.

Cheese: serve with 25 g/1 oz grated cheese sprinkled on top of the potato.

Chives: crush 1 garlic clove, mix with 1 tablespoon of soured cream and add 2 teaspoons of chopped fresh chives.

Bacon: top the potato with a rasher of crisply fried bacon.

Onion: chop a spring onion and mix it with a tablespoon of crème fraîche.

SPINACH, BACON AND MUSHROOM SALAD

Serves 4
Preparation time: 5 minutes
Cooking time: 20 minutes

INGREDIENTS

225 g/8 oz baby spinach leaves

225 g/8 oz lardons or streaky bacon, snipped into 1 cm/
½ inch strips

2 garlic cloves, peeled and finely chopped

225 g/8 oz button mushrooms

2 tbsp olive oil

4 slices thick wholemeal bread, cut into 1 cm/½ inch cubes

Dressing
2 tbsp balsamic vinegar

4 tbsp extra-virgin olive oil

1 tsp Dijon mustard

½ tsp sugar

1 tbsp chopped fresh parsley

salt and pepper

4 tbsp freshly grated Parmesan, to garnish

You will need a frying pan, a chopping board, a cook's knife, a bread knife, a small roasting tin, a grater, a wooden spatula and 4 salad bowls for serving.

WINE SUGGESTION
Try a cold, white Pouilly Fuissé with this salad.

METHOD

1 Make sure the spinach leaves are clean and dry and divide them between the serving bowls.

2 Fry the lardons in a dry frying pan, with the garlic, over a medium heat for 3–4 minutes until they are cooked and crispy. Add the mushrooms and cook for about 2 minutes until just soft. Set aside to keep warm.

3 To make croûtons, heat the olive oil in the frying pan and fry the bread cubes over a high heat for 4–5 minutes until they are crisp and golden brown. Move them around the pan quickly to ensure even colouring.

4 Scatter the bacon and mushroom mixture over the spinach and top with the fried croûtons.

5 Mix all the dressing ingredients together in a small screw-top jar, season to taste and shake well. Pour over the salad and garnish with the Parmesan.

ROASTED WINTER VEGETABLES

Roasted vegetables are very popular, especially since they all cook together and need little attention once prepared. You can use a mixture of whatever is available and vary the mix according to choice. Try to cut all the vegetables to roughly the same size.

Serves 6
Preparation time: 25 minutes
Cooking time: 1 hour

INGREDIENTS

3 red onions

3 medium parsnips

4 baby turnips

3 medium carrots

350 g/12 oz butternut squash, peeled and cut into chunks (prepared weight)

350 g/12 oz sweet potato, peeled and cut into chunks (prepared weight)

2 garlic cloves, peeled and chopped

2 tbsp chopped fresh rosemary

1 tbsp chopped fresh thyme

2 tsp chopped fresh sage

3 tbsp olive oil

salt and pepper

2 tbsp chopped fresh mixed herbs, such as parsley, thyme and rosemary, to garnish

You will need a large roasting tin, a sharp knife, a chopping board, and a wooden spatula.

METHOD

1 Cut the onions into quarters through the root (this will hold them together during the cooking).

2 Peel and cut the parsnips into even-sized pieces, about 5 cm/2 inches long.

3 Cut the turnips into quarters.

4 Scrub or peel the carrots as necessary and cut into pieces like the parsnips. Put all the vegetables, including the squash and sweet potato, in one layer in a roasting tin. Scatter over the garlic and herbs.

5 Pour over the oil and season well.

6 Toss all the ingredients together until they are well mixed and coated with the oil (you can leave them to marinate at this stage for 1–2 hours to allow the flavours to be absorbed).

7 Preheat the oven to 220°C/425°/Gas 7. Roast the vegetables at the top of the preheated oven for 45 minutes to 1 hour until they are cooked and nicely browned. Turn the vegetables over halfway through the cooking time.

8 Serve the vegetables with a good handful of fresh mixed herbs scattered on top and a final sprinkling of salt and freshly grated pepper.

MASHED POTATO

Serves 4
Preparation time: 10 minutes
Cooking time: 35 minutes

INGREDIENTS

900 g/2 lb floury potatoes, such as King Edwards, Maris Piper or Desirée
4 tbsp butter
3 tbsp hot milk
salt and pepper

You will need a large lidded saucepan, a potato peeler, a colander, a small milk pan and a potato masher

METHOD

1 Peel the potatoes carefully using a potato peeler. Place them in cold water while you prepare the others to prevent them from going brown.

2 Cut the potatoes into even-sized chunks and cook them in boiling salted water over a medium heat, covered, for 20–25 minutes until they are tender. Test that they are cooked by piercing them with the point of a knife, but do make sure you test that they are soft right to the middle to avoid lumps later. Remove the pan from the heat and drain through a colander.

3 Return the potatoes to the hot pan and mash with a potato masher until smooth. Add the butter and continue to mash until it is all mixed in. Then add the milk (it is better hot because the potatoes absorb it more quickly and produce a creamier mash.

4 Taste the mash and season to taste. Serve at once.

Variations

Herb mash: mix in 3 tablespoons chopped fresh parsley, thyme or mint.

Mustard mash: mix in 2 tablespoons of wholegrain mustard.

Horseradish mash: mix in 2 tablespoons horseradish sauce.

Pesto mash: stir in 4 tablespoons fresh pesto.

PERFECT ROAST POTATOES

Perfect roast potatoes are what many people try to achieve. Without a crisp potato to accompany the joint, the whole meal can be a disappointment. Make sure you choose the right potatoes: floury King Edwards, Maris Piper, Romano or Desirée are the best.

Serves 6
Preparation time: 15 minutes
Cooking time: 1 hour

INGREDIENTS

1.3 kg/3 lb large, floury potatoes
3 tbsp olive oil
salt and pepper

You will need a lidded saucepan, a potato peeler, a pointed knife, a colander, a heavy roasting tin and a serving dish

METHOD

1 Preheat the oven to 220°C/425°F/Gas 7. Peel the potatoes carefully using a potato peeler. Place them in cold water while you prepare the others to prevent them from going brown.

2 Cut the potatoes into even-sized chunks (the size you prefer) and cook in boiling salted water over a medium heat, covered, for 5–7 minutes. They should still be firm.

3 Whilst the potatoes are boiling, pour the oil into a roasting tin and place in the hot oven.

4 Remove the potatoes from the heat, drain well and return them to the saucepan. Cover with the lid and firmly shake the pan so that the surface of the potatoes is roughened (this helps to give a much crisper texture).

5 Remove the tin from the hot oven carefully and tip the potatoes into the hot oil, basting them carefully to ensure that they are all coated with the oil.

6 Put the tin back into the oven and roast at the top for 45–50 minutes until the potatoes are browned all over and thoroughly crisp. Turn the potatoes once only during the process or the crunchy edges will be destroyed.

7 Transfer the potatoes from the roasting tin carefully into a hot serving dish. Sprinkle with a little more salt and serve at once. Any potatoes left over (most unlikely) are delicious cold.

SPECIAL CAULIFLOWER CHEESE

Serves 4
Preparation time: 15 minutes
Cooking time: 25 minutes

INGREDIENTS

1 cauliflower, about 675 g/1 lb 8 oz prepared weight, trimmed and cut into florets

1 tbsp olive oil

1 onion, peeled and thinly sliced

1 garlic clove, peeled and finely chopped

115 g/4 oz streaky bacon, cut into 1 cm/½ inch strips

3 tbsp butter

3 tbsp plain flour

450 ml/16 fl oz milk

115 g/4 oz Cheddar cheese, finely grated

a good grating of nutmeg

1 tbsp grated Parmesan

salt and pepper

To serve
tomato salad or green salad
crusty bread

You will need a 1.4 litre /2½ pint au gratin dish, a cook's knife, a chopping board, a frying pan, a measuring jug, a medium saucepan, a grater and a wooden spatula

WINE SUGGESTION

A sturdy red Merlot or oaky Australian Chardonnay would go well with this dish.

METHOD

1 Cook the cauliflower in a saucepan of boiling salted water for 4–5 minutes; it should still be firm. Drain and place in the hot serving dish, then keep it warm.

2 Heat the olive oil in a frying pan over a medium heat and fry the onion, garlic and bacon for 5–6 minutes until the onion is caramelised and golden and the bacon is crisp.

3 Melt the butter in a saucepan over a medium heat. Stir in the flour. Cook for 1 minute, stirring continuously. Remove from the heat and stir in the milk gradually until smooth. Return to a low heat and stir until the sauce comes to the boil and thickens. Simmer gently, stirring constantly, for about 3 minutes, until the sauce is creamy and smooth. Remove from the heat and stir in the Cheddar cheese and nutmeg. Taste, and season well.

4 Spoon the onion and bacon over the cauliflower and pour over the hot sauce. Top with the Parmesan and place under a hot grill to brown. Serve immediately with a small tomato salad or green salad and some crusty bread.

MINTED NEW POTATOES

Potatoes have been staple fare in Britain for ages, but began to wane in popularity due to the growing use of rice and pasta. However, today the potato is back in fashion. It can be served in various ways, as an accompaniment or as a meal in its own right. Make sure you buy the correct variety of potato for the method of cooking. These potatoes can also be served cold, without the butter, as a salad.

Serves 4
Preparation time: 5 minutes
Cooking time: 15–20 minutes

INGREDIENTS

900 g/2 lb new potatoes, Jersey Royals if possible
sprig fresh mint
1 tbsp butter
salt and pepper
2 tbsp chopped fresh mixed herbs, such as parsley, chives and mint, to garnish

You will need a lidded saucepan, a colander and a small pointed knife

METHOD

1 Wash the potatoes, or just wipe them if they are not dirty. Put the potatoes and the mint in a covered saucepan of boiling salted water and cook, covered, for 15–20 minutes until tender. Test with the point of a sharp knife (the timing will vary according to the size of the potatoes).

2 Drain the potatoes well and remove the mint. Return to the saucepan with the butter. Allow the butter to melt and mix with the potatoes until they are well covered.

3 Tip the potatoes into a serving dish, season well, particularly with lots of freshly ground pepper, and toss over the herbs. Serve at once.

Note: new potatoes can also be served 'crushed'. Simply break them up roughly with a fork in the saucepan and add more herbs or a few leaves of rocket or spinach until they are wilted.

GRILLED SUMMER VEGETABLES

Grilling summer vegetables enhances their flavour and allows you to eat them hot, with grilled meats or fish, or cold as a salad with a herb dressing. They are versatile and can be prepared ahead. Cook them under a conventional grill, on a griddle on top of the cooker or on a barbecue.

Serves 6–8
Preparation time: 25 minutes
Cooking time: 30 minutes–1 hour

INGREDIENTS

2 red peppers, deseeded and cut into quarters

2 yellow peppers, deseeded and cut into quarters

2 red onions, peeled and sliced into thick rings

3 courgettes, sliced lengthways into 3 or 4 pieces

1 aubergine, sliced across into 8 pieces

2 bulbs fennel, trimmed and sliced

3 tbsp olive oil

2 tbsp extra-virgin olive oil

1 lemon, cut in half

salt and pepper

To garnish
2 tbsp chopped fresh mixed herbs, such as parsley, chives and lemon thyme

55 g/2 oz Parmesan cheese, shaved with a potato peeler

You will need a grill, a cook's knife, a chopping board, a pastry brush, some kitchen tongs, a potato peeler and a serving dish

METHOD

1 Brush the vegetables well with the 3 tablespoons of olive oil.

2 Cook under a grill preheated to high for 4–5 minutes on each side. Alternatively, cook on a griddle over a medium heat for 5–7 minutes on each side. The vegetables should have a good brown colour. If you are using a barbecue, the vegetables will need to cook for about 4–6 minutes on each side. Cooking times will vary depending on the thickness. Transfer the vegetables to a serving dish. You will need to cook them in different batches until all the vegetables are cooked.

3 Sprinkle with the extra-virgin olive oil and squeeze the lemon halves over the vegetables. Season well and scatter over the herbs and cheese.

PEAR AND AVOCADO SALAD

Serves 4

Preparation time: 15–20 minutes

INGREDIENTS

4 small pears, Rocha or French William

2 tbsp lemon juice

2 ripe avocados

1 bunch of watercress

55 g/2 oz rocket

2 tbsp finely chopped walnuts

115 g/4 oz dolcelatte or Roquefort cheese

walnut bread, sliced, to serve

Dressing
3 tbsp balsamic vinegar

2 tbsp extra-virgin olive oil

2 tbsp walnut oil

1 tsp Dijon mustard

½ tsp light soft brown sugar

1 tbsp chopped fresh parsley

salt and pepper

You will need a chopping board, a cook's knife, a pastry brush, a screw-top jar and 4 serving plates

METHOD

1 Halve the pears, then core and cut them carefully into thin slices. Brush with lemon juice to prevent discoloration.

2 Cut the avocados in half, remove the stones and peel them. Carefully cut each half into about five slices. Also brush with lemon juice.

3 Put the watercress and rocket on four serving plates and arrange the pears and avocados on top. Scatter over the chopped walnuts.

4 For the dressing, mix all the ingredients together in a small screw-top jar and shake well.

5 Spoon the dressing over the salad and crumble the cheese over the top.

6 Serve at once with some sliced walnut bread.

DRESSINGS

A basic dressing is essential for a good salad. Good olive oil and a fine vinegar or lemon juice should be used. Vary the oil and vinegar according to the salad ingredients and add appropriate herbs at the last minute. Salads should only be dressed immediately before eating or else the leaves will go soggy. For the simplest dressing, just sprinkle over some freshly squeezed lemon juice and some olive oil.

Preparation time: 5–10 minutes

BASIC DRESSING

INGREDIENTS

2 tbsp lemon juice, or red or white wine vinegar
4–6 tbsp extra-virgin olive oil
1 tsp Dijon mustard
pinch of caster sugar
1 tbsp freshly chopped parsley
salt and pepper

You will need a screw-top jar or a small basin and a fork

METHOD

1 Place all the ingredients in a jar, secure the top and shake well. Alternatively, beat all the ingredients together in a small basin. Use as much oil as you like. If you have just salad leaves to dress, then 4 tablespoons of oil will be sufficient, but if you have heavier ingredients like potatoes, you will need 6 tablespoons of oil.

2 Use the dressing at once. If you want to store it, do not add the herbs – it will then keep for 3–4 days in the refrigerator.

Variations

Oriental dressing: replace 1 tablespoon of the oil with sesame oil and add 1–2 teaspoons of soy sauce. Add chopped coriander instead of the parsley.

Tomato dressing: use balsamic vinegar instead of lemon juice and add 1 tablespoon of chopped sun-dried tomatoes. Replace the parsley with torn basil leaves.

Cheese dressing: add 1 tablespoon of crumbled strong blue cheese, or fork in 1 tablespoon of garlic-flavoured soft cheese. A few chopped walnuts, say 25 g/1 oz, would be a nice addition.

Sweet/sour dressing: add 1 tablespoon of honey and 1 teaspoon finely grated fresh ginger. Some toasted sesame seeds, about 1 tablespoon, would add a good crunch.

PASTA, NOODLES, RICE, GRAINS AND PULSES

This section covers pasta and noodles (mainly made from wheat), the oriental varieties (made from other grains), other varieties of rice and quickly cooked grains, and pulses. Collectively, they may be called cereals and have a place in the diet on their own or as accompaniments to other foods.

PASTA

There really are hundreds of types of pasta, some made simply from wheat flour and water and some richer ones made with egg. You can make pasta at home but there are so many easily available that I prefer to put the effort into the sauce making. Fresh pasta is now more widely obtainable but the staple is dried pasta, which you can always keep in your cupboard. There are two main types of pasta: long and short.

Spaghetti
This is the basic long pasta, and all kitchens should have a packet. Use it for bolognese and carbonara sauces, and as an accompaniment to meat and vegetable dishes.

Macaroni
This is a basic short pasta and is often used for macaroni cheese – a quickly made, economical supper dish.

Lasagne
These are large sheets of pasta, which are used with layers of fillings – such as meat sauce and cheese sauces – and then baked in the oven.

Cannelloni
Large tubes of pasta, which need cooking first before being stuffed with either a meat or vegetable filling.

Fusilli
These are thin spiral shapes, which are particularly good with sauces because they hold the sauces well. They also make good pasta salads.

Farfalle
This is a bow-shaped pasta. It is very attractive in salads and good with meat sauces.

Vermicelli
A very fine pasta – the finest is called 'angel's hair'. It is best used with fine ingredients, such as prawns and crab. It is also good with wild mushrooms.

Tagliatelle
Long, flat noodles, known as ribbon noodles. The ribbons also come in different widths, known as linguine, fettuccine and pappardelle (this is the widest).

Conchiglie
Shell-shaped pasta, which comes in all sizes from tiny, for soups, to large, which can be stuffed. This is a good, short pasta for use with all sorts of sauces.

Stuffed pasta
Ravioli and tortellini are stuffed pastas with a variety of fillings, including meat, mushrooms and cheese. They can form the basis of a quick meal and they only need cooking and tossing in melted butter or cream for an easy dish. They are available made from plain or flavoured pasta.

Storage
Store dried pasta in a cool, dry place for up to 1–2 years. Egg pastas will not keep as long as the plain varieties, so check labels for storage. Use fresh pasta within 1–2 days of purchase.

LASAGNE

Lasagne is a quick, satisfying and versatile dish. You can use chicken or vegetables instead of the beef in this recipe.

1 Heat 1 tbsp olive oil in a pan. Add 1 chopped onion and 1 chopped garlic clove. Cook over a medium heat for 4 minutes. Add 100 g/3½ oz chopped mushrooms and 350 g/12 oz minced beef and cook, stirring, for 4 minutes.

2 Add 150 ml/5 fl oz red wine, 100 ml/3½ fl oz water, 250 g/9 oz passata and 1 tsp sugar; cook for 5 minutes. Put 3 sheets of dried 'no-cook' lasagne in the bottom of a baking dish, add half of the sauce, top with 3 sheets, then the remaining sauce, then 3 more sheets.

3 Melt 5 tbsp butter in a pan, stir in 50 g/1¾ oz plain flour, and cook for 2 minutes. Remove from the heat, and gradually stir in 600 ml/1 pint milk. Bring to the boil, stirring until thickened. Cool slightly.

4 Stir in 75 g/2¾ oz grated Parmesan and 1 beaten egg. Season, then pour over the lasagne. Sprinkle with 75 g/ 2¾ oz grated Parmesan, then bake at 190°C/375°F/Gas 5 for 30 minutes until golden.

You can replace the beef with the same quantity of chicken or turkey, or make a vegetarian version by replacing the beef with the same quantity of soya mince. Cook in the same way as the beef.

NOODLES

Under this heading we are dealing with oriental noodles, not the Italian variety.

Egg noodles

These are the most common noodles used in Chinese and Thai cooking. They are available in various thicknesses and are very quick to cook (from 1–5 minutes). They can be served with stir-fry dishes or can be a quick meal in themselves mixed with some shellfish and vegetables and a dash of soy sauce and sesame oil. They can also be stir-fried after cooking.

Rice noodles

These are available as very fine noodles; most of them only need soaking before use, but check the pack for instructions because they vary. Rice noodles can be added to soups and to stir-fries.

Japanese noodles

These are egg noodles like the Chinese noodles, but there are also two specific varieties of Japanese noodles. Soba noodles are made from buckwheat: they have a darker colour and are quite thin – they are usually used in soups and broths. Udon noodles are thicker and made from wheat flour – they are used in stir-fries.

Storage

Keep in a cool, dry place and use by the date on the packs.

RICE

Again, there is a large variety available but a small range opens up a wide area of savoury and sweet dishes.

Long-grain rice

This is the easiest to cook and the most easily available. Most of it comes from America. Long-grain rice is quick to cook and can be the basis of many dishes. It is also cheap. Use it as an accompaniment to meat, fish and chicken dishes. It is also good in kedgeree. It makes a quick storecupboard meal – keep some rice into which you can stir some grated cheese, or some tuna and chopped spring onion.

Basmati rice

This is long-grain rice from the Punjab region of India. It is the best rice in the world with the best flavour. Use it in the same way as long-grain rice, to accompany delicious food. It is available in white, brown and as a mixture with 'wild rice'. Wild rice is not a rice but a grass – it is black and gives a good, nutty flavour.

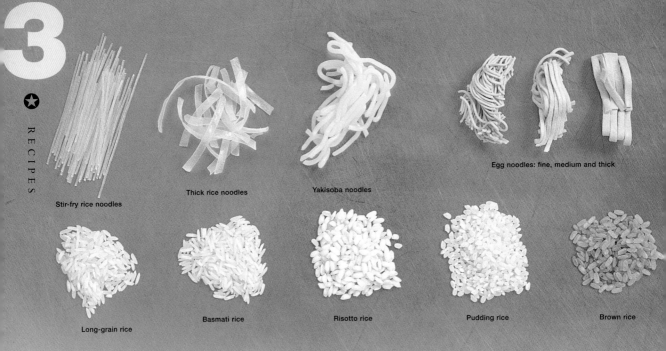

Stir-fry rice noodles

Thick rice noodles

Yakisoba noodles

Egg noodles: fine, medium and thick

Long-grain rice

Basmati rice

Risotto rice

Pudding rice

Brown rice

Risotto rice

This is a short-grain rice, which is specially grown for risotto. Arborio is most widely available, but carnaroli is thought to be superior because it has a creamier texture. Due to the fashion of Italian food at the moment, risotto is very popular. It is a very soothing dish, both to make and to eat, and can be flavoured with different shellfish, meats and vegetables, along with a few herbs and some grated Parmesan cheese.

Pudding rice

This short-grain rice is suitable for long, slow cooking in milk to make rice pudding. Rice pudding is still a popular dessert with all age groups.

Brown rice

This is available as long-grain or basmati. It is much nuttier than white rice and retains the bran layer and germ of the rice; it therefore has a higher nutritional value. It does take longer to cook, so check the packet for instructions.

Storage

Store in airtight containers in a dry, cool place. Rice will keep for up to three years, so it is a long term storecupboard item. If you have enough space and containers, it is a good idea to buy large packs because they are more economical (but only if you are going to use them).

GRAINS

Due to their availability now in instant form, I suggest you try both of the following grains and keep them as basics in your storecupboard.

Couscous

This is a fine-grained semolina and is produced from durum flour. It has a mild flavour but a good, nutty texture, which mixes well with other salad ingredients. Now that instant couscous is available, it is really useful in the storecupboard for a quick meal. Instant couscous just needs a quick soak in hot water or stock for 2–3 minutes and then you can serve it hot with meat, fish or vegetables. Alternatively, mix it with chopped tomatoes, cucumber, spring onions and lots of herbs for a delicious cold salad. In this case, you will need to soak it in cold water or cooled stock instead.

Polenta

This is another almost instant accompaniment. It is a fine granular cornmeal, which can be made by mixing with boiling stock or water in a saucepan and cooking for 1–2 minutes. Check packets for instructions because they vary. Polenta can be served hot and soft, like mashed potato with a good knob of butter or some olive oil, or it can be poured into a baking tray and left to cool. It is then cut into slices and grilled to serve in place of bread.

Storage

Keep in an airtight container in a cool, dry place. Storage times vary, but are often up to 18 months.

BEANS, CHICKPEAS AND LENTILS

These are all known as pulses and are a good, economical source of protein. They are available dried and in cans. Cans cut out the soaking and cooking time and make pulses a useful instant convenience food.

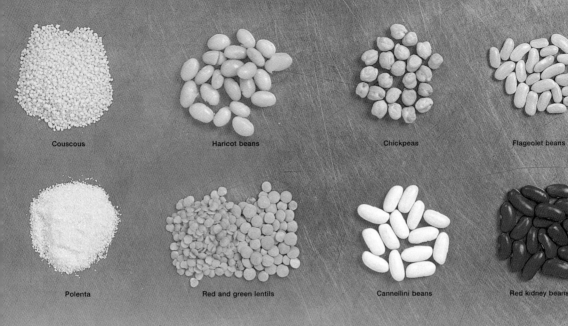

Couscous   Haricot beans   Chickpeas   Flageolet beans

Polenta   Red and green lentils   Cannellini beans   Red kidney beans

Haricot beans

These are probably the most versatile, because they can be used for cassoulet and other casserole dishes such as Boston Baked Beans. They are white, medium-sized beans and are best known tinned as baked beans in tomato sauce. The tinned varieties are easier to use because they eliminate the need for soaking overnight and cooking for 1–1½ hours.

Chickpeas

These are another good, basic food. Chickpeas are round and beige and can quickly be made into a mash to serve with fish or meat. They can also be made into hummus with olive oil and garlic. They need to be soaked overnight and then cooked for anything up to 4 hours (depending on their age). I always use the ready-cooked tinned variety, but enthusiasts will say that the flavour of the soaked and cooked chickpeas is superior. You will need to make your own choice.

Lentils

These are available in yellow, red, green, grey and continental brown varieties. Since lentils do not need soaking and do not take much time to cook, I would always use the dried type. However, if you are short of time, then the tinned type might suit you better. The red and yellow lentils are actually split, so they are very quick to cook: they become very soft and break down to a creamy purée. These lentils form the basis of Indian dhal, and are also used in stuffings and in vegetarian burgers. The green variety are whole and take a little longer to cook. Serve them in salads, thick soups and casseroles. Puy lentils are grey/green and are considered to be the finest. They are best served as an accompaniment to meat or fish.

Butter beans

These large, flat, white beans have a lovely buttery flavour. They are good served as an accompaniment with a sprinkling of chopped herbs. They are also good as a purée or roughly forked with a little garlic and chilli flavouring. Butter beans can be a useful addition to soups.

Cannellini beans

These beans are popular in Italian cooking, particularly in minestrone. They are also used cold in salads, and hot in some pasta dishes.

Flageolet beans

These are delicate, small, green beans, which can be served cold in salads. Traditionally, they are also served hot with lamb.

Red kidney beans

The red kidney bean is the favourite bean of Mexico. It is used in chilli con carne, and is also mashed to make refried beans.

Other beans you might like to try include soya beans, pinto beans, borlotti beans, black-eyed beans, black beans and aduki beans. They all have a different shape and colour and can be used to add bulk to a casserole or soup. Use them dried or tinned for convenience.

Storage

Buy dried beans, chickpeas and lentils in small quantities from a source that has a quick turnover. The longer you keep these dried pulses the longer you will need to cook them because they toughen with age. Store in airtight containers in a cool, dry place. Check the packets for storage times.

CHEESY PASTA BAKE

Serves 4

Preparation time: 15 minutes
Cooking time: 35 minutes

INGREDIENTS

3 tbsp olive oil

1 onion, peeled and thinly sliced

2 garlic cloves, peeled and finely chopped

3 courgettes, cut into 5 cm/2 inch batons

2 red peppers, deseeded and sliced

800 g/1 lb 12 oz canned chopped tomatoes

3 tbsp fresh torn basil leaves

100 g/3½ oz button mushrooms, sliced finely

350 g/12 oz dried fusilli or rigatoni pasta

350 g/12 oz mascarpone cheese

3 tbsp freshly grated Parmesan cheese

salt and pepper

4 sprigs fresh basil, to garnish

You will need a cook's knife, a chopping board, a large saucepan, a large frying pan, a wooden spatula, a 1.7 litre / 3 pint baking dish, and a baking sheet

METHOD

1 Preheat the oven to 200ºC/400ºF/Gas 6. Heat the oil in the frying pan and fry the onion and garlic over a medium heat for 2–3 minutes until golden. Add the courgettes and peppers and continue to cook for a further 3–4 minutes.

2 Lower the heat, add the tomatoes and basil, and simmer for 5 minutes until the vegetables are starting to soften. Season well. Stir in the mushrooms and cook for 2 minutes.

3 In the meantime, cook the pasta in the saucepan in boiling salted water, for 8–10 minutes, or according to the instructions on the packet. When it is 'al dente' (tender but still firm to the bite), remove from the heat and drain well.

4 Pour the drained pasta into the baking dish and pour over the tomato mixture. Stir well.

5 Top with the mascarpone cheese and sprinkle over the grated Parmesan.

6 Bake in the centre of the preheated oven on a baking sheet for 20–25 minutes until bubbling and golden brown. Serve at once garnished with the basil.

WINE SUGGESTION

Try a rich red Montepulciano d'Abruzzo from Italy with this bake.

CHICKPEA SALAD

Dried chickpeas need soaking overnight and then up to four hours' cooking. The canned variety are very good as long as you rinse them thoroughly before use.

Serves 4
Preparation time: 15 minutes
Cooking time: 15 minutes

INGREDIENTS

400 g/14 oz canned chickpeas
1 red onion, peeled
1 tbsp olive oil
2 garlic cloves, peeled and crushed
1 tsp coriander seeds
1 tsp cumin seeds
1 tsp paprika
4 tomatoes, deseeded and roughly chopped
salt and pepper

Dressing
2 tbsp olive oil
juice of 1 lemon
2 tbsp chopped fresh flat-leaf parsley

To serve
115 g/4 oz baby spinach leaves, washed and dried well
125 ml/4 fl oz Greek yoghurt
1 tbsp chopped fresh mint

You will need a cook's knife, a chopping board, a frying pan, a wooden spatula, a bowl and four serving plates

METHOD

1 Drain and rinse the chickpeas thoroughly.

2 Halve the onion vertically and cut each half into small slices, from root to stem.

3 In a frying pan, fry the onion in the oil over a medium heat for about 8 minutes until soft but not coloured. Add the garlic and cook for 2 minutes. Meanwhile, place the coriander and cumin seeds in a pestle and mortar and grind until fine (or crush with the end of a rolling pin in a bowl). Add these to the pan with the paprika and continue to cook for 1 minute, stirring all the time. Remove from the heat.

4 Add the chickpeas to the pan and stir well to ensure they are coated with the spices. Add the tomatoes. Season well.

5 Pour the warm salad into a bowl. Shake the dressing ingredients together in a screw-top jar and pour over the salad. Serve warm or allow to stand for 1 hour to allow the flavours to develop.

6 Arrange the spinach leaves on the serving plates and top with the chickpea salad.

7 Mix the yoghurt with the mint and serve separately.

COUSCOUS SALAD

Serves 6

Preparation time: 10 minutes

Cooking time: 10 minutes

INGREDIENTS

350 g/12 oz couscous

600 ml/1 pint vegetable stock, made with Marigold vegetable bouillon powder if possible

225 g/8 oz cherry tomatoes

225 g/8 oz piece of cucumber

6 spring onions

55 g/2 oz pine kernels

1 tbsp chopped fresh mint

salt and pepper

1 tbsp chopped fresh mint, to garnish

Dressing

juice and grated rind of 1 lemon

5 tbsp extra-virgin olive oil

You will need a measuring jug, a cook's knife, a chopping board, a mixing bowl, a small frying pan and a serving bowl

METHOD

1 Put the couscous in the mixing bowl and pour over the hot stock. Fork through and soak for 2–3 minutes until all the stock has been absorbed, then leave to cool.

2 Cut the tomatoes into quarters.

3 Quarter the cucumber lengthways and remove the seeds, then dice finely.

4 Cut the spring onions into 5 mm/¼ inch lengths.

5 Dry-fry the pine kernels over a medium heat for 1–2 minutes until they are golden brown. Stir well to avoid burning and remove from the heat once they are ready. Leave to cool.

6 Place the dressing ingredients in a screw-top jar, season and shake well.

7 Add all the vegetables to the couscous and stir well. Pour over the dressing and toss together with the pine kernels and mint. Check for seasoning and adjust if necessary.

8 Put the salad into a large serving bowl and scatter the mint over the couscous.

LENTILS WITH SAUSAGES

Puy lentils are available in tins, but since they are quite quick to cook and do not need any soaking, I find the dried variety better.

Serves 4
Preparation time: 15 minutes
Cooking time: 35 minutes

INGREDIENTS

250 g/9 oz Puy lentils, rinsed

2 tsp Marigold Swiss vegetable bouillon powder or a vegetable stock cube

1 carrot, peeled and cut into 4 large chunks

2 shallots, peeled and left whole

4 cloves

2 bay leaves

sprig fresh thyme

700 g/1 lb 9 oz good-quality sausages (about 12)

1 tbsp vegetable oil

2 shallots, peeled and finely chopped

2 garlic cloves, peeled and finely chopped

2 tbsp chopped fresh parsley

salt and pepper

You will need a large saucepan, a cook's knife, a chopping board, a frying pan, a wooden spatula, a slotted spoon and a serving dish

METHOD

1 Put the lentils in the saucepan and cover well with water, about 2.5 cm/1 inch above their level. Stir in the stock powder and add the carrot. Make two small holes in each of the whole shallots and push in the cloves. Add these to the pan with the bay leaves and thyme.

2 Bring to the boil, reduce the heat and simmer gently, with the lid half on, for 15–20 minutes. The lentils should be tender but still whole and firm.

3 Meanwhile, in a frying pan, fry the sausages in the oil over a medium heat for about 15 minutes until they are crusty and brown. Use a slotted spoon to lift them out into a hot serving dish.

4 Add the chopped shallots and garlic to the pan and fry quickly over the same heat for 2–3 minutes until soft, stirring the sediment from the bottom of the pan.

5 Drain the lentils and remove the vegetables and bay leaves. Tip the lentils into the frying pan and mix well. Adjust the seasoning to taste.

6 Stir in the parsley and serve at once with the sausages.

WINE SUGGESTION
Try a strong red Côtes du Rhône with these sausages.

PASTA, NOODLES, RICE, GRAINS AND PULSES

PEA AND BEAN RISOTTO

Serves 4
Preparation time: 10 minutes
Cooking time: 35 minutes

INGREDIENTS

3 tbsp butter

1 tbsp olive oil

1 onion, peeled and finely chopped

1 garlic clove, peeled and finely chopped

350 g/12 oz risotto rice (arborio or carnaroli)

150 ml/5 fl oz dry white wine

850 ml/1½ pints hot vegetable stock

115 g/4 oz shelled broad beans (you can use frozen)

115 g/4 oz fresh or frozen peas

115 g/4 oz freshly grated Parmesan

grated rind of 2 lemons

2 tbsp chopped fresh mint leaves

2 tbsp chopped fresh parsley

salt and pepper

You will need a cook's knife, a chopping board, a large, deep frying pan, a saucepan and ladle, a measuring jug, a wooden spatula and a grater

WINE SUGGESTION

A cold white Sauvignon matches the flavours of this risotto well.

1 Put 1 tablespoon of the butter and 1 tablespoon oil in the frying pan and melt together over a low heat. Add the chopped onion and garlic and cook for about 5 minutes until soft but not coloured.

2 Stir in the rice and fry for 1 minute. Pour in the wine and keep stirring until the rice has absorbed all the liquid. Keep the vegetable stock simmering in a pan. Add one ladleful of stock to the rice and stir constantly. Wait until the liquid has been absorbed before adding the next ladleful. Gradually use all the stock, stirring constantly. This is a slow process; it will take about 15–20 minutes.

3 After you have added half the stock, add the broad beans and the peas (if using fresh) and allow to cook with the rice. When all the stock is absorbed, the rice should be very creamy in texture. Taste to see if the rice is cooked: it should still be a little chewy, but not hard. Season to taste. If you are using frozen beans and peas, add them now and heat through for 1 minute.

4 Remove the pan from the heat and stir in the remaining butter and half of the grated Parmesan. Cover the pan and then allow to stand for 2–3 minutes for the risotto to become even creamier. Stir in the grated lemon rind and chopped mint and parsley and serve at once on hot plates. Serve the remaining Parmesan separately.

3

FRUIT AND NUT PILAF

Serves 6
Preparation time: 10 minutes
Cooking time: 30 minutes

INGREDIENTS

1 tbsp butter
1 tbsp olive oil
1 onion, peeled and finely chopped
1 garlic clove, peeled and finely chopped
350 g/12 oz long-grain (basmati) rice
pinch ground cinnamon
pinch ground cloves
700 ml/1¼ pints chicken or vegetable stock
55 g/2 oz raisins
55 g/2 oz pistachio nuts
salt and pepper

You will need a cook's knife, a chopping board, a lidded saucepan, a measuring jug, a wooden spatula and a serving dish

METHOD

1 Heat the butter and the oil in the saucepan over a low heat. Fry the onion and garlic for about 10 minutes until soft but not coloured.

2 Gently stir in the rice and fry for a further minute. Stir in the ground spices.

3 Pour in the stock, bring to the boil over a medium heat, cover and simmer gently for 15–20 minutes until the rice is tender and the stock has all been absorbed.

4 Season to taste and stir in the raisins and nuts.

5 Remove from the heat, and serve at once in a warm serving dish as an accompaniment to any meat, poultry or fish dish.

SPAGHETTINI WITH CRAB

Serves 2
Preparation time: 10 minutes
Cooking time: 15 minutes

INGREDIENTS

225 g/8 oz dried spaghettini or linguine
1 tbsp butter
1 tbsp olive oil
225 g/8 oz courgettes, thinly sliced
1 garlic clove, peeled and crushed
pinch chilli powder or crushed chillies
175 g/6 oz fresh crabmeat (or frozen and defrosted)
2 tbsp mayonnaise
2 tbsp crème fraîche
salt and pepper
1 tbsp chopped fresh parsley, to garnish

You will need a cook's knife, a chopping board, a large saucepan, a frying pan, a wooden spatula and 2 serving plates

METHOD

1 Put the linguine in a saucepan of boiling water and cook for 8–10 minutes, or according to the pack instructions, until 'al dente' (tender but still firm to the bite).

2 Meanwhile, heat the butter and oil in a frying pan and quickly fry the courgettes over a high heat for 2–3 minutes, stirring continuously, until they are quite brown.

3 Add the garlic and chilli and stir well.

4 Carefully mix in the crabmeat, allow it to warm through for about 1 minute and season well.

5 Drain the pasta, then return it to the hot saucepan. Stir in the mayonnaise and crème fraîche.

6 Turn the pasta onto two serving plates and pour over the crab mixture.

7 Serve at once garnished with parsley.

WINE SUGGESTION

A light Italian Pinot Blanco or a Portuguese Vinho Verde would go well with this crab dish.

WARM CHICKEN NOODLE SALAD

Serves 4
Preparation time: 20 minutes, plus marinating
Cooking time: 25 minutes

INGREDIENTS

350 g/12 oz skinless chicken breast
½ tsp ground ginger
½ tsp turmeric
½ tsp medium curry powder
½ tsp mustard powder
3 tbsp olive oil
2 courgettes, cut into 5 cm/2 inch batons
1 red pepper, deseeded and sliced
1 yellow pepper, deseeded and sliced
115 g/4 oz mangetouts, topped and tailed
1 garlic clove, peeled and finely chopped
2 cm/¾ inch fresh root ginger, peeled and finely chopped
3 tbsp honey
2 tbsp lemon juice
175 g/6 oz medium egg noodles
salt and pepper
2 tbsp chopped fresh coriander, to garnish

You will need a cook's knife, a chopping board, a basin, a large saucepan, a frying pan, a wooden spatula, a slotted spoon and a serving dish

METHOD

1 Cut the chicken into thin strips and place in a basin.

2 Mix in the ground ginger, turmeric, curry powder and mustard and season well. Cover with clingfilm and allow to marinate for 1–2 hours.

3 Heat 2 tablespoons of the oil in a frying pan and cook the courgettes over a high heat for 2–3 minutes until they are well coloured. Using a slotted spoon, lift them from the pan and place in the heated serving dish. Put the peppers in the pan and cook for 2–3 minutes until slightly softened and just taking on some colour. Add the mangetouts and cook for another minute. Remove from the heat and add these to the courgettes.

4 Add the remaining oil to the pan and cook the chicken over a high heat until golden brown. Add the garlic and chopped ginger and stir well. Spoon in the honey and lemon juice and allow to bubble for 2–3 minutes until the chicken is tender. Adjust the seasoning to taste.

5 Cook the noodles for about 3 minutes or according to the instructions on the packet, and drain well.

6 Mix the noodles with the vegetables in the serving dish and pour in the chicken mixture.

7 Serve at once, garnished with the chopped coriander.

WINE SUGGESTION
Try a light, white, unoaked Chardonnay or Pinot Grigio with this salad.

POLENTA

Polenta is the northern Italian equivalent to pasta and can be served soft, like mashed potato, to accompany meat and fish. It can also be served, as here, in a thicker form which is grilled or fried and served with a variety of toppings.

Serves 4
Preparation time: 10 minutes, plus chilling
Cooking time: 10 minutes

INGREDIENTS

1 litre/1¾ pints water
1 tsp salt
250 g/9 oz quick-cook polenta
2 garlic cloves, peeled and crushed
55 g/2 oz sun-dried tomatoes, roughly chopped
½ tsp dried oregano
2 tbsp freshly grated Parmesan
3 tbsp olive oil
salt and pepper

You will need a large saucepan, a measuring jug, a cook's knife, a chopping board, a frying pan or a griddle pan, a wooden spatula and a small baking sheet

METHOD

1 Pour the water into a saucepan, bring to the boil, then add the salt.

2 Pour the polenta, in a steady stream, into the pan, stirring continuously. Lower the heat and simmer for 1 minute (or according to the instructions on the packet).

3 Beat in the garlic, sun-dried tomatoes, oregano and Parmesan, and season well.

4 Use 2 teaspoons of the oil to grease the baking sheet, and spoon on the polenta mixture. Smooth over the surface and leave to cool for about 1 hour.

5 Cut into eight slices or wedges and brush with the remaining olive oil.

6 Cook under a grill preheated to medium, or on a griddle pan over a medium heat, for 2–3 minutes each side until golden.

7 Serve two slices per person with any cooked meat or fish, or grilled summer vegetables (see page 177).

3

FRUIT

*W*e are exhorted to eat five pieces of fruit and vegetables each day – what a delight! We are so lucky to have our shops overflowing with wonderful fruit all year round. Some people think this is sad and that we should still eat according to season. I certainly believe that when it comes to summer berries – raspberries and strawberries – Britain has some of the best. British apples are good at the start of the season but towards the end of their storing time they get rather tired, so it is good to have new season varieties from Australia and New Zealand.

Some seasonal fruits are around for a short time, like tangerines or satsumas, and the season for peaches and nectarines passes very swiftly, so we are limited to eating those in season. Home-grown rhubarb also has a limited season – it is one of the only fruits that cannot be eaten raw – it needs cooking and sweetening to make it edible. Here is a selection of the most popular fruits.

TREE FRUITS

These include apples, pears, plums, peaches, nectarines, apricots and cherries.

Apples
These are the best-known fruit. There are many varieties, divided into two types – eating apples and cooking apples. Eating apples are best bought when they are not too large – their flavour is best when they are small. Well-known varieties include Cox's Orange Pippins, Golden Delicious, Granny Smith, Egremont Russet and Worcester Pearmain. The best known cooking apple is Bramley's Seedling – a large green apple that is too tart for eating. When they are cooked, they 'fall' and reduce to a soft pulp, which makes them useful for sauces and other desserts.

Pears
These are a softer fruit than apples, and need careful buying. It is difficult to buy ripe pears for eating, so it is best to buy ahead and allow 3–4 days for ripening at home. There are quite a few varieties available, but some are very hard and are better for cooking. Conference pears are quite large and hard – peel and poach them for eating. Comice pears can be eaten

raw or cooked, and the newer types of Rocha and French William are smaller and can be eaten for dessert, perhaps with some cheese. They are also good cooked.

Plums
Plums vary in size and colour and are available in dessert and cooking varieties. Buy plums that have smooth skins and no blemishes and make sure they are not too soft. The Victoria plum is the traditional British plum and is large and oval in shape. When it is ripe, it is delicious to eat raw, and it also cooks well. Damsons are small plums with dark-blue skins: they are rather sour and should only be eaten cooked and used for jelly and jam.

Peaches and nectarines
Again, it is difficult to buy these fruits when they are ripe – often they are picked before they are ripe and then only soften rather than ripen. Make sure you choose the ripest ones available – they should have a good, pink colour, without any green tinge. If they haven't softened in a couple of days, it would be best to cook them. A ripe peach or nectarine is a delight, but a soft 'cotton wool' texture is unpleasant. Both

peaches and nectarines come with white and yellow flesh. A peach has a downy skin and the nectarine a smooth skin; if you prefer, you can also remove the skin by blanching (see page 14). Peaches and nectarines can be eaten raw, whole, cut in half and stoned, mixed in a fruit salad or cooked by poaching or baking.

Apricots

These are small, orange-coloured fruits with downy skins. They are popular in eastern countries, where they are used in both sweet and savoury dishes. They have a very short season and it is difficult to find really good ones because they do not travel well. If you find good apricots, eat them as they are – they have a lovely sharp/sweet taste. Otherwise, use them in recipes or simply poach them with a little cinnamon and serve them hot or cold.

Cherries

Some very good cherries are available now but the season is quite short. Choose even-sized cherries with their stalks still attached. The sweet cherries are large and particularly

delicious: just eat them as they are – they will keep in the refrigerator for 2–3 days. Morello cherries are small and very dark and cannot be eaten without cooking. They are often made into jam, or poached and preserved in brandy.

SOFT FRUITS

This category includes all the fresh currants, strawberries, raspberries, blackberries, cranberries and gooseberries.

Currants

These are available white, red and black. We can now buy them easily, albeit for a short season. They are available in small punnets and should look plump and shiny. Black ones are too sour to eat raw but the red and white varieties can be served in summer puddings or fruit salads, or are good for decorating pavlovas or cheesecakes.

Strawberries

Eat strawberries just as they are with some sugar and cream if desired. Choose small to medium-sized strawberries, which

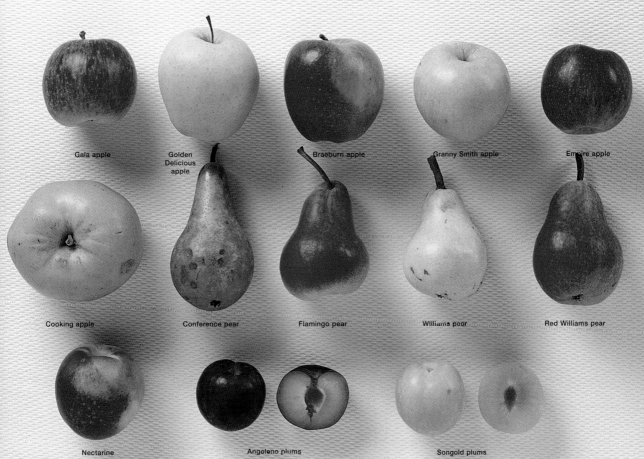

Gala apple

Golden Delicious apple

Braeburn apple

Granny Smith apple

Empire apple

Cooking apple

Conference pear

Flamingo pear

Williams pear

Red Williams pear

Nectarine

Angeleno plums

Songold plums

are not too soft. Always buy British because they really are the best. They are not usually cooked, but some people serve them with a dash of black pepper or a splash of balsamic vinegar. Serve them with ice-cream or on top of a pavlova, in fruit salads and in tarts or flans. They also make excellent jam. Do not attempt to freeze them.

Raspberries
These are the most delicious of all the small fruits. They have a wonderful flavour and look attractive. Again, they are best eaten as they are, simply with sugar and cream. However, they can also form part of a summer pudding, or they can be used to decorate desserts. They are also popular as a modern sauce or 'coulis', made by simply sieving the fruit and mixing the purée with a little icing sugar. Unlike strawberries, raspberries freeze very well. They also make delicious jam.

Blackberries
Cultivated blackberries are available in the shops, but they may also grow wild in hedgerows. The cultivated ones are larger and sweeter: choose ones that are completely ripe. Blackberries can be served in fruit salads. More usually, and certainly this is the case with the wild ones, they are better

cooked – in crumbles, pies, fools, mousses and summer puddings. They can also be made into jam.

Gooseberries
Green gooseberries are a traditional British fruit, and have gone in and out of favour over the years. Buy berries that are large and plump, and store them in the refrigerator for up to 4–5 days. They are not often eaten raw, although some varieties are sweet enough to eat uncooked. Cook them in crumbles and pies. You can also make a gooseberry sauce and serve it with oily fish such as mackerel or trout.

CITRUS FRUITS

Oranges
Oranges are available throughout the year. There are many varieties, mostly sweet, as well as the bitter Seville orange, which is used to make marmalade. Eating oranges should be firm with a clean skin and no blemishes. They will keep for a week at room temperature or longer if stored in the refrigerator. Eat them simply peeled, or segment them and use them in salads. Orange slices can be used for decorating

Currants

Navel orange

Lemon

Strawberries

Mandarin

Lime

Raspberries

Satsuma

Grapefruit

and garnishing all kinds of food. Squeeze out the juice for drinking or to make sorbets, ice-cream, mousses, tarts and puddings. Grate the zest to flavour cakes, pastries and stuffings (it is best to buy unwaxed fruit or organic if you are using the skin). Seville oranges are in the shops in January to February. The season is short, so buy some as soon as you see them and make some marmalade with them (see page 253).

Lemons

These are also available throughout the year. Buy lemons that are firm with good, yellow skins. Store them in the same way and for the same length of time as oranges. They are very versatile and can be used in many ways. Gin and tonic, for example, would not be the same without a slice of lemon. Many foods benefit from the sharp taste and flavour of lemon. Lemon juice is squeezed over food before serving and lemon zest is added to cakes, stuffings and fish dishes (use unwaxed ones). Recipes for lemons include lemon tart, lemon curd, lemon sorbet and ice-cream. They can also be used with other citrus fruits to make marmalade.

Limes

These green fruits are like small lemons. They are used in similar ways and are popular in Thai and South American cooking.

Grapefruit

These can be bought all year round. They have different coloured flesh, from pale yellow and pink to ruby red. The pinker the fruit, the sweeter the taste. They are usually eaten as a breakfast food, with or without sweetener. The zest is not used because it is too pungent. Grapefruit juice is popular, and the fruit can be segmented and served in some savoury salads. It can also be made into mixed fruit marmalades.

Tangerines, satsumas, clementines and mandarins

All of these are available around Christmas time. They are small, orange-coloured fruits and taste rather like oranges. They vary in sweetness and in the thickness of their skins. Some are easy to peel, which makes them ideal for children, and they are practically seedless. They are usually eaten uncooked but they can be served in a flavoured syrup.

OTHER FRUITS

These fruits are put together because they do not fall into a particular category.

Rhubarb

This is available in the spring as forced rhubarb, when it is at its tenderest and needs only a little cooking. Buy stems that are slim and a pale pink colour – they should be firm. Baking the rhubarb stems in the oven will allow them to stay in shape and to retain their colour. First remove the leaves and the bases of the stems before cutting into 5 cm / 2 inch lengths, then sweeten to taste. Rhubarb can also be used for crumbles and pies, as well as jam.

Grapes

Green and red varieties are available, and they can be either seeded or seedless. Grapes can be eaten on their own at any time of day, but they are also a good accompaniment for cheese at the end of a meal. Choose grapes that look dry and firm, and avoid those that are soft and look sticky. Always choose a well-shaped bunch. Grapes can also be used in fruit salads, or as a garnish.

Melons

Melons are best in late summer but they can be bought all year round. There are a variety of colours and flavours available. Honeydew is a largish melon, very sweet with a pale yellow colour. Galia is a pale-green, slightly smaller melon and is medium sweet. Cantaloupe is small and round with a brownish skin and sweet orange flesh. Charentais is very small with a strong flavour and deep-orange flesh. Look for melons that have unblemished skins. To test for ripeness, use a finger to press the stalk end of the melon – it should just yield slightly. Do not store melons in the refrigerator – I find they taint all the other foods with their smell. Serve melon cut into segments as a starter or light lunch dish. You can also serve it with a little Parma ham. Alternatively, serve it for dessert with some soft fruits. Melon flesh can also be cut into balls and served in a fruit salad.

Bananas

These are starting to become the most popular fruit, and are eaten a lot by sportspeople. Choose yellow bananas for immediate eating or green ones for ripening at home. Do not store them in the refrigerator because they will go black. They are usually peeled and eaten as an instant snack, but they can also be sliced onto breakfast cereal or in fruit salads. Bananas can be baked or grilled and can be used to flavour cakes and ice-cream. They are also good with bacon: I was brought up on fried banana with bacon for breakfast.

Kiwi fruit

These are small, dark, rough-skinned fruits, and are bright-green inside. They are a very attractive fruit when sliced and have a very particular flavour. They can be sliced in half and eaten with a teaspoon (like a boiled egg), or peeled and sliced to serve on pavlovas or cheesecakes. The peeled slices can also be added to fruit salads.

APPLE AND BLACKBERRY CRUMBLE

This is one of the simplest desserts — it is easy to make and delicious to eat. Any fruit or combination of fruit can be used to ring the changes.

Serves 6
Preparation time: 20–25 minutes
Cooking time: 25–30 minutes

INGREDIENTS

450 g/1 lb Bramley apples
450 g/1 lb blackberries
115 g/4 oz caster sugar
4 tbsp water
cream, yoghurt or custard, to serve

Crumble
175 g/6 oz wholemeal flour
85 g/3 oz unsalted butter
85 g/3 oz soft brown sugar
1 tsp mixed spice

You will need a potato peeler, a small, sharp knife, a chopping board, a mixing bowl, a fork, a baking sheet and a 1.7 litre/ 3 pint ovenproof dish (an au gratin dish would be good)

METHOD

1 Preheat the oven to 190°C/375°F/Gas 5. Prepare the apples by cutting them into quarters, then peeling and coring them. Thinly slice them into an ovenproof dish.

2 Add the blackberries and then stir in the sugar. Pour over the water.

3 Make the crumble by placing the flour in a mixing bowl and rubbing in the butter until the mixture resembles breadcrumbs. Stir in the sugar and mixed spice.

4 Spread the crumble evenly over the fruit and use a fork to press down lightly.

5 Put the dish on a baking sheet and bake in the centre of the preheated oven for 25–30 minutes until the crumble is golden brown.

6 Serve warm with cream, yoghurt or custard.

POACHED PEARS IN CASSIS

Serves 4
Preparation time: 15 minutes, plus chilling
Cooking time: 30 minutes–1 hour

INGREDIENTS

4 firm Comice pears
55 g/2 oz caster sugar
100 ml/3½ fl oz Cassis
125 ml/4 fl oz crème fraîche, to serve

You will need a wide-based, lidded saucepan, a wooden spoon, a sharp knife, a chopping board, a measuring jug, a potato peeler, a slotted spoon and a serving dish

METHOD

1 Peel the pears carefully, then cut them in half and remove the cores. Place them in the saucepan and just cover them with water, then add the sugar.

2 Slowly bring to the boil over a gentle heat, making sure the sugar dissolves.

3 Reduce the heat, cover and simmer for 15–45 minutes until the pears are tender. The cooking time will depend on the ripeness of the fruit.

4 Remove from the heat and use a slotted spoon to lift out the pears. Transfer to a serving dish.

5 Return the saucepan to the heat and simmer for about 4–6 minutes until the syrup has thickened.

6 Stir in the Cassis, and then pour over the pears.

7 Cover the dish with clingfilm and chill well for up to 2–4 hours before serving. Serve with crème fraîche.

APPLE AND GINGER MERINGUE

This spicy baked dessert is full of flavour and is equally good served hot or cold.

Serves 6
Preparation time: 25 minutes
Cooking time: 20–25 minutes

INGREDIENTS

115 g/4 oz sponge fingers
2 tbsp brandy (optional)
900 g/2 lb Bramley apples
2 tbsp unsalted butter
½ tsp cinnamon
4 tbsp soft brown sugar
3 pieces stem ginger in syrup, finely diced
3 egg whites
175 g/6 oz caster sugar
cream, to serve

You will need a 25 cm/10 inch round ovenproof serving dish, a saucepan, a sharp knife, a wooden spoon, a hand whisk, a mixing bowl and a flexible spatula

1 Preheat the oven to 180°C/350°F/Gas 4. Place the sponge fingers in an ovenproof serving dish and sprinkle over the brandy (if using). Peel, core and thinly slice the apples.

2 Melt the butter in a saucepan over a gentle heat and add the apples, cinnamon and sugar. Cover and cook over a medium heat for 6–8 minutes until the apples are cooked and soft. Stir in the chopped ginger, remove from the heat and allow to cool a little. Spoon the mixture over the sponge fingers.

3 Whisk the egg whites in a mixing bowl until thick and glossy, and then carefully whisk in the sugar gradually, a tablespoon at a time. Continue until all the sugar is added.

4 Immediately spoon the meringue over the apple mixture and swirl into soft peaks. Make sure the meringue goes right up to the edge of the dish to cover the apple completely.

5 Bake in the centre of the preheated oven for 10–15 minutes until the meringue is pale golden brown.

6 Remove the meringue from the oven and serve hot or cold with a little cream.

BAKED STICKY BANANAS

Serves 2
Preparation time: 5 minutes
Cooking time: 12–14 minutes

INGREDIENTS

4 ripe bananas
4 tbsp unsalted butter
juice of ½ lemon
3 tbsp soft, light-brown sugar
½ tsp crushed cardamom seeds
25 g/1 oz flaked almonds
3 tbsp chilled crème fraîche, to serve

You will need a small, sharp knife, a lemon squeezer, a chopping board and an ovenproof dish (an au gratin dish is good), which is large enough to hold the bananas

METHOD

1 Preheat the oven to 200°C/400°F/Gas 6. Peel the bananas and then cut them diagonally into 1 cm/½ inch slices.

2 Use 1 tablespoon of the butter to grease an ovenproof dish.

3 Place the bananas in the prepared dish and sprinkle with the lemon juice. Add the sugar and the cardamom seeds.

4 Bake in the centre of the preheated oven for 6–7 minutes until the sugar has melted.

5 Remove the dish from the oven and baste the fruit with the juices from the dish. Dot on the remaining butter and sprinkle over the almonds.

6 Return to the oven and bake for a further 6–7 minutes at the same temperature until the bananas are cooked and the almonds are browned.

7 Serve immediately with the crème fraîche.

BAKED STUFFED PEACHES

Serves 4
Preparation time: 15 minutes
Cooking time: 20–25 minutes

INGREDIENTS

4 ripe peaches
4 tbsp unsalted butter
2 tbsp soft brown sugar
55 g/2 oz amaretti or macaroon biscuits, crushed
2 tbsp Amaretto liqueur
125 ml/4 fl oz single cream, to serve

You will need a small, sharp knife, a chopping board, a basin, a wooden spoon, and an ovenproof dish (an au gratin dish is good), which is large enough to hold the peaches

METHOD

1 Preheat the oven to 180°C/350°F/Gas 4. Prepare the peaches by cutting them in half and removing the stones (if you want to skin them, just dip them into boiling water for 10–15 seconds and then plunge them into cold water).

2 Use 1 tablespoon of the butter to grease an ovenproof dish.

3 In a basin, mix together the remaining butter and sugar until creamy, then add the amaretti and mix well.

4 Place the peach halves in the greased ovenproof dish, cut sides up, and stuff them with the biscuit filling.

5 Bake them in the centre of the preheated oven for 20–25 minutes until the peaches are soft.

6 Pour over the liqueur and serve hot with some single cream.

CARAMELISED ORANGES

Serves 4
Preparation time: 20–30 minutes, plus chilling
Cooking time: 5–7 minutes

INGREDIENTS

4 large oranges
115 g/4 oz caster sugar
225 ml/8 fl oz water

You will need a citrus zester or grater, a small, sharp knife, a chopping board, a heavy-based saucepan, a measuring jug, a wooden spoon, a basin, 4 cocktail sticks and 4 serving dishes

METHOD

1 Using a citrus zester, carefully remove the rind in strips from two of the oranges, then set aside.

2 Use a sharp knife to peel the remaining oranges. To peel and segment an orange, cut the top and bottom off the orange and place it on a board, then cut down onto the board, removing the peel and all the pith. Slice the oranges horizontally into 5 thick slices and then secure them through the centre with a cocktail stick to reform. Place them in individual serving dishes.

3 In a saucepan, melt the sugar over a medium heat for about 1–2 minutes until it dissolves. Continue to heat for another 2–3 minutes until it turns a good caramel colour.

4 Remove the pan from the heat and, holding it at arm's length, slowly and carefully pour in the water. It will bubble and spit. Use an oven glove or a cloth to hold the jug of water.

5 Stir well to dissolve any lumps. If there are still lumps, you might need to heat it again very gently. Allow it to cool thoroughly for 15–20 minutes before pouring the syrup over the oranges.

6 Cover with clingfilm and chill in the refrigerator for up to 24 hours until needed.

7 Just before serving, scatter over the prepared orange peel.

ORIENTAL GREEN FRUIT SALAD

Serves 6
Preparation time: 20 minutes, plus chilling
Cooking time: 5 minutes

INGREDIENTS

175 g/6 oz lychees

225 g/8 oz green, seedless grapes

1 small melon (Honeydew or Ogen)

2 kiwi fruit, peeled and thinly sliced

2 green apples (Granny Smith), cored and sliced

juice of 1 lemon

1 pear, cored and sliced

sprigs fresh mint, to decorate

Syrup
115 g/4 oz granulated sugar

300 ml/10 fl oz water

2 tsp China tea leaves

You will need a saucepan, a wooden spoon, a sharp knife, a chopping board, a measuring jug, a potato peeler and a melon baller

METHOD

1 For the syrup, put the sugar and water into a saucepan and bring slowly to the boil over a low heat. Stir to ensure the sugar is dissolved. Pour over the tea leaves in a basin and leave to cool.

2 To prepare the fruit, peel the lychees and remove the stones. Wash the grapes and cut in half if large. Cut the melon in half and scoop out the seeds. Using a melon baller, make small spheres of fruit. (If you have not got a baller, cut the fruit into even-sized chunks.)

3 Use a potato peeler to peel the kiwi fruit, then slice thinly with a sharp knife.

4 Carefully cut the apples into halves and then quarters and remove the core. Slice thinly into equal slices. Sprinkle the slices with lemon juice to prevent browning.

5 Repeat with the pear: you can peel this if you prefer.

6 Place all the fruit, and any remaining lemon juice, in a serving bowl and strain the cold tea syrup over it.

7 Chill well for up to 2–4 hours before serving. Serve decorated with the mint sprigs.

RHUBARB FOOL

Serves 6
Preparation time: 15 minutes, plus chilling
Cooking time: 8–10 minutes

INGREDIENTS

700 g/1 lb 9 oz rhubarb, cut into 2.5 cm/1 inch lengths
about 115 g/4 oz caster sugar
grated rind and juice of 1 orange
300 ml/10 fl oz double cream
2 tbsp grated dark chocolate, to decorate

You will need a sharp knife, a chopping board, a medium
saucepan, a wooden spoon, a grater, a hand whisk, a basin,
a metal spoon and 6 glass serving dishes

METHOD

1 Put the rhubarb in a saucepan with the sugar and the
orange juice.

2 Over a gentle heat, slowly bring to the boil, stirring well to
make sure the sugar dissolves.

3 Reduce the heat and simmer very gently for about
5 minutes until the rhubarb is tender. Do not overcook
because you need to retain a good colour.

4 Remove from the heat and allow to cool. Taste for
sweetness and add a little more sugar if necessary.

5 If the rhubarb is too liquid strain it into a basin, then beat it
with a wooden spoon until smooth or process it in a blender
if you prefer your fool absolutely smooth.

6 In a separate bowl, whip the cream until it is thick but not
too dry. Using a metal spoon, fold in the cold rhubarb
carefully, then add the orange rind. Only just combine the two –
the fool looks more attractive if it has a marbled effect.

7 Spoon into the serving dishes, cover with clingfilm and chill
well for up to 2 hours. Just before serving, decorate with
the grated chocolate.

SUMMER PUDDING

This traditional pudding is made with slices of bread and summer fruits, hence the name. You can vary the fruits according to what you can buy at the time.

Serves 6
Preparation time: 15 minutes, plus chilling
Cooking time: 5 minutes

INGREDIENTS

675 g/1 lb 8 oz mixed soft fruits, such as redcurrants, blackcurrants, raspberries and blackberries
140 g/5 oz caster sugar
6–8 slices day-old white bread, crusts removed
175 ml/ 6 fl oz double cream, to serve

You will need an 850 ml/1½ pint pudding basin, a large saucepan, a wooden spoon, a bread knife and a chopping board

METHOD

1 First prepare the fruit. Remove any stalks from the currants and blackberries – there is no need to wash them. Put the fruit in a large saucepan with the sugar.

2 Over a low heat, very slowly bring to the boil, stirring carefully to ensure that the sugar has melted. Cook over a low heat for only 2–3 minutes until the juices run but the fruit still holds its shape.

3 Line the pudding basin with some of the slices of bread (cut them to shape so that the bread fits well). Spoon in the cooked fruit and juice, reserving a little of the juice for later.

4 Cover the surface with the remaining bread.

5 Place a saucer or small plate on top of the pudding. Use a large can of food or scale weights to weigh it down for at least 8 hours or overnight in the refrigerator.

6 Turn out the pudding and pour over the reserved juice to colour any white bits of bread that may be showing.

7 Serve with the thick cream.

PUDDINGS AND DESSERTS

Puddings are where British cooking comes into its own. The British are masters of the art of pudding making. Puddings were originally cooked and made from flour. They were first steamed, and then baked when ovens became the norm. The 'steamed pudding' as we know it now has made a revival and is usually made from a suet pudding mix or a creamed 'cake' mix and can be cooked either by steaming (which gives a moist sponge) or by baking (for a drier result). There are also some healthier puddings, which are not cooked – for example summer pudding (see page 207). Sweet dishes that are served hot include crumbles, pies, tarts, milk puddings and meringues. Lighter, cold desserts may contain fruit or cream and may be set with gelatine or frozen, such as mousses and soufflés, ice creams and sorbets, custards and trifles. Recipes for hot and cold puddings and desserts can be found in this section. But in the sections devoted to Eggs, Dairy Produce, and Fruit you will find other sweet dishes, which can be served at the end of a meal.

INGREDIENTS USED IN PUDDINGS AND DESSERTS

Flour
Plain and self-raising flour are used. For buying and storage, see page 36.

Fats
Butter is usually used because of its good flavour and colour.

Sugar
Caster sugar is used in the same way in puddings and desserts as it is in baking. Also syrup, honey and different types of brown sugar are used in various ways.

Eggs
These are an important ingredient in puddings and desserts.

Cream
Single or double cream can be used in many desserts.

Other ingredients
Fruit, nuts, dried fruit, cocoa powder, chocolate, gelatine, honey, syrup and jam all play an important part in preparing and cooking puddings and desserts.

EQUIPMENT

Pudding basins
Different sizes are needed, from individual dariole moulds to 600ml/1 pint and 1.2 litre/2 pint basins for steamed puddings and moulded desserts.

Baking dishes
Oval or round ceramic dishes are useful for baked puddings and crumbles.

Soufflé dishes
Individual ramekins are good for individual desserts and large, ovenproof dishes are useful for serving large mousses and soufflés and for baking sponge puddings.

Glass dishes
Individual sundae glasses and large glass bowls are good for serving smaller desserts and fruit salads. Large, heatproof glass dishes are good for baking crumbles and other fruit desserts.

LEMON SURPRISE PUDDING

Serves 4–6
Preparation time: 20 minutes
Cooking time: 45 minutes

INGREDIENTS

4 tbsp butter
grated rind and juice of 2 lemons
115 g/4 oz caster sugar
2 eggs, separated
55 g/2 oz self-raising flour
225 ml/8 fl oz milk

You will need a wooden spoon, a grater, an electric hand mixer or a wooden spoon, 2 mixing bowls, a flexible spatula, an 850 ml/1½ pint ovenproof baking dish (a pie dish or a soufflé dish is best), a measuring jug, and a roasting tin

METHOD

1 Preheat the oven to 180°C/350°F/Gas 4. Using a little of the butter, grease an ovenproof baking dish.

2 In a mixing bowl, beat the remaining butter with the lemon rind and sugar until it is soft and creamy. Beat in the egg yolks one at a time.

3 Sift the flour and then fold it in alternately with the lemon juice and milk.

4 In a separate bowl, whisk the whites until stiff, then fold into the lemon mixture.

5 Pour the mixture into the baking dish and place in a roasting tin half-filled with water. Transfer to the preheated oven and bake in the centre for about 45 minutes until the pudding is golden brown and set on the top. Underneath the sponge topping there will be a lovely layer of lemon sauce, hence the surprise. Serve warm.

QUEEN OF PUDDINGS

This is a very traditional and popular pudding. Simply make it from breadcrumbs, eggs and milk, then top it with jam and meringue – delicious!

Serves 4–6
Preparation time: 20 minutes, plus 15 minutes standing
Cooking time: 45 minutes

INGREDIENTS

2 tbsp butter
600 ml/1 pint milk
115 g/4 oz fresh white breadcrumbs
115 g/4 oz caster sugar
grated rind of 1 lemon
3 eggs, separated
3 tbsp raspberry jam, warmed
1 tsp golden granulated sugar

You will need a small saucepan, a wooden spoon, a grater, an electric hand mixer or a balloon whisk, a mixing bowl, a flexible spatula, and a 1 litre/1½ pint ovenproof baking dish (a pie dish or a soufflé dish is best) or 4 individual baking dishes

METHOD

1 Using a little of the butter, grease an ovenproof baking dish.

2 Heat the remaining butter and the milk in a saucepan over a medium heat and gently bring to the boil.

3 Remove from the heat and then stir in the breadcrumbs, 1 tablespoon of the caster sugar, and the lemon rind. Allow to stand and cool for 15 minutes, then beat in the egg yolks.

4 Preheat the oven to 180°C/350°F/Gas 4. Pour the mixture into the baking dish and smooth the surface. Bake in the centre of the preheated oven for about 30 minutes (20 minutes for individual puddings) until set. Spread over the jam.

5 Whisk the egg whites in a mixing bowl until very thick, then gradually add the remaining caster sugar. Continue, whisking, until all the caster sugar is added.

6 Spoon the meringue mixture over the pudding and make sure the meringue covers it completely. Swirl the meringue into attractive peaks and sprinkle with the granulated sugar.

7 Bake again in the centre of the oven at the same temperature for about 10–15 minutes until the meringue is golden brown. Serve whilst still warm.

BAKED ALASKA

A simple dessert, which looks spectacular yet is really easy to make; you can even prepare it ahead and freeze it.

Serves 8–10
Preparation time: 20 minutes, plus freezing
Cooking time: 4–5 minutes

INGREDIENTS

one 25 cm/10 inch sponge flan
500 ml/18 fl oz double chocolate-chip ice-cream, slightly softened
500 ml/18 fl oz vanilla ice-cream, slightly softened
225 g/8 oz fresh raspberries
85 g/3 oz mint chocolates, chopped
4 egg whites
225 g/8 oz caster sugar
2 tsp golden granulated sugar

You will need an ice-cream scoop or a spoon, a cook's knife, a chopping board, a mixing bowl, an electric hand mixer or a balloon whisk, a flexible spatula and a large, ovenproof plate

METHOD

1 Place the sponge on an ovenproof plate and scoop spoonfuls of the ice-cream onto the sponge. Alternate the flavours and push the raspberries and the pieces of chocolate into the spaces; pile it up high into a mound. Put the plate into the freezer for 20 minutes so that the ice-cream can firm up.

2 Preheat the oven to 220°C/425°F/Gas 7. Whisk the egg whites in a mixing bowl until very thick, then gradually add the caster sugar. Continue until all the sugar is added.

3 Immediately spoon the meringue mixture over the ice-cream. Make sure the meringue covers the ice-cream completely and makes a seal with the sponge base. Swirl the meringue into attractive peaks and then sprinkle with the granulated sugar.

4 Bake in the centre of the preheated oven for about 4–5 minutes until the meringue is golden brown and the tips of the peaks are well coloured. Serve immediately.

* Suitable for freezing. Prepare up to the end of step 3 and freeze for up to 2 days. Only keep it for 1–2 days because it is impossible to cover and will take up rather a lot of space in the freezer. When serving, remove from the freezer and allow about 15 minutes for the ice-cream to soften a little before cooking.

TOFFEE NUT PUDDING

Serves 6–8
Preparation time: 20 minutes
Cooking time: 1½ hours

INGREDIENTS

2 tsp melted butter

Sauce
115 g/4 oz butter
140 g/5 oz light muscovado sugar
150 ml/5 fl oz double cream
12 whole pecan nuts

Pudding
115 g/4 oz butter, softened
115 g/4 oz light muscovado sugar
2 eggs, lightly beaten
175 g/6 oz self-raising flour
2 tbsp milk
55 g/2 oz pecan nuts, chopped
55 g/2 oz pecan nuts, to decorate

You will need a small saucepan, a wooden spoon, an electric hand mixer or a wooden spoon, a mixing bowl, a flexible spatula, a 1.2 litre/2 pint pudding basin, some aluminium foil, a large, lidded saucepan and a serving dish

METHOD

1 Use the melted butter to grease a pudding basin.

2 To make the sauce, place the butter, muscovado sugar and cream in a small saucepan. Bring to the boil over a medium heat, stirring constantly. Lower the heat and simmer for 2 minutes until slightly thickened. Pour 2 tablespoons of the sauce into the pudding basin and add 12 whole pecan nuts.

3 To make the pudding, beat together the butter and sugar in a mixing bowl until soft and creamy, then beat in the eggs a little at a time.

4 Fold in the flour carefully and then stir in the milk to make a soft dropping consistency. Fold in the chopped pecan nuts.

5 Turn the mixture into the pudding basin. Cover the surface with a circle of greaseproof paper or baking paper and top with a pleated sheet of foil. Secure with some string or crimp the edges of the foil to ensure a tight fit round the basin.

6 Place the pudding in a large saucepan and half-fill the saucepan with boiling water. Cover the pan and bring back to the boil over a medium heat. Reduce the heat to a slow simmer and steam for 1½ hours until risen and firm. Keep checking the water level and top up with boiling water when necessary.

7 Remove the pan from the heat and lift out the pudding. Turn out onto a warm serving dish and decorate with pecan nuts. Reheat the remaining sauce over a medium heat for 2–3 minutes. Serve the pudding immediately and pass the sauce separately.

CONTEMPORARY CHRISTMAS PUDDING

This is a wonderful pudding: it has no suet or added fat, and is deliciously rich and fruity. It could become a family tradition.

Serves 10–12
Preparation time: 30 minutes
Cooking time: 5 hours, then 2 hours to reheat

INGREDIENTS

250 g/9 oz day-old wholemeal breadcrumbs
500 g/1 lb 2 oz mixed dried fruits
250 g/9 oz no-soak dried apricots, roughly chopped
115 g/4 oz almonds, slivered
115 g/4 oz almond macaroons or amaretti, crushed
2 tsp mixed spice
2 Cox's apples, cored and chopped
4 eggs
5 tbsp brandy
150 ml/5 fl oz Marsala
grated zest and juice of 1 orange
2 tbsp coarse marmalade (see page 253)
2 tsp vegetable oil
sprig of holly, to decorate

To serve
thick cream, or brandy butter (see opposite)
2 tablespoons brandy (to flame the pudding), optional

You will need a blender (or grater), a large mixing bowl, a basin, an electric hand mixer or a balloon whisk, a measuring jug, a flexible spatula, one 2.4 litre/4 pint pudding basin (or two 1.2 litre/ 2 pint basins), some greaseproof paper and aluminium foil, and a large, lidded saucepan

METHOD

1 Prepare the breadcrumbs by processing in a blender or grate the bread using a grater.

2 Put the breadcrumbs, dried fruits, nuts and crushed almond biscuits into a mixing bowl, along with the mixed spice and prepared apples.

3 Break the eggs into a separate bowl and mix well until frothy. Pour in the brandy and Marsala and add the orange zest and juice. Mix well. Stir in the marmalade.

4 Pour the liquid over the dry ingredients, stir well, then make a wish – to do this, get all the household together so that everyone can make a wish!

5 Cover the bowl with clingfilm and leave to stand for at least 3 hours, or overnight is ideal.

6 Use the oil to grease the pudding basin, and spoon in the mixture. Cover with greaseproof paper or baking paper and then with a layer of foil. Crimp the edges of the foil to ensure a tight fit round the basin.

7 Place the pudding in a saucepan. It is a good idea to make a long, folded piece of foil on which the basin will stand in the pan – this makes it easier to lift out at the end of the cooking time. Half-fill the saucepan with boiling water, cover and bring back to the boil over a medium heat. Reduce the heat to a low simmer and leave to steam for 5 hours. Keep checking the water level and top it up with boiling water when necessary.

8 Remove the pan from the heat and lift out the pudding. Remove the cooking paper and foil and replace with new pieces. Store in the refrigerator for up to 2 months until you want to serve it. To serve, steam for 2 hours (see step 7 above).

9 Now flame the pudding and decorate it with a sprig of holly. Serve with thick cream or brandy butter. To flame the pudding, heat 2 tablespoons of brandy in a small saucepan and pour over the hot pudding. Light and stand back – the flames will die out after 30–60 seconds.

BRANDY BUTTER

This rich butter makes the most delicious accompaniment to Christmas pudding and mince pies.

Serves 6–8
Preparation time: 10 minutes

INGREDIENTS

115 g/4 oz butter, softened
175 g/6 oz soft brown sugar
4 tbsp brandy

You will need a basin, a wooden spoon or an electric hand mixer, a flexible spatula, and a serving dish

METHOD

1 Beat the butter until pale and creamy – it will take 2 minutes if using an electric mixer and 4 minutes by hand. Add the sugar and continue to beat for a further 2 minutes until very light and fluffy. Gradually beat in the brandy.

2 Turn into a serving bowl and chill until required.

3 To store, cover with clingfilm or put in a lidded plastic container and keep in the refrigerator for up to 2 weeks.

BROWN BREAD ICE-CREAM

Serves 6
Preparation time: 15 minutes, plus freezing
Cooking time: 10 minutes

INGREDIENTS

125 g/4½ oz day-old wholemeal bread
1 tsp vegetable oil
125 g/4½ oz muscovado sugar
450 ml/16 fl oz double cream
2 tbsp caster sugar
½ tsp vanilla extract
4–6 tbsp rum or brandy, to serve (optional)

You will need a blender (or grater), a baking sheet, a mixing bowl, an electric hand mixer or a balloon whisk, a flexible spatula, and a lidded, rigid container or a loaf tin

METHOD

1 Preheat the oven to 200ºC/400ºF/Gas 6. Prepare the breadcrumbs by processing them in a blender, or grate the bread using a grater.

2 Brush a baking sheet with oil and scatter over the breadcrumbs. Sprinkle with the sugar.

3 Bake in the preheated oven for 8–10 minutes until the sugar caramelises with the crumbs. Stir from time to time to prevent the crumbs sticking together.

4 When the crumbs are a good colour, remove from the oven, break up with a fork and allow to cool thoroughly.

5 In a separate bowl, whip the cream and sugar together lightly until just thickening. Fold in the vanilla extract. Carefully fold in the cold crumbs and turn into a rigid container. Cover and freeze until firm.

6 Before serving, allow the ice-cream to soften slightly in the refrigerator for 1 hour. Spoon out onto individual serving plates or turn out the loaf shape and serve in slices. For extra flavour, pour a tot of rum or brandy over each serving.

* Suitable for freezing. This ice-cream will keep for 2 months in the freezer.

LEFT Brown Bread Ice-cream

EVE'S PUDDING

Serves 6–8
Preparation time: 30 minutes
Cooking time: 45 minutes

INGREDIENTS

675 g/1 lb 8 oz Bramley cooking apples
175 g/6 oz demerara sugar
175 g/6 oz butter
175 g/6 oz golden caster sugar
3 eggs, beaten
175 g/6 oz self-raising flour
55 g/2 oz ground almonds
3 tablespoons milk
1 tbsp flaked almonds
cream or custard, to serve

You will need a mixing bowl, a hand-held electric mixer or a wooden spoon, a flexible spatula, a deep pie dish or an oval au gratin dish (about 1.7 litre/3 pint capacity), and a baking sheet

METHOD

1 Preheat the oven to 180°C/350°F/Gas 4. Peel and core the apples and slice thinly into a large, ovenproof dish. Sprinkle over the demerara sugar.

2 In a separate bowl, cream together the butter and caster sugar until pale and fluffy, then beat in the eggs gradually. Fold in the flour and the ground almonds together with the milk. Spread the mixture evenly over the apples and scatter the flaked almonds on top.

3 Place the dish on a baking sheet and bake in the centre of the preheated oven for about 45 minutes, until the pudding is golden brown and well risen.

4 Serve hot with cream or custard.

* Suitable for freezing. Prepare up to the end of step 3, cool well, then cover and freeze for up to 3 months. To use, allow to thaw and then reheat gently for 15–20 minutes at the same temperature.

QUICK CHOCOLATE MOUSSE

*This mousse is very rich and therefore needs to be served
in small portions.*

Serves 6
Preparation time: 15 minutes, plus chilling

INGREDIENTS

300 ml/10 fl oz single cream
**200 g/7 oz continental dark chocolate (should have at least
52% cocoa solids), such as Meunier**
2 eggs, lightly beaten
2 tbsp Marsala
2 tbsp grated white chocolate, to decorate

You will need a small saucepan, a blender, a small basin, a
fork, a flexible spatula and 6 small ramekins or glass dishes

METHOD

1 Heat the cream in a saucepan over a low heat for about
3–4 minutes until almost boiling.

2 Break up or chop the chocolate into small pieces and place
in a blender.

3 Pour the hot cream into the blender and then blend together
until smooth.

4 Pour in the eggs and blend again until well mixed. Add the
Marsala and give the mixture a final blend.

5 Pour into 6 ramekin dishes and allow to cool. Cover with
clingfilm and chill for about 2 hours. Serve decorated with
the grated white chocolate.

** Suitable for freezing. Make up to the end of step 5, but do not decorate
with the grated chocolate. Cover the dishes with clingfilm and freeze for
up to 1 month. To serve, allow to thaw in the refrigerator overnight and
then decorate with the grated white chocolate.*

PASTRY

The range of traditional pastry is quite wide. You need to learn how to make pastry and it takes some practice. It is best to start with the simpler pastry and to progress to others when you have mastered the techniques. For this book, we are concentrating on making shortcrust pastry only, and the use of ready-made puff pastry and filo pastry. The ready-made varieties are increasing all the time and now come ready-rolled and in different shapes so that you do not even need a rolling pin.

TYPES OF PASTRY

Shortcrust

This is the basic pastry for everyday items such as pies and flans. It is very simple to make and can also be made with wholemeal flour for a healthier version. It can also be bought ready-made, both fresh and frozen.

Rough Puff

This is also known as flaky pastry. It is simple to make when you want a raised, layered pastry. Use it to top savoury pies.

Puff

This is layered during the making process and is very time consuming to make. In manufacturing, ready-made puff pastry is rolled and folded many times, resulting in many layers that allow the pastry to puff up on cooking. This gives a light, crisp-textured pastry.

Suet

This is pastry made using suet, to give a soft, spongy pastry. It is used for steamed puddings and dumplings.

Choux

Unlike all the other pastries, choux pastry is made by melting the fat in water and then adding it to the flour. It is used to make profiteroles and éclairs.

Filo

This Greek 'strudel' pastry is widely available ready made. It consists of many wafer-thin sheets, which when assembled are brushed with butter and layered or rolled to make Greek dishes such as Baklava (a sweet pastry with honey and nuts) or German varieties of strudel. Filo pastry can be used for a variety of pastries and for pies.

INGREDIENTS

Flour

Plain white and wholemeal flour can be used for shortcrust pastry. For puff pastry, strong white flour is used because the gluten content gives the dough more elasticity and helps the rising. For buying and storage, see page 36.

Fats

The type of fat used affects the texture and flavour of the pastry. Butter is the best fat for flavour and lard is the best for texture. Traditionally, half butter and half lard were used for shortcrust pastry, but today people prefer to use either all butter or half butter and half vegetable shortening.

Sugar

Caster sugar is often used to sprinkle over the top of pastry dishes before baking. This gives a crisp, crunchy appearance and texture.

Eggs

These are used only in the preparation of choux pastry, but they are also used as glazes for savoury pastry. To make a glaze, use a whole egg and beat well. For a richer brown colouring, add a pinch of salt. Brush it over the pastry before cooking and again during cooking if a really rich crust is desired.

RULES FOR PASTRY MAKING

Cold temperature
Everything should be cold for pastry making, especially the hands. Use fat directly from the refrigerator and freshly drawn cold water.

Proportions
Weigh everything accurately; the ratio of fat to flour is especially important.

Light touch
Rub the fat into the flour very carefully, using only the fingertips. Gather the pastry together gently, and handle it as little as possible. Do not knead. When rolling out, use a light touch with the rolling pin and do not stretch the pastry.

Relaxing
After mixing, leave the dough in the refrigerator for at least half an hour to reduce shrinkage. You can also repeat this once the pastry has been rolled if you have time.

Oven temperature
Always preheat the oven to the correct temperature (check your cooker instructions to see how long it will take). Pastry needs a hot oven to set it into shape.

EQUIPMENT

Pie dishes
Pie dishes of different sizes, preferably metal, are necessary to produce good pies.

Loose-based flan tins
These are ideal for quiches and sweet and savoury flans.

Bun tray
This is necessary for jam tarts and mince pies.

Baking sheet
This is necessary for sausage rolls and other small items.

Rolling pin
This is an essential item.

Flour dredger
This makes life easier when rolling out pastry dough.

BAKING BLIND

Pastry cases are sometimes baked without their filling to ensure a crisp base, especially if the filling needs little or no cooking.

1 Roll out the pastry to a size large enough to fill the base of the tin. It should overhang the tin by at least 5 cm/2 inches all round. Press the pastry gently into the shape of the tin, then use a knife to trim off the edges.

2 Prick the bottom of the pastry all over with a fork. This will let any trapped air escape during baking. Cut out a piece of baking parchment or foil large enough to line the pastry case and overhang by 5 cm/2 inches all round.

3 Line the pastry case with the baking parchment, then fill it with ceramic baking beans, or dried beans or peas from your storecupboard.

4 Bake at 200°C/400°F/ Gas 6 for 10 minutes until the pastry is set and golden. Remove the beans and paper, then bake the empty pastry case for another 5–10 minutes at the same temperature. Let it cool in the tin.

Whether you decide to use commercially made baking beans, or dried beans and peas from your storecupboard, they can be used over and over again.

SPINACH FILO PIE

This pie is also good served cold — it makes a good dish for a picnic or for eating in the garden.

Serves 4–6
Preparation time: 20 minutes
Cooking time: 35–40 minutes

INGREDIENTS

250 g/9 oz fresh spinach
1 onion, peeled and finely chopped
1 tbsp olive oil
2 eggs
200 g/7 oz feta cheese, crumbled
1 tsp dried oregano
2 spring onions, sliced (optional)
whole nutmeg, for grating
10 sheets filo pastry (about 175 g/6 oz)
4 tbsp butter, melted
salt and pepper
mixed salad, to serve

You will need a 23 cm/9 inch diameter pie tin, a cook's knife, a chopping board, a wooden spatula, a small basin, a fork, a grater, a large saucepan, a pastry brush and a baking sheet

WINE SUGGESTION
A light Sauvignon, perhaps from New Zealand, would go well with this pie.

1 Wash the spinach and remove any tough stalks. Dry well. Cook the onion and oil in a large saucepan over a low heat for 1–2 minutes until soft but not coloured. Add the spinach and cook for 1–2 minutes until wilted. Remove from the heat and cool. In a separate bowl, beat the eggs well and season (but remember the cheese is salty already). Add the eggs, cheese and oregano, spring onions if using and a good grating of nutmeg.

2 Preheat the oven to 180°C/350°F/Gas 4. Lay one sheet of filo pastry in the dry pie tin and brush well with melted butter. Keep the filo pastry covered with a damp tea towel as you use it or it will dry out. Repeat using a further 3 sheets, arranging them round the tin and brushing them with butter, until the tin is fully covered.

3 Place the spinach filling in the dish and cover with 4 more sheets of pastry, brushing well with butter between each layer. Press the edges well together and trim the edges with a sharp knife.

4 Butter the top of the pie and scrunch up the two remaining sheets of pastry and arrange over the surface to give an attractive top. Brush with the remaining butter. Bake on a heated baking sheet in the preheated oven for 35–40 minutes until the top is golden brown. Allow to stand for 10 minutes before serving in wedges accompanied by a mixed salad.

QUICHE LORRAINE

This quiche can be made without baking blind as long as you are going to eat it hot straight away; in this case bake at the hotter temperature for 30–40 minutes.

Serves 6–8
Preparation time: 20 minutes, plus chilling
Cooking time: 1 hour

INGREDIENTS

175 g/6 oz plain flour, plus extra for dusting
pinch of salt
85 g/3 oz butter (or use half butter and half vegetable shortening)
2–3 tbsp cold water, to mix
225 g/8 oz lardons, or bacon rashers, snipped into small slices
1 onion, finely chopped
3 eggs
300 ml/10 fl oz single cream
salt and pepper

You will need a 25 cm/10 inch diameter fluted flan tin, a cook's knife, a chopping board, a frying pan, a wooden spatula, a rolling pin, a flour dredger, a mixing bowl, a sheet of baking paper, some baking beans and a baking sheet

WINE SUGGESTION
A white Alsace or an oaky Chardonnay would go well with this quiche.

METHOD

1 Sift the flour and salt into a bowl and gently rub in the butter until the mixture resembles breadcrumbs. Sprinkle in the cold water and stir well using a round-bladed knife. Continue to mix until you have a smooth dough.

2 Wrap in clingfilm and allow to rest in the refrigerator for 1–2 hours.

3 Preheat the oven to 200°C/400°F/Gas 6. Fry the bacon in a dry frying pan until the fat runs. Add the onion and continue to cook for 5 minutes until the bacon is crispy and the onion soft and just turning golden.

4 On a lightly floured work surface, roll out the pastry into a circle 5 cm/2 inches larger then the flan tin. Fold the pastry over the rolling pin and lift the pastry over the tin. Ease the pastry into the tin without stretching and press down lightly into the corners. Roll off the excess pastry to neaten the pastry case. Prick the base of the flan case and chill, uncovered, in the refrigerator for about 30 minutes.

5 Line the pastry case with baking paper and fill with baking beans. Bake on a heated baking sheet in the preheated oven for 10–15 minutes. This process is 'baking blind'. Remove the paper and beans and return the pastry case to the oven for another 10 minutes until quite dry. Reduce the oven temperature to 180°C/350°F/Gas 4.

6 Beat the eggs and cream together in a bowl. Season well.

7 Put the bacon and onion into the flan case and carefully pour in the egg mixture.

8 Put it on the baking sheet and then bake in the oven for 30–35 minutes until set and golden brown; it will be quite puffed up. Serve immediately. Alternatively, to serve cold, allow to cool, cover with clingfilm and then store in the refrigerator for up to 48 hours until needed.

* Suitable for freezing. Cool first in a refrigerator for 2–4 hours, then open freeze on a baking tray. Remove from the freezer, discard the baking tray and wrap well in foil or a large plastic bag. To use, thaw at room temperature for 5–6 hours and warm through in an oven at 180°C/350°F/Gas 4 for 20 minutes before serving.

STEAK AND MUSHROOM PIE

Serves 4–6
Preparation time: 30 minutes, plus standing
Cooking time: 2½ hours

INGREDIENTS

700 g/1 lb 9 oz braising steak, cut into 4 cm/1½ inch pieces
4 tbsp plain flour
3 tbsp vegetable oil
1 onion, peeled and roughly chopped
1 garlic clove, peeled and finely chopped
350 g/12 oz mushrooms, wiped and sliced
125 ml/4 fl oz red wine
450 ml/16 fl oz stock, shop-bought or made from powder
1 bay leaf
400 g/14 oz puff pastry
1 egg, beaten
salt and pepper

You will need a large 2.25 litre/4 pint flameproof casserole dish, a measuring jug, a rolling pin, a flour dredger, a pie funnel, a pastry brush, a slotted spoon, a sharp knife and a 1.2 litre/ 2 pint pie dish

METHOD

1 Preheat the oven to 170°C/325°F/Gas 3. Put the prepared meat with 2 tablespoons of the flour in a large plastic bag and season. Shake well until all the meat is well floured.

2 Heat the oil in a flameproof casserole dish over a high heat and cook the meat until brown. Brown the meat in batches. Remove it from the dish with a slotted spoon and keep it warm.

WINE SUGGESTION
Try a red Tempranillo or Rioja from Spain with this.

3 Fry the onion and garlic in the casserole dish over a medium heat for 2–3 minutes until softening and then add the mushrooms. Continue to cook for about 2 minutes, stirring constantly, until they start to wilt.

4 Carefully stir in the wine and scrape the bottom of the pan to release all the sediment. Pour in the stock, stirring constantly, and bring to the boil; let the mixture simmer for 2–3 minutes.

5 Add the bay leaf and return the meat to the casserole.

6 Cover and cook in the centre of the preheated oven for 1½–2 hours until the meat is tender. Check for seasoning and adjust if necessary.

7 Remove from the oven, discard the bay leaf and allow to cool in a refrigerator, preferably overnight (this allows the flavours to develop).

8 Preheat the oven to 200°C/400°F/Gas 6. Roll out the pastry on a lightly floured work surface to about 5 cm/2 inches larger than the pie dish (use the inverted dish as a measure). Cut off a strip, 1 cm/½ inch wide, from around the edge. Moisten the rim of the dish with water and press the pastry strip onto it. Place a pie funnel in the centre of the dish and spoon in the steak and mushroom filling. Do not overfill, and keep any extra gravy to serve separately.

9 Moisten the pastry collar with a little water and put on the pastry lid, taking care to fit it carefully round the pie funnel. Crimp the edges of the pastry firmly and glaze with the egg. You can use some leftover dough to make leaf shapes to garnish the pie; stick these on using the egg and glaze well with egg.

10 Place the pie on a baking sheet and bake near the top of the preheated oven for about 30 minutes. If the pastry is getting too brown, cover it with foil and reduce the oven temperature to 180°C/350°F/Gas 4. The pie should be golden brown and the filling bubbling hot.

* Suitable for freezing. At the end of step 9, open freeze without covering until the pastry is firm, then wrap well in foil or a large, sealed plastic bag. Freeze for up to 3 months. To use, thaw overnight in a cool place and cook as above.

SAUSAGE ROLLS

These sausage rolls are delicious eaten straight from the oven but can be stored in an airtight container and reheated in the oven at 180°C/350°F/Gas 4 for 10 minutes when needed.

Makes 18–24
Preparation time: 20 minutes
Cooking time: 20–25 minutes

INGREDIENTS

2 tbsp plain flour, for dusting

450 g/1 lb puff pastry

450 g/1 lb good quality sausage meat or sausages (casings removed)

1 egg, beaten

You will need 2 heavy baking sheets with a raised edge, a rolling pin, a flour dredger, a pastry brush, a sharp knife, a pair of scissors and a cooling tray

1 Preheat the oven to 220°C/425°F/Gas 7. Sprinkle a work surface or pastry board with a little of the flour and flour a rolling pin. Roll out the pastry into a large rectangle, about 45 cm x 23 cm/18 inches x 9 inches. Cut into two strips 45 cm/18 inches long and 12 cm/4½ inches wide.

2 Divide the sausage meat in half and roll into two long shapes the length of the pastry; use a little of the flour to help in the shaping.

3 Place the sausage meat on the pastry. Moisten the long edges of the pastry with a little water. Fold the pastry over and seal the two moist edges together. Press well down and use a sharp knife to trim the pastry to a good, firm edge. Make cuts horizontally into the sealed edge so that it will flake and rise well.

4 Brush the pastry with egg, then cut into 9 or 12 smaller rolls per piece, whichever you prefer. Snip the tops of the rolls twice with scissors to give two attractive cuts and place on baking sheets. Bake near the top of the oven for 20–25 minutes until well risen and golden brown (swap the trays over half way through cooking). Remove from the oven and cool on a wire rack.

Suitable for freezing. Allow to cool, then open freeze on a baking tray, uncovered, for 1–1½ hours. Transfer to sealed rigid containers and freeze for up to 3 months. Reheat from frozen in an oven at 180°C/350°F/Gas 4 for 10–15 minutes until warm.

FAMILY APPLE PIE

Serves 6
Preparation time: 25 minutes, plus chilling
Cooking time: 30–35 minutes

INGREDIENTS

225 g/8 oz plain flour, plus 2 tbsp, for dusting
pinch of salt
55 g/2 oz butter
55 g/2 oz vegetable shortening
2–3 tbsp cold water, to mix
700 g/1 lb 9 oz cooking apples, peeled, cored and finely sliced
115 g/4 oz caster sugar, plus 1 tsp, for sprinkling
1 tsp ground cinnamon
¼ nutmeg, freshly grated
55 g/2 oz raisins
1 tbsp semolina
2 tsp milk
custard or ice-cream, to serve

You will need a 23 cm/9 inch (top diameter) pie tin, a potato peeler, a sharp knife, a small palette knife, a rolling pin, a flour dredger, a mixing bowl and a baking sheet

METHOD

1 Place the flour and salt in a bowl. Gently rub in the butter and vegetable shortening until the mixture resembles breadcrumbs. Sprinkle in the cold water and stir well using a palette (round-bladed) knife. Continue to mix until you have a smooth dough.

2 Wrap in clingfilm and leave to rest in the refrigerator for 1–2 hours.

3 Preheat the oven to 190°C/375°F/Gas 5. In a mixing bowl, combine the apples, sugar, spices, raisins and semolina.

4 Divide the dough into two, one piece slightly larger than the other. On a lightly floured work surface, roll out the larger piece of pastry into a circle just larger than the pie tin, and use it to line the ungreased tin. Press the pastry down well and make sure no air is trapped.

5 Put the fruit filling into the pastry case.

6 Roll out the remaining pastry to a circle just larger then the top of the tin. Moisten the pastry round the rim of the tin with water, and lay the rolled out pastry on top. Press down well round the rim to seal, and cut any excess pastry away. Crimp the edges of the pastry with your fingers or use a fork.

7 Glaze with a little milk and sprinkle with sugar.

8 Put the tin on a baking sheet and bake near the top of the preheated oven for 30–35 minutes until golden brown. Serve whilst still hot with lots of custard or some ice-cream.

* Suitable for freezing. Open freeze, uncovered, on a baking sheet for 2 hours when cooked and chilled, then wrap well in foil or a large plastic bag. Freeze for up to 3 months. To use, thaw at room temperature for 4–5 hours and warm through in the oven at 190°C/375°F/Gas 5 for 20 minutes before serving.

MINCE PIES

These pies make a delicious, quick dessert.

Makes 24
Preparation time: 40–45 minutes, plus chilling
Cooking time: 25 minutes

INGREDIENTS

350 g/12 oz plain flour
½ tsp salt
85 g/3 oz butter
85 g/3 oz vegetable shortening
3–4 tbsp cold water, to mix
450–550 g/1–1¼ lb mincemeat
2 tbsp brandy
4 tbsp milk
2 tbsp caster sugar
thick cream or brandy butter (see page 215), to serve

You will need a bun tray with 12 patty tins (two tins would be a good idea to save time), two fluted cutters (one 7.5 cm/ 3 inches and one 6 cm/2½ inches), a mixing bowl, a round-bladed knife, a rolling pin, a flour dredger, a pastry brush, a fork, a palette knife and a cooling tray

METHOD

1 Sift the flour and salt into a bowl and gently rub in the butter and vegetable shortening until the mixture resembles breadcrumbs. Sprinkle in the cold water and stir well using a round-bladed knife. Mix until you have a smooth dough.

2 Wrap in clingfilm and allow to rest in the refrigerator for 1–2 hours.

3 Preheat the oven to 200°C/400°F/Gas 6. Divide the dough into two, one piece slightly larger then the other. Roll the larger piece out as thinly as possible on a lightly floured work surface and cut out circles using the larger cutter. Gather together the trimmings, re-roll and cut out into 24 circles.

4 Carefully place the dough circles in the ungreased patty tins and press down gently.

5 In a separate bowl, mix the mincemeat with the brandy and spoon a good teaspoonful into each pie.

6 Roll out the remaining pastry and cut out more circles, using the smaller cutter this time. Gather the trimmings, re-roll and cut out until you have 24 circles.

7 Brush the edges of these circles with water and place them, damp side down, on top of the pies, pressing gently round the edges to seal the top and bottom pastry circles together.

8 Glaze the top of the mince pies with milk and sprinkle with a little sugar.

9 Bake near the top of the preheated oven (if you are cooking 2 trays together, change positions on the shelves at half-time) for 20–25 minutes, until lightly golden brown.

10 Remove the trays from the oven and carefully remove the pies with a small palette knife. Transfer them to a cooling tray for about 1 hour. When cool, store in an airtight tin for about a week. To serve, warm through gently in an oven at 180°C/350°F/Gas 4 for 10 minutes, and serve sprinkled with a little more sugar and some thick cream or brandy butter.

* Suitable for freezing. Open freeze, uncovered, on a baking tray for 1½–2 hours, then transfer to rigid sealed containers. Freeze for up to 3 months. To serve, reheat in an oven at 180°C/350°F/Gas 4 for 10 minutes.

TREACLE TART

Serves 6
Preparation time: 25 minutes, plus resting time
Cooking time: 25 minutes

INGREDIENTS

175 g/6 oz plain flour, plus extra for dusting

a pinch of salt

85 g/3 oz butter

2–3 tbsp cold water

225 g/8 oz golden syrup

115 g/4 oz white or wholemeal breadcrumbs

4 tbsp double cream

2 tbsp milk, for glazing (optional)

cold single cream, to serve

You will need a 20 cm/8 inch flan tin or metal pie dish, a mixing bowl, a rolling pin, a flour dredger, a small saucepan, a round-bladed knife, a wooden spoon and a pastry brush

METHOD

1 Make the pastry by placing the flour and salt in a mixing bowl and rubbing in the butter until the mixture resembles breadcrumbs. Sprinkle in 2–3 tablespoons of cold water and stir into the flour using a round-bladed knife. Cut through the mixture until it starts to cling together. Using a floured hand bring the mixture together in the centre of the bowl and form a smooth ball. Handle very carefully because pastry needs a delicate hand. Pop the pastry into a plastic bag and rest in the refrigerator for 30 minutes.

2 Meanwhile, warm the syrup gently in the saucepan until it is runny. Add the breadcrumbs and cream and stir well. Set aside for about 15 minutes for the breadcrumbs to swell.

3 Preheat the oven to 190ºC/375ºF/Gas 5. On a lightly floured work surface, roll out the chilled pastry into a circle large enough to line a flan tin. Press it gently into the ungreased tin and cut off any excess.

4 Pour the syrup filling into the pastry case. Roll out the remaining pastry trimmings to make a lattice decoration, lay it on top of the tart and glaze with the milk, if using, or otherwise leave it plain.

5 Place the tart on a baking sheet and bake in the centre of the preheated oven for about 25 minutes until the pastry is golden brown. The filling should still be soft as it sets.

6 Remove from the oven and allow to stand for 5 minutes. Remove the flan tin and serve whilst still warm, with some cold single cream.

* Suitable for freezing. Open freeze, uncovered, on a baking sheet for 1–1½ hours and then wrap well with foil or a large sealed plastic bag. To use, allow to thaw at room temperature for 3–4 hours, then warm in an oven at 180°C/350°F/Gas 4 for 10–15 minutes before serving.

PEAR TARTE TATIN

Serves 6
Preparation time: 30 minutes
Cooking time: 20 minutes

INGREDIENTS

85 g/3 oz butter

115 g/4 oz caster sugar

6 pears (Rocha or French William), peeled, halved and cored

flour, for dusting

225 g/8 oz ready-made puff pastry

clotted cream, to serve (optional)

You will need a 25 cm/10 inch heavy-based ovenproof frying pan, a wooden spoon, a sharp knife, a chopping board, a potato peeler, a rolling pin, a flour dredger, a large, deep serving dish and a pair of thick oven gloves

METHOD

1 Preheat the oven to 200°C/400°F/Gas 6. Melt the butter and sugar in an ovenproof frying pan over a medium heat. Stir carefully for 5 minutes until it turns to a light caramel colour. Take care because it gets very hot.

2 Remove the pan from the heat, place on a heatproof surface and arrange the pears, cut side up, in the caramel. Place one half in the centre and surround it with the others.

3 On a lightly floured work surface, roll out the pastry to a circle, slightly larger than the pan, and place it on top of the pears. Tuck the edges down into the pan.

4 Bake near the top of the preheated oven for 20–25 minutes until the pastry is well risen and golden brown.

5 Remove from the oven and allow to cool for 2 minutes.

6 Invert the tart onto a serving dish that is larger than the pan and has enough depth to take any juices that may run out. Remember that this is very hot so take care with this manoeuvre and use a pair of thick oven gloves.

7 Serve warm, with clotted cream if using.

BAKING

*T*he term 'baking' covers the method of making cakes and biscuits with a flour base (breadmaking is covered in a separate section). It also refers to the method of cooking in the oven, although some scones are cooked on a griddle pan.

INGREDIENTS

The ingredients used in baking include:

Flour

Plain white flour, self-raising flour (which contains baking powder as a raising agent), wholemeal flour, granary flour (which is a mixture of brown and rye flours and malted grains) and brown flour (which contains 85% of the grain). For buying and storing flour, see page 36.

Raising agents

Bicarbonate of soda is a raising agent which, when mixed with an acid, produces carbon dioxide to raise cakes and scones. Baking powder is a mixture of bicarbonate of soda and tartaric acid which, when moistened, also produces carbon dioxide.

Sugar

Caster, granulated, icing, soft light- and dark-brown, light and dark muscovado, and demerara sugar should all be used according to recipe instructions. For buying and storage, see page 37.

Eggs

For more information on eggs, see pages 72–75.

Fats

Oils and butter, lard and shortening are used in baking. For more information on fats, please see pages 38 and 91.

Nuts

For more information on nuts, please see page 43.

Dried fruits

For more information on dried fruits, please see page 42.

METHODS

In cake and biscuit making four methods are used:

Creaming method

This is where the fat and sugar are creamed together, using either a wooden spoon or an electric mixer. For an example of the creaming method, see the Victoria Sandwich recipe on pages 232–3. The eggs are then added and the flour folded in. Cakes made by this method keep well due to the amount of fat in the mixture.

Whisking method

This is when the eggs and sugar are first whisked together to form a fat/sugar foam. This technique entraps the air, which, when heated in the oven, expands and raises the cake. The flour is then carefully folded in. These cakes are often called fatless sponges or sponge cakes and do not keep as well as creamed cakes.

Rubbing-in method

These cakes and biscuits are less rich and the fat content is usually below half that of the flour. The fat is incorporated by rubbing it into the flour using the fingertips until the mixture resembles breadcrumbs. This method is used for scones, shortbread, rock cakes and tea breads.

Melting method

This is the method used to make moist, heavy cakes like gingerbread and parkin, and biscuits such as flapjacks. The fat and sugar, together with any other ingredients, are heated until all are dissolved before the addition of the eggs, flour, raising agent and any spices. These cakes keep well due to their high fat and sugar content; wrap them well in clingfilm to maintain their moist texture.

EQUIPMENT

Here is a list of the main items you will need for baking.
Other baking equipment is mentioned in the equipment
section (see pages 28–29).

Baking sheet

A good-quality baking sheet is essential to cook biscuits and
small cakes.

Sandwich tins

A pair of sandwich tins are useful for Victoria sandwiches and
sponge cakes.

Deep, round tin

This kind of tin is needed to cook a Christmas cake or other
rich fruit cake.

Medium-sized square tin

This is good for gingerbreads (see pages 28–29 for further
advice regarding baking tins).

Baking paper (or silicone paper)

This is more reliable than greaseproof paper and can be used
for meringues as well.

Bun tray

This will be needed if you want to make small cakes.

VICTORIA SANDWICH

Victoria sandwiches are delicious when freshly baked.
However, you can store any remaining in an airtight tin for
up to one week.

Serves 8–10 slices
Preparation time: 25 minutes, plus cooling
Cooking time: 30 minutes

INGREDIENTS

175 g/6 oz unsalted butter, softened at room temperature
175 g/6 oz caster sugar
3 eggs, beaten
175 g/6 oz self-raising flour

To serve
3 tbsp jam or lemon curd
1 tbsp caster or icing sugar

You will need two 20 cm/8 inch sponge tins, greased, and
bases lined with greaseproof paper or baking paper, a hand-held
electric mixer or a wooden spoon, a mixing bowl, a flexible
palette knife or a metal spoon, and a cooling rack

1 Preheat the oven to 180°C/350°F/Gas 4. Put the butter and 175 g/6 oz caster sugar in a mixing bowl and cream together until the mixture is pale and light and fluffy. Cream for 1–2 minutes if using a hand-held mixer, or 5–6 minutes by hand. Add the eggs, a little at a time, beating well after each addition.

2 Sift the flour and carefully add it to the mixture, folding it in with a metal spoon or a palette knife.

3 Divide the mixture between the two prepared sponge tins and smooth over with the palette knife. Bake on the same shelf in the centre of the preheated oven for 25–30 minutes until well risen, golden brown and beginning to shrink from the sides of the tins. Remove from the oven and let them stand for 1 minute. Use a palette knife to loosen the cakes from the edge of the tins.

4 Turn the cakes out onto a clean tea towel and remove the papers. Invert the cakes onto a cooling tray (this prevents the cooling tray from marking the top of the cakes). Leave for 30–45 minutes in a cool place to cool completely. Sandwich together with jam or lemon curd, and sprinkle over the sugar.

* Suitable for freezing. Open freeze, uncovered, on a baking sheet for 1 hour. Transfer to a sealed freezer bag, or freeze in a rigid plastic container. Freeze for up to 3 months. To use, thaw at room temperature for about 4 hours.

CHRISTMAS CAKE

This delicious cake is a wonderful treat during the festive season. Try to use natural coloured glacé cherries if possible. They are available from many health food stores.

Makes 20–24 portions
Preparation time: 45 minutes, plus 15 minutes marzipan and 25 minutes icing
Cooking time: 2–2½ hours

INGREDIENTS

175 g/6 oz unsalted butter, softened
175 g/6 oz dark muscovado sugar
3 eggs, beaten well
225 g/8 oz plain flour
1 tsp baking powder
2 tsp mixed spice
225 g/8 oz sultanas
225 g/8 oz raisins
100 g/3½ oz glacé cherries, roughly chopped
100 g/3½ oz candied mixed peel, finely chopped
100 g/3½ oz no-soak dried apricots, roughly chopped
100 g/3½ oz almonds, chopped
grated zest of 1 lemon
grated zest of l orange
125 ml/4 fl oz sherry or brandy

Decoration
750 g/1 lb 10 oz marzipan
3 tbsp apricot jam
3 egg whites
650 g/1 lb 7 oz icing sugar

You will need a 20 cm/8 inch round cake tin, baking paper, a mixing bowl, an electric hand mixer, a sieve, a flexible palette knife, a grater, some aluminium foil and greaseproof paper, a metal skewer, 26 cm/10½ inch silver cake board, a wooden spoon, a pastry brush, a small saucepan, a piece of string and a cook's knife

METHOD

1

4

TO DECORATE THE CAKE

9

13

1 Prepare the tin carefully, by lining with a double thickness of baking paper.

2 Cream the butter and sugar together in a mixing bowl until creamy and fluffy. Add the eggs, a little at a time, beating well between each addition.

3 In a separate bowl, sift together the flour, baking powder and mixed spice, then carefully fold into the egg mixture using a metal spoon or a spatula.

4 Add all the dried fruit, the nuts and the grated zest, and fold in together with the sherry or brandy until everything is well mixed. (If you have time, you could soak the fruit in the sherry or brandy overnight). The mixture should be a soft consistency, which will drop easily from a spoon.

5 Preheat the oven to 160°C/325°F/Gas 3. Turn the mixture into the prepared tin, use a palette knife to smooth the top, then cook in the centre of the preheated oven for about 2 hours until the cake is firm in the centre. Test by inserting a skewer into the middle: if it comes out clean it is done. Check the cake from time to time and if it is getting too brown, cover it with a piece of aluminium foil. Remove from the oven and allow to cool in the tin for 1–1½ hours. You can feed the cake with a little more brandy at this stage to ensure a moist cake. Prick the surface all over and pour on 2–3 tablespoons brandy.

6 Remove the cake from the tin, wrap it in greaseproof paper and then store it in an airtight container in a cool place for up to 2 days.

7 Divide the marzipan into three equal-sized pieces. Roll out one piece of marzipan into a circle large enough to cover the top of the cake.

8 Roll out the remaining marzipan to a rectangle, twice the depth of the cake and half the circumference (measure this with a piece of string). Cut the rectangle in half so you have two pieces that will fit round the cake.

9 Warm the jam in a saucepan over a low heat for 1–2 minutes, then brush the edges of the cake with it. Position the cake on its edge and roll it onto the marzipan, then press firmly. Repeat with the other piece and smooth over the joins. Trim any rough edges.

10 Brush the underside of the cake with the remaining jam (this way you have a smoother surface). Place the round of marzipan over the top and smooth the edges. At this stage it is a good idea to allow the marzipan to dry in a cool place for up to 1 week but if there is not time, continue with the icing.

11 Make the icing by placing the egg whites in a large bowl and adding the icing sugar a little at a time, beating well until the icing is very thick and will stand up in peaks.

12 Use 1 tablespoon of the icing to secure the cake to a cakeboard.

13 For a simple finish, spread the remaining icing over the cake and swirl it around so that you have attractive peaks all over the sides and top. You can leave the cake just as it is or arrange decorations of your choice over the top. Store in an airtight tin or rigid plastic container for up to 2 months.

CARROT CAKE

Makes 16 pieces
Preparation time: 30 minutes
Cooking time: 40–50 minutes

INGREDIENTS

2 eggs
175 g/6 oz muscovado sugar
200 ml/7 fl oz sunflower oil
200 g/7 oz carrot, coarsely grated
225 g/8 oz wholemeal flour
1 tsp bicarbonate of soda
2 tsp ground cinnamon
whole nutmeg, grated (about 1 tsp)
115 g/4 oz walnuts, roughly chopped

Topping
115 g/4 oz half-fat cream cheese
4 tbsp butter, softened
85 g/3 oz icing sugar
1 tsp grated lemon rind
1 tsp grated orange rind

You will need a grater, a mixing bowl, a wooden spoon, a
cook's knife, a sieve, a chopping board, a 23 cm/9 inch square
cake tin (lined with baking paper) and a cooling rack

METHOD

1 Preheat the oven to 190°C/375°F/Gas 5. In a mixing bowl,
beat the eggs until well blended and add the sugar and oil.
Mix well. Add the grated carrot.

2 Sift in the flour, bicarbonate of soda and spices, then add
the walnuts. Mix everything together until well incorporated.

3 Spread the mixture into the prepared cake tin and bake in
the centre of the preheated oven for 40–50 minutes until the
cake is nicely risen, firm to the touch and has begun to shrink
away slightly from the edge of the tin.

4 Remove from the oven and leave to cool in the tin until just
warm, then turn out onto a cooling rack.

5 To make the topping, put all the ingredients into a mixing
bowl and beat together for 2–3 minutes until really smooth.

6 When the cake is completely cold, spread with the topping,
smooth over with a fork and leave to firm up a little before
cutting into 16 portions. Store in an airtight tin in a cool place for
up to 1 week.

** Suitable for freezing. Open freeze, uncovered, on a baking sheet for 1½
hours until the top is firm, then transfer to a rigid container and freeze
for up to 3 months. To use, allow to thaw at room temperature for at least
3–4 hours.*

BANANA CHOCOLATE CHIP COOKIES

Makes about 18 cookies
Preparation time: 15 minutes
Cooking time: 15–20 minutes

INGREDIENTS

125 g/4½ oz unsalted butter

5 tbsp demerara sugar

2 tbsp granulated sugar

1 large egg

½ tsp vanilla extract

1 small, ripe banana, mashed

175 g/6 oz plain flour

¼ tsp bicarbonate of soda

pinch of salt

2 tbsp milk

115 g/4 oz good-quality dark chocolate (with at least 50% cocoa solids), roughly chopped

55 g/2 oz walnuts, chopped

You will need a mixing bowl, a hand-held electric mixer or a wooden spoon, a cook's knife, a chopping board, a metal spoon or palette knife, 2 or 3 solid baking trays (lined with baking paper) and a cooling rack

METHOD

1 Preheat the oven to 190°C/375°F/Gas 5. In a mixing bowl, cream the butter and sugars together until the mixture is pale in colour and light and fluffy.

2 In a separate bowl, beat the egg and vanilla extract together.

3 Add the egg mixture to the butter mixture, a little at a time, beating well between each addition.

4 Finally, beat in the mashed banana until the mixture is completely smooth.

5 In a separate bowl, sift together the flour, bicarbonate of soda and salt and add to the mixture, carefully folding it in with a metal spoon or a palette knife. Stir in 2 tablespoons of milk, then fold in the chocolate and walnuts.

6 Drop a dessertspoon of the mixture onto the lined baking trays, spaced well apart (about 6 per sheet). (If you only have one baking tray, you will need to do this in batches.)

7 Bake in the preheated oven for 15–20 minutes until lightly golden. Remove from the oven and leave to firm up slightly before placing onto a cooling rack to cool completely.

8 Repeat with the remaining mixture if necessary.

9 Store in an airtight tin in a cool place for up to 1 week.

* Suitable for freezing. Open freeze, uncovered, on a baking sheet for about 1 hour, then transfer to rigid containers and freeze for up to 3 months. To use, allow to thaw at room temperature for 3–4 hours or warm in an oven at 180°C/350°F/Gas 4 for 10 minutes.

CHOCOLATE BROWNIES

Makes 12–16 pieces
Preparation time: 20 minutes
Cooking time: 25–30 minutes

INGREDIENTS

140 g/5 oz continental dark chocolate (with at least 52% cocoa solids) such as Meunier

140 g/5 oz unsalted butter

3 eggs

175 g/6 oz caster sugar

115 g/4 oz plain flour

1 tsp baking powder

pinch of salt

1 tsp vanilla extract

55 g/2 oz walnuts, chopped

crème fraîche or ice-cream, to serve

You will need a basin, a small saucepan, a mixing bowl, an electric hand mixer, a sieve, a flexible palette knife, a 25 cm/10 inch square tin (lined with baking paper) and a cooling rack

METHOD

1 Preheat the oven to 180°C/350°F/Gas 4. Melt the chocolate and butter together in a basin over a saucepan of just simmering water, then remove from the heat and allow to cool for 5 minutes.

2 In a mixing bowl, whisk together the eggs and sugar until thick and creamy.

3 In a separate bowl, sift together the flour, baking powder and salt, then fold into the egg mixture. Add the vanilla. Carefully fold in the cooled chocolate mixture and the chopped nuts.

4 Turn the mixture into the tin and bake in the preheated oven for 25–30 minutes. Do not overcook. The top will be crusty but the centre should be slightly gooey.

5 Remove from the oven and then immediately cut into 12–16 pieces (depending on preference), but leave to cool for a while in the tin. Remove from the tin and peel off the paper before transferring to a cooling rack.

6 Serve warm for dessert with crème fraîche or ice-cream, or allow to cool completely and store in an airtight container for up to 1 week, to eat as biscuits.

* Suitable for freezing. Open freeze, uncovered, on a baking sheet for 1 hour, then transfer to a rigid container and freeze for up to 3 months. To use, allow to thaw at room temperature for at least 3–4 hours.

SCONES

Makes 10–12
Preparation time: 10 minutes
Cooking time: 10–12 minutes

INGREDIENTS

225 g/8 oz self-raising flour, plus extra for dusting
½ tsp salt
1 tsp baking powder
2 tbsp caster sugar
55 g/2 oz butter, plus extra for greasing
55 g/2 oz mixed fruit
150 ml/5 fl oz milk
3 tbsp milk, to glaze

To serve
strawberry jam
clotted cream

You will need a solid, greased baking sheet, a mixing bowl,
a measuring jug, a round-bladed knife, a flour dredger, a
6 cm/2½ inch pastry cutter, a pastry brush and a cooling rack

METHOD

1 Preheat the oven to 220°C/425°F/Gas 7. Sift together the
flour, salt, baking powder and sugar into a bowl. Rub in the
butter and add the fruit. Stir in 150 ml/5 fl oz milk, using a
round-bladed knife, and make into a soft dough.

2 Turn the mixture onto a floured surface and lightly flatten the
dough until it is of an even thickness, about 1 cm/½ inch.
Do not be heavy handed – scones need a light touch.

3 Using a pastry cutter, cut out the scones and place on the
prepared baking sheet. Glaze with a little milk.

4 Bake in the preheated oven for 10–12 minutes until golden
and well risen.

5 Remove from the oven and cool on a cooling rack. Serve
freshly baked, with strawberry jam and clotted cream. Serve
them warm, if possible, but certainly on the same day.

Variation

To make cheese scones, omit the sugar and fruit and replace
with 55 g/2 oz finely grated cheese (Cheddar or Gloucester) and
1 teaspoon of any mustard. Sprinkle with 1 tablespoon of finely
grated Parmesan before baking.

** Suitable for freezing. Freeze in a rigid plastic container, or open freeze,
uncovered, on a baking sheet for 1–1½ hours and then transfer to a well-
sealed freezer bag. Freeze for up to 3 months. To use, thaw at room
temperature for 3–4 hours. Reheat in an oven at 180°C/350°F/Gas 4
for 10 minutes from thawed or 15–20 minutes from frozen.*

SHORTBREAD

Makes 8 pieces
Preparation time: 15 minutes
Cooking time: 40–50 minutes

INGREDIENTS

115 g/4 oz plain flour, plus 1 tbsp for dusting
55 g/2 oz fine semolina
pinch of salt
55 g/2 oz caster sugar
115 g/4 oz butter
2 tsp golden caster sugar, for dredging

You will need a mixing bowl, a rolling pin, a flour dredger,
a 20 cm/8 inch sandwich tin lined with baking paper or a
20 cm/8 inch fluted flan tin and a cooling rack

METHOD

1 Preheat the oven to 150°C/300°F/Gas 2. In a mixing bowl,
mix 115 g/4 oz flour with all the semolina, salt and sugar.

2 Cut the butter into small pieces and rub it into the dry
ingredients. Continue to work at the mixture until it forms
a soft dough.

3 Gently roll out the dough into a circle on a lightly floured
work surface and then place it carefully in the tin. Lightly
press it into the tin and prick all over with a fork.

4 Bake in the centre of the preheated oven for 1 hour to
1 hour 10 minutes until the shortbread is firm and pale golden.

5 Remove from the oven and mark into 8 wedges with a
knife. Allow to cool in the tin for about 1 hour. Dredge with
the sugar. Cut into wedges following the markings made earlier,
then transfer to a cooling rack for another 30 minutes to cool
completely Store in an airtight container in a cool place for up to
1 week until needed.

*Suitable for freezing. Open freeze, uncovered, on a baking sheet for
1 hour, then transfer to a rigid container and freeze for up to 3 months.
To use, allow to thaw at room temperature for 2–3 hours.*

FLAPJACKS

Makes 21 pieces
Preparation time: 10–15 minutes
Cooking time: 30–35 minutes

INGREDIENTS

225 g/8 oz butter
225 g/8 oz light muscovado sugar
85 g/3 oz golden syrup
450 g/1 lb porridge oats

You will need a 20 x 30 cm/8 x 12 inch deep baking tin, baking paper, a large saucepan, a wooden spoon and a sharp knife

METHOD

1 Preheat the oven to 180°C/350°F/Gas 4. Line the tin with the baking paper.

2 Put the butter, sugar and syrup into a saucepan and heat over a low heat for 2–3 minutes until melted. Mix in the porridge oats and stir well.

3 Pour the mixture into the prepared tin, press down well and bake in the centre of the preheated oven for 30–35 minutes until golden brown but still moist and slightly soft when pressed.

4 Remove from the oven and leave to cool for 5 minutes. Cut into about 21 squares and leave to cool completely for about 30 minutes in the tin.

5 Carefully remove the flapjacks from the tin and store in an airtight container in a cool place for up to 3–4 days.

* Suitable for freezing. Pack carefully into a rigid container and freeze for up to 3 months. To use, allow to thaw at room temperature for at least 2–3 hours.

BREAD

There are times in our lives when we want to make a special effort and really treat our family and friends to some very special home cooking. Breadmaking is probably the epitome of this: it is very simple and very therapeutic to make and results in something very special.

Once you have confidence, the timing can be controlled by you and can be fitted into any schedule; it does not have to be made, risen, kneaded, proved and baked all on the same occasion. First mixing and rising can be done as quickly or as slowly as you wish; in a warm place or even in the refrigerator overnight. There is nothing better to greet your family or guests than the smell of home baked bread and nothing more that can make any house feel more like home.

The use of easy-blend yeast has contributed to the simplicity of breadmaking – no longer do you have to cream the yeast and sugar together and wait for the dough to start rising. The yeast is simply added to the flour and mixed in. A 7 g/¼ oz sachet is usually enough to raise 450 g/1 lb of strong white flour. To use dry yeast, sprinkle the dried granules into a little warmed water and add a little sugar, stir well and leave to act. Exact quantities and times depend on the recipe. It is ready when the surface is covered with froth. Note that with wholemeal flour and rich recipes (those containing eggs and fruit) the amount of yeast needs to be increased.

There is also a better selection of flours available for breadmaking – organic, strong plain white, granary and wholemeal flour to enable you to bake good-quality, well-flavoured loaves. Always make sure you buy 'strong' flour for breadmaking because it has a high gluten content and becomes elastic, allowing the dough to rise to give a good loaf.

MAKING BREAD
You can make bread simply by mixing it by hand in a mixing bowl, turning out onto a floured surface and kneading well before shaping. Otherwise you can use a free-standing mixer, which takes all the heavy work out of kneading. Some people will say that this takes all the fun and enthusiasm out of making bread, but for those with weak hands or arthritis it is a very good way to make the dough. The newer, popular way to make bread is to use an electronic breadmaker; this allows you to put all the ingredients into the machine and the machine

does all the work – the mixing, kneading, proving and baking all in one go. The downside of these machines, apart from the cost, is that you get a uniform loaf every time and that shape is not ideal. Making your own dough allows you greater individuality in terms of size and shape.

RULES FOR BREADMAKING
There are a few rules concerned with breadmaking, as follows. Everything needs to be warm; it is a good idea to warm the bowl and the flour so that the rising time will be shorter. Do take care how hot the ingredients become because if they are above 30°C/86°F the yeast will be killed and the bread will not rise. The answer is to make sure everything is hand-hot, that is, comfortable to touch and feeling just warm.

Kneading is essential: this is how the gluten is developed to give structure to the bread. To knead properly by hand you need to use the heel of your hand and push the dough down onto the surface and away from you – almost a rolling action. Once you get into the rhythm you will enjoy the sensation and it is a good method of ridding yourself of any tension you might have.

Bread is always baked at a high temperature in order to kill the yeast. In breadmaking, it is always better to overcook rather than undercook because undercooking results in a rather mealy flavour. If the bottom of the loaf is not cooked sufficiently when tested, you can replace the loaf in the oven without its tin to crisp up the base.

This section contains a few simple recipes for basic breadmaking: a basic white loaf, seeded wholemeal bread, fruit and nut rolls (which are ideal to serve with soup), focaccia, and pizzas (which are easily made).

OPPOSITE FROM TOP: Wholemeal bread, fruit bread, rye bread with sunflower seeds, whole-grain rye bread, fruited soda bread.

BASIC WHITE BREAD

Although we know that wholemeal bread is supposed to be healthier for us, there are times when a good loaf of white bread suits the occasion, especially for toast.

Makes 1 large loaf
Preparation time: 20 minutes, plus rising
Cooking time: 25–30 minutes

INGREDIENTS

450 g/1 lb strong white flour, plus 2 tbsp for dusting

1 tsp salt

one 7 g/¼ oz packet easy-blend yeast

1 tbsp vegetable oil or melted butter, plus 1 tsp for greasing

300 ml/ 10 fl oz warm water

You will need a large mixing bowl, a wooden spoon, a measuring jug, a flour dredger, a 900 g/2 lb loaf tin, and a cooling rack

1 Mix the flour, salt and yeast together in a mixing bowl. Add the oil and water and stir well to form a soft dough.

2 Turn the dough out onto a lightly floured board and knead well by hand for 5–7 minutes. Alternatively, use a free-standing electric mixer for this and knead the dough with the dough hook for 4–5 minutes. The dough should have a smooth appearance and feel elastic.

3 Return the dough to the bowl, cover with clingfilm and leave to rise in a warm place for 1 hour. When it has doubled in size, turn it out onto a floured board and knead again for 30 seconds; this is known as 'knocking back'. Knead it until smooth.

4 Shape the dough into a rectangle the length of the tin and three times the width. Grease the tin well, fold the dough into three lengthways and put it in the tin with the join underneath for a well-shaped loaf. Cover and leave to rise in a warm place for 30 minutes until it has risen well above the tin.

5 Preheat the oven to 220°C/425°F/Gas 7. Bake in the centre of the preheated oven for 25–30 minutes until firm and golden brown. Test that the loaf is cooked by tapping it on the bottom – it should sound hollow. Cool on a cooling rack for 30 minutes. Store in an airtight container in a cool place for 3–4 days.

Suitable for freezing. When thoroughly cooled, wrap in a plastic bag, seal well and freeze for up to 3 months. To use, allow to thaw at room temperature for 4–5 hours before using.

FOCACCIA

Focaccia is delicious with any Italian food, but particularly with antipasto, soups and salads.

Makes 1 loaf
Preparation time: 15 minutes, plus rising
Cooking time: 20–25 minutes

INGREDIENTS

450 g/1 lb strong, white bread flour, plus 2 tbsp for dusting
1½ tsp easy-blend yeast
½ tsp salt
5 tbsp good-quality Italian extra-virgin olive oil
300 ml/10 fl oz warm water
1 tsp olive oil, for greasing
2 tbsp coarse sea salt

You will need a large mixing bowl, a wooden spoon, a measuring jug, a flour dredger, a baking sheet and a cooling rack

METHOD

1 Mix together the flour, yeast and salt in a mixing bowl.

2 Pour in 3 tablespoons of the extra-virgin olive oil and add the warm water. Mix well with a wooden spoon or your hands until you have a soft dough.

3 Turn the dough out onto a lightly floured surface and knead for 8–10 minutes until very smooth.

4 Place the dough in a bowl, cover with a clean cloth and leave to rise in a warm place for 45 minutes–1 hour until doubled in size.

5 Turn the dough out onto a lightly floured surface and knead gently, taking care not to knock out all the air.

6 Grease a baking sheet with the olive oil. Gently roll out the dough until it is 2 cm/¾ inch thick and about 30 cm/ 12 inches in diameter: it does not need to be a perfect circle – a slightly rounded rectangle is good.

7 Place the dough on the baking sheet, cover with a clean tea towel or a piece of greased clingfilm and leave to rise again in a warm place for 20–30 minutes. With the handle of a wooden spoon, make holes about 5 cm/2 inches apart all over the surface of the dough.

8 Drizzle over the remaining oil and scatter over the sea salt.

9 Preheat the oven to 200°C/400°F/Gas 6. Bake in the centre of the preheated oven for 20–25 minutes until well risen and golden brown. Transfer to a cooling rack for a few minutes, but serve the bread while still warm. Store in an airtight container in a cool place for 2–3 days or in a sealed plastic bag in the refrigerator for 4–5 days.

Variations

• Add an extra 2 tablespoons olive oil and 2 tablespoons chopped fresh herbs such as basil, rosemary or thyme before cooking.

• Fold 115 g/4 oz Parma ham and 115 g/4 oz mozzarella into the dough before the second rising to give a savoury snack loaf.

• Scatter fried onion rings and garlic over before cooking. Use 1 onion and 1 garlic clove.

• Add 55 g/2 oz sun-dried tomatoes and 55 g/2 oz chopped olives before the final rising, or just scattered on top, for a wonderful Mediterranean flavour.

Suitable for freezing. Allow to cool thoroughly and wrap well in a plastic bag, then seal well and freeze for up to 3 months. To use, allow to thaw at room temperature for 2–3 hours and warm gently before serving.

HAZELNUT AND RAISIN ROLLS

These are delicious served with cheese. The fruit just adds a little sweetness and makes an ideal accompaniment to strong varieties of cheese such as Stilton and Gorgonzola.

Makes 16–20 rolls
Preparation time: 20 minutes, plus rising
Cooking time: 15 minutes

INGREDIENTS

450 g/1 lb wholemeal flour, plus 3 tbsp for dusting
225 g/8 oz strong white flour
1 tsp salt
two 7g/½ oz packets easy-blend yeast
3 tbsp olive oil or hazelnut oil
450 ml/16 fl oz warm water
115 g/4 oz hazelnuts, coarsely chopped
100 g/3½ oz raisins

You will need a large mixing bowl, a wooden spoon, a measuring jug, a flour dredger, 2 baking sheets and a cooling rack

METHOD

1 In a mixing bowl, mix together the flours, salt and yeast. Add 2 tablespoons of the oil and all the warm water and stir well to form a soft dough.

2 Turn the dough out onto a lightly floured board and knead well for 5–7 minutes. The dough should have a smooth appearance and feel elastic. Add the nuts and raisins and mix well.

3 Return the dough to the bowl, cover with a clean cloth or with some clingfilm, and leave in a warm place for 1–1½ hours to rise.

4 When the dough has doubled in size, turn it out onto a lightly floured board and knead again for 1 minute.

5 Divide the dough into 20–24 even pieces and shape into good rounds. Grease the baking sheets well with the remaining oil. Place the rolls on the sheets, leaving enough space between them to allow for growth whilst they prove (rise).

6 Cover again (a large bin liner is ideal) and leave to rise again for about 30 minutes, until the rolls are risen and have doubled in size.

7 Preheat the oven to 200°C/400°F/Gas 6. Bake in the preheated oven for about 15 minutes, swapping their positions halfway through. The buns should be golden brown and their bases should sound hollow when tapped.

8 Cool on a cooling rack and eat on the same day, or store for 2–3 days in a sealed container in the refrigerator.

*Suitable for freezing. When thoroughly cooled, place in a plastic bag or rigid box. Seal well and freeze for up to 3 months. To use, remove as many rolls as you need from the freezer and reheat in an oven at 180°C/350°F/Gas 4 for 10–15 minutes before serving.

PIZZA

Serves 2

Preparation time: 15 minutes, plus rising
Cooking time: 20–25 minutes

INGREDIENTS

225 g/8 oz strong, white bread flour or strong wholemeal flour, plus 2 tbsp for dusting

2 tsp easy-blend yeast

½ tsp salt

1 tbsp olive oil, plus 1 tsp for greasing

175 ml/6 fl oz warm water

Topping
400 g/14 oz canned chopped tomatoes, drained well

1 red onion, peeled, sliced and fried in 1 tbsp olive oil for 5–10 minutes

1 tsp chopped fresh oregano

4 slices salami, halved

140 g/5 oz mozzarella cheese, sliced

55 g/2 oz Parmesan, freshly grated

salt and pepper

You will need a large mixing bowl, a wooden spoon, a measuring jug, a flour dredger and a baking sheet

METHOD

1 In a mixing bowl, mix together the flour, yeast and salt.

2 Pour in 1 tablespoon of the oil and all the warm water. Mix well with a wooden spoon or your hands until you have a soft dough. If you are using wholemeal flour, you may need a little more water.

3 Turn the dough out onto a lightly floured surface and knead for 8–10 minutes until very smooth and elastic.

4 Grease a baking sheet with oil. Gently roll out the dough into a circle about 30 cm/12 inches in diameter and place it on the baking sheet. Allow to rise whilst you make the topping.

5 Spread the tomatoes and onion on top of the pizza. Add the oregano, season well and arrange the salami slices round the edge. Place the mozzarella on top and scatter over the Parmesan.

6 Preheat the oven to 220°C/425°F/Gas 7. Leave for a further 10–15 minutes until the edges are beginning to rise.

7 Bake in the centre of the preheated oven for 20–25 minutes until golden brown. Serve immediately.

Variations

• Sun-dried tomatoes and chopped olives can be added, with a few torn basil leaves.

• Roasted peppers can be sliced and added on top of the tomatoes; omit the salami and add a few sliced green olives.

• Drain a can of tuna and flake the fish onto the tomato, onion and oregano base (omit the salami). Add the cheese and top with 4 sliced anchovy fillets and some black olives.

• Sauté 115 g/4 oz button mushrooms with a crushed clove of garlic in 1 tbsp olive oil, spread over the tomatoes and cover with 4 slices of Parma ham; top with the cheese before cooking.

* Suitable for freezing. Allow to cool thoroughly and wrap well in a plastic bag, then seal well and freeze for up to 3 months. To use, allow to thaw at room temperature for 3–4 hours and heat in an oven at 220°C/425°F/Gas 7 for 10–15 minutes before serving.

WALNUT AND SEED BREAD

If you are making bread, it always seems sensible to make more than one loaf. The extra effort involved in making three loaves instead of one is negligible. And, after all, if you are having the oven on it is more economical to utilise the whole space.

Makes 1 large and 2 small loaves
Preparation time: 20 minutes, plus rising
Cooking time: 25–30 minutes

INGREDIENTS

450 g/1 lb wholemeal flour
450 g/1 lb granary flour
115 g/4 oz strong white flour
2 tbsp sesame seeds
2 tbsp sunflower seeds
2 tbsp poppy seeds
115 g/4 oz walnuts, chopped
2 tsp salt
two 7 g/⅛ oz packets easy-blend yeast
2 tbsp olive oil or walnut oil
700 ml/1¼ pints warm water
1 tbsp melted butter or oil, for greasing

You will need a large mixing bowl, a wooden spoon, a measuring jug, a flour dredger, a 900 g/2 lb loaf tin and two 450 g/1 lb loaf tins or alternatively two 900 g/2 lb loaf tins and a cooling rack

METHOD

1 In a mixing bowl, mix together the flours, seeds, nuts, salt and yeast. Add 2 tablespoons of oil and all the warm water and stir well to form a soft dough.

2 Turn the dough out onto a lightly floured board and knead well for 5–7 minutes. The dough should have a smooth appearance and feel elastic.

3 Return the dough to the bowl, cover with a clean cloth or clingfilm and leave in a warm place for 1–1½ hours to rise. On top of the boiler, on an Aga or in an airing cupboard works well.

4 When the dough has doubled in size, turn it out onto a lightly floured board and knead again for 1 minute.

5 Divide the dough into two. Shape one piece into a rectangle the length of the tin and three times the width. Grease the tins well with melted butter or oil. Fold the dough into three lengthways. Place in a large tin with the join underneath for a well-shaped loaf. Repeat with the other piece, divided into two for two small loaves.

6 Cover and leave to rise again in a warm place for about 30 minutes, until the bread is well risen above the tins.

7 Preheat the oven to 230°C/450°F/Gas 8. Bake in the centre of the preheated oven, with the larger tin towards the back, for 25–30 minutes. If the loaves are getting too brown, reduce the temperature to 220°C/425°F/Gas 7. To test that the bread is cooked, tap the loaf on the bottom – it should sound hollow.

8 Cool on a cooling rack for 30 minutes to 1 hour; this enables the steam to escape and prevents a soggy loaf. When cool, seal in a plastic bag and keep in the refrigerator for up to 1 week.

*Suitable for freezing. When thoroughly cooled, wrap in a plastic bag, then seal well and freeze for up to 3 months. To use, allow to thaw at room temperature for 4–5 hours. It is always nice to warm the loaf before serving, so heat in an oven at 180°C/350°F/Gas 5 for 10–15 minutes.

PRESERVING

*P*reserving was carried out over the centuries to ensure that there was always a good supply of food when the weather became inclement and to make use of all the fruit and vegetables when there was a glut. Nowadays, methods have changed as technology has improved – we no longer salt our meat or fish, or bottle fruit, because freezing has superseded these methods.

Although we no longer use all the preserving methods our ancestors used, the making of jams, marmalades and chutneys has stayed with us. They produce not only useful commodities, they also give us pleasure to make and provide us with lovely gifts for friends and neighbours who may not have the time or the inclination to make their own. And great satisfaction is to be had from looking at a row of labelled jars of preserves in the pantry or storecupboard.

Home-made chutneys are a delicious accompaniment to cold meats, cheese and salads and for adding to sandwiches; you cannot have too much. You can use almost any fruit or vegetable together with lots of sugar, vinegar and spices to produce a well-flavoured chutney.

The making of marmalade is a good way to spend half a day when the days are very short and cold; an ideal time to stand near a warm stove preparing a great pan of bubbling,

sweet, pungent Seville orange marmalade – something to look forward to during January when the fruit comes into the shops. You do not need any special equipment: a very large saucepan is all that is needed. However, a long-handled wooden spoon to avoid any burns caused by splashing is useful, and safe.

I would also recommend a jam funnel; this enables you to fill the jars quickly and gives a cleaner result, which will save the time of wiping the jars.

Do not buy special jars – collect them throughout the year and ask friends and neighbours to keep them for you. I try to keep all sorts of jars throughout the year, particularly those special jars you may be given for Christmas; it does not really matter about the size. In fact, it is nice to have a variety of sizes to give as presents. Jars with lids are particularly useful for chutneys: basic cellophane covers are not good enough because they let the chutney dry out.

SPICY TOMATO CHUTNEY

1 Heat 3 tbsp sesame oil in a preserving pan. Add 300 g/10 oz chopped onions, 2 red chillies (deseeded and chopped), and 1 chopped head of garlic. Cook over a low heat for 4–5 minutes. Add 1 kg/2 lb tomatoes (skinned, deseeded and chopped). Cook for 15 minutes.

2 In a separate pan, melt 125 g/4 oz brown sugar in 250 ml/8 fl oz distilled spice vinegar over a low heat, then pour it into the tomato mixture. Bring to the boil, then simmer for 40–45 minutes, stirring frequently, until thick. Remove the pan from the heat.

3 Make sure the jars have been warmed in an oven at 180°C/350°F/Gas 4 for 10 minutes first. Using a jam funnel, ladle the hot chutney into the jars carefully. Top with waxed paper discs and cover with a layer of cellophane to prevent the lids from corroding. Screw on the lids, wipe the jars and cool. Label with contents and date. Store in a cool, dry, dark place for up to 2 years. Once opened, refrigerate and use within 3 months.

RIPE TOMATO CHUTNEY

I have made this chutney very successfully using tinned tomatoes (cheap supermarket brands work well and are very economical). They are very useful when fresh tomatoes are expensive and out of season.

Makes 3.6 kg/8 lb
Preparation time: 45 minutes, plus potting
Cooking time: 2–3 hours

INGREDIENTS

2.7 kg/6 lb tomatoes
450 g/1 lb onions, peeled and finely chopped
600 ml/1 pint distilled spice vinegar
½ tsp paprika
pinch of cayenne pepper
3 tbsp salt
700 g/1 lb 9 oz granulated sugar

You will need a large saucepan, a colander, a bowl, a wooden spoon, eight 450 g/1 lb jam jars with lids, a ladle, a jam funnel, waxed paper discs, cellophane covers and labels

METHOD

1 Remove the skins of the tomatoes by dipping in boiling water for 1–2 minutes and then covering in cold water. This will make the skins easier to remove and is kinder to the hands.

2 Cut the tomatoes into quarters and remove the seeds. Roughly chop the flesh.

3 Put the tomatoes and onions in a saucepan and cook over a medium heat without a lid for 1–2 hours until a thick pulp is obtained. The cooking time will depend on the type of tomatoes used and the size of the pan.

4 Add half the vinegar, the spices and salt and simmer for about 20 minutes until thick.

5 In a separate bowl, dissolve the sugar in the remaining vinegar and add to the pan. Cook for 40–45 minutes until a good, thick consistency is achieved. The liquid should have all been absorbed but the chutney should still be moist and not dry. Bottle whilst still hot.

6 Make sure the jars have been warmed in an oven at 180°C/350°F/Gas 4 for 10 minutes and then fill them carefully using a ladle and a jam funnel. Top with the waxed discs and cover with a layer of cellophane to prevent the lids corroding. Screw on the lids. Wipe the jars clean and leave to cool. Label with the type of chutney and the date.

7 Chutney is better if it is stored before use to develop its flavour. Label and store in a cool, dry, dark place for up to 2 years before use. Once opened, keep in the refrigerator and use within 3 months.

SEVILLE ORANGE MARMALADE

This recipe is adapted from a very old 'HMSO' book, but it is the best I have used. Only Seville oranges are suitable.

Makes 4.5 kg/10 lb
Preparation time: 3 hours, plus potting
Cooking time: 20–30 minutes

INGREDIENTS

1.3 kg/3 lb unpeeled Seville oranges, washed
2.5–3.5 litres/4½–6 pints boiling water
2.7 kg/6 lb granulated or preserving sugar
juice of 2 lemons

You will need a large preserving pan or a large saucepan, a large heatproof casserole dish, a colander, a sieve, a measuring jug, a wooden spoon, a sugar thermometer or a saucer, ten 450 g/1 lb jam jars with lids, a ladle, a slotted spoon, a jam funnel, waxed paper discs and labels

METHOD

1 Put the whole fruit in the casserole dish and cover with the boiling water. Bring to the boil, cover, and simmer gently for 2 hours, or cook in an oven at 150°C/300°F/Gas 2 for 2 hours.

2 Remove the pan from the stove or oven. Using a slotted spoon, carefully lift out the fruit from the water and put it into a colander. Leave to cool.

3 When cool enough to handle, cut the fruit in half, separating the flesh and pips from the peel. Use a sharp knife and a fork to cut the orange peel into strips to the size you like – thin strips or chunky depending on your preference.

4 Add the pips and flesh to the cooking water in the casserole, return it to the stove and bring back to the boil. Boil briskly for 5 minutes with the lid off. This helps to set the marmalade.

5 Strain this liquid through a sieve and press the pulp through using a wooden spoon.

6 Place the sliced peel and the strained liquid in a preserving pan and add the sugar.

7 Place the pan over a gentle heat and stir well for 4–5 minutes until the sugar is dissolved. Turn up the heat and boil rapidly for 20–30 minutes until the marmalade has reached setting point. Test that it is setting by using a sugar thermometer (if you have one). When it reads 105°C/221°F it is a good setting point. Alternatively, use the saucer test: drop a small spoonful of marmalade onto a cold saucer, refrigerate to cool it, then push it with a finger. If it forms a wrinkled skin it is ready. If not, boil for a further 5 minutes and repeat the test.

8 Remove the pan from the heat and cool for 10 minutes. Skim any scum off the surface with a tablespoon.

9 Warm the jars in an oven at 180°C/350°F/Gas 4 for 10 minutes, then fill them carefully using a ladle and a jam funnel. Top with waxed discs and screw on the lids. Wipe the jars clean and leave to cool. Label with the type of marmalade and the date and store in a cool, dry place for up to 2 years. Once opened, keep in the refrigerator and use within 3 months.

INDEX

INDEX